READING VÁCLAV HAVEL

Reading Václav Havel

DAVID S. DANAHER

UNIVERSITY OF TORONTO PRESS
Toronto Buffalo London

Toronto Buffalo London
www.utppublishing.com

ISBN 978-1-4426-4992-7 (cloth)

Library and Archives Canada Cataloguing in Publication

Danaher, David S., author
Reading Václav Havel / David S. Danaher.

Includes bibliographical references and index.
ISBN 978-1-4426-4992-7 (bound)

1. Havel, Václav – Criticism and interpretation. I. Title.

PG5039.18.A9Z75 2015 891.8′655 C2014-907981-8

University of Toronto Press acknowledges the financial assistance to its publishing program of the Canada Council for the Arts and the Ontario Arts Council, an agency of the Government of Ontario.

Canada Council for the Arts
Conseil des Arts du Canada

University of Toronto Press acknowledges the financial support of the Government of Canada through the Canada Book Fund for its publishing activities.

Contents

Acknowledgments

I am indebted to a great many people, institutions, and places for their support in the process of researching and writing this book. My greatest debt is to the students in my monograph course on Havel's writings that I have offered regularly at UW-Madison since 2002. They have collectively taught me more about Havel than any scholarly book possibly could, and it is to them that I dedicate this book. In particular, I am grateful to Paul and Tommy Atwell, Jerrie Ceplina, Katie Peplinski Coffin, Soren Larsen-Ravenfeather, Abby Panozzo, Rachel Parker, and Wyl Schuth. Two former students, Megan Munroe and Ruth Ann Stodola, have done heroic work in reading, editing, and commenting on drafts of the book, and I am deeply grateful to them for their generosity of time and spirit. Graduate students in the Slavic Department at UW-Madison – especially Colleen Lucy, Naomi Olson, and Joey Vergara – also deserve my thanks.

I am fortunate to have had input from careful readers of a draft of the full manuscript – Greg Bettwy, Judith Kornblatt, Hana Pichova, and Tom McCarthy – whose kindness in agreeing to take on an additional project in the midst of their already busy professional and personal lives overwhelms me.

Special thanks go out to my colleagues in Prague for their unwavering support of my work on Havel, and in particular to Jasňa Pacovská and Daniel Vojtěch. I am forever in the debt of Irena Vaňková (and the members of her informal discussion *kroužek*) for her (their) unwavering and enthusiastic support of my research over the years. I am also grateful to Kim Strozewski, whose help at various stages of my Prague-based research has been much appreciated.

Jonathan Bolton, Craig Cravens, and Kieran Williams are US-based colleagues who have been generous with their time in critiquing parts of the manuscript and in sharing with me their ideas about Havel and his larger context. James Pontuso has been extremely generous over the years in this regard, and to him I owe a particular debt of gratitude.

Personal discussions with Christopher Ott (and not only or even especially about Havel) have made this a much better book than it otherwise would have been.

Institutions and organizations to which I am grateful for support include: the UW Foundation for support in the form of a Vilas Fellowship; the Davis Center at Harvard University for an affiliation that, among other benefits, allowed me access to the stacks at Widener Library; and the Kruh přátel českého jazyka, the Filozofická fakulta of Charles University, and the Prague-based Václav Havel Library for generously inviting me to present on my research. For providing internet infrastructure and a quiet place to write, I am grateful to the Cambridge Public Library, the former Lyndell's Bakery in Cambridge's Central Square, Top Pot in Seattle's Capitol Hill, and Fair Trade on Madison's State Street.

I gratefully acknowledge the following journals and edited volumes in which some of the material in this book has previously appeared: *The Linguistic Worldview: Ethnolinguistics, Cognition, and Culture* (Versita 2013), *Česká literatura, Ročenka textů zahraničních profesorů 4* (Charles University 2010), *Slovo a slovesnost*, *Between Texts, Languages, and Cultures: A Festshrift for Michael Henry Heim* (Slavica 2008), *Slovo a smysl / Word and sense*, and *Czech Language News*. For full citations of the articles and chapters in question, see the bibliography.

Two anonymous reviewers of the book manuscript also made valuable suggestions for improving the book's arguments as well as its readability, and I thank them for their input. Any errors that remain in the book are naturally my own responsibility.

READING VÁCLAV HAVEL

Introduction: Approaches to Reading Havel

"You must change your life," says Rilke's sculpture of Apollo to the beholder. So says every major work of intellect and imagination, but in the university now – as in the culture at large – almost no one hears.

– Mark Edmundson, *Why Read?*[1]

Who was Václav Havel? In what way or ways do we – his twenty-first century readers from all over the world who may already know something, or perhaps very little, about Havel's life and context – typically think about him? How do we read Havel, both in the literal sense of reading his remarkably diverse set of writings in translation, or perhaps even in the original Czech, as well as in the figurative sense of interpreting his writings and his life? How do we make sense of Havel as one of the most prominent and arguably most influential intellectual figures (if not also political figures) in world history from the second half of the twentieth century through the end of the first decade of the twenty-first? With Havel's death in December 2011 comes another question, one tightly bound up with the preceding ones: what shape will Havel's legacy take?

Václav Havel was born in 1936 to an affluent, educated, and well-connected family. His childhood took place against the backdrop of geopolitical turbulence. Within several years of his birth, the democratic First Czechoslovak Republic (1918–38) would come to an end with the signing of the Munich Agreement by the great European powers. An attempt to appease Germany, the agreement allowed Hitler to annex the ethnically German borderlands of Czechoslovakia, which would result in German occupation of the country beginning in March 1939. When the war ended in 1945, the Czechoslovak government-in-exile returned from London and founded the Third Republic, but this political entity lasted for only three years. Most of the country had been liberated by Stalin's army and, before Havel was twelve years old, Czechoslovakia had been taken over by the Communist Party. The country remained in the Soviet sphere of influence from 1948 to 1989, that is, for what would prove to be the majority of Havel's life.

Although Havel, as a child of "bourgeois" parents under a communist regime, was denied access to educational opportunities that befitted his interests and talents, he nonetheless managed to establish himself as a promising writer and engaged intellectual before the age of thirty. By the mid-1960s, he had begun what would develop into a brilliant career as a playwright, and in the process had brought the techniques of French theatre of the absurd, in conjunction with the Czech theatre of the appeal, to his country.[2] Throughout the 1960s, he was also a leading figure in the cultural and political movement that eventually culminated in the 1968 Prague Spring and the national tragedy of the Soviet invasion of Czechoslovakia in August of the same year. The post-invasion regime, under the leadership of Gustáv Husák, banned Havel (along with other reformist writers and cultural figures) from publication and public life as part of a campaign of repression that came to be known as "normalization." Despite his "normalized" status, Havel continued to write, and gradually became a key figure in the so-called dissident movement that led to the founding of Charter 77.[3]

Founded in 1977 and extant as an organization until several years after the fall of communism in Central Europe, Charter 77 was a civic initiative composed largely of dissidents or "intellectual oppositionists" (Goldfarb 1998: 85). Technically speaking, the Charter focused on questions of human rights under Husák's regime, but it also served, more broadly speaking, as a cultural space for a community of people who wanted to think and live outside the "normalized" box. Havel was one of the leading theorizers of the oppositionist intellectuals not only in Czechoslovakia's Charter movement – he was one of the Charter's founders and among its original spokespeople – but also in the Soviet bloc as a whole. Because of these activities, the regime tried Havel (and others) on trumped-up criminal charges, and Havel spent almost four years in prison from 1979 to 1983.

As the communist regimes began to crumble across Central and Eastern Europe in the late 1980s, and in the aftermath of dramatic events in

Czechoslovakia in November 1989, a Prague-based organization called the Civic Forum was established to unite opposition to the regime and push for its end. Havel was a founder, and the nominal leader, of the Civic Forum, and most of the Forum's leading representatives came from Charter circles. The Forum was successful in negotiating a non-violent end to the communist regime in Czechoslovakia, and the Velvet Revolution, as it came to be known, transformed Havel nearly overnight from a publicly vilified "dissident" to the unanimously elected president of his country on 29 December 1989.[4]

Havel served as president of Czechoslovakia from 1989 to 1992, and then of the newly independent Czech Republic from 1993 to 2003. During his presidential years, Havel also travelled the world to receive awards and honorary degrees; he gained global renown as an intellectually oriented politician and leading thinker. He cemented this reputation during his presidency and beyond both by concerning himself with questions of human rights across the world and by organizing global initiatives to confront the challenges faced by humanity in the twenty-first century.[5] After a long illness, Havel died on 18 December 2011 at his country home in northern Bohemia.

A commentator writing on Havel's philosophical or "dissident" essays once described him as a "relentless thinker," observing that "there's something exhilarating about the dogged way Havel sniffs and digs at his ideas until every bony chip has been unearthed" (Schiff 1999: 87). This is a feature of his writing that any serious reader of Havel, or at least someone who has tried to take notes on his essays, will immediately recognize; the notes often end up reproducing nearly every detail of the original text. In a not-unrelated characterization, Paul Wilson, Havel's English-language translator, called him a "visionary tinkerer" who had "a mind as much at home with the minutiae of a state banquet or designing improvements to Prague Castle as with NATO expansion or the New World Order" (Wilson 2006: 15). What some may be quick to consider a quirk of Havel's personality seems, in a different light, more integral to his persona. The big picture can never be divorced from the procedural details – those "bony chips" – that comprise it, and small details are not incidental to the outcome of great events.

Although it is useful to trace the outlines of Havel's life, this book is not intended as a biography. My ambition is instead to develop an approach to reading Havel that reassembles the "bony chips" and tinkered pieces of his visionary project into a coherent whole. Over the course of his life, Havel engaged in a remarkably diverse range of genres, both literary and non-literary; he presented a variety of "faces" to the public at different stages of his life. He was, for example, a productive and accomplished writer of essays devoted to literary and film criticism, visual poetry, plays, philosophical (and political) essays, short philosophical reflections written and sent as letters from prison, and political speeches (as well as other texts); he was a writer and also simultaneously a political figure both as a pre-1989 so-called dissident and the post-1989 president of his country.[6] Across all of these various genres or faces, Havel was nothing if not a consistent thinker. His ideas and themes – and, as we will see, the conceptual strategies he exploits in engaging with them – remain constant across these faces, genres, and time periods. It should be possible, then, to read Havel in a way that does not fragment but rather integrates the diversity of his writings and political contributions. In other words, Havel's artistic and literary versatility as well as his role as a leading actor in the culture and society of his time ought to have a direct bearing on how we read him. In order to make sense of Havel as a writer, a thinker, and a politician, and also to initiate a discussion of his legacy, we are in need of a holistic evaluation of Havel's contributions.

One path to realizing an integrative approach to reading Havel consists in identifying and describing key conceptual threads running through his thought. These threads cut across the various genres and time periods that characterize his career, and are therefore crucial to understanding Havel as a coherent thinker. Moreover, and as will become evident, these threads represent forms that Havel himself uses as an engaged writer while simultaneously functioning as crucial elements of Havel's message; in reading Havel, the *how* cannot be easily separated from the *what*. The crux of Havel's project is to map the topography of human identity in the modern world, and the strategies that he exploits in realizing the mapping turn out to be crucial features of the topography itself. In other words, the strategies that Havel uses to analyse the crisis of modern human identity – the very ones that we encounter again and again while reading his works – also prove useful as conceptual tools for analysing ourselves. Reading Havel thus becomes a way in which to "read" ourselves also.

I explore four of these strategies/tools over the course of this book. The first of these is suggested by a recurring image in Havel's oeuvre, the image of the mosaic (or the related image of the collage), which symbolizes for Havel the structural complexity of modern human identity at both personal and societal levels.[7] The second is a recurrent opposition found in Havel's thinking between, on one hand, *explaining*, and, on the other, *understanding*; the former is, in Havel's treatment, a way of relating to the world that privileges rationality at the cost of depersonalizing and fragmenting human experience, while the latter represents an integrative way of being in the world that is grounded in everyday human experience. The third thread that I will consider, and which has been underappreciated in the scholarly literature on Havel to date, is his radical reconceptualization of the East/West dynamic during the Cold War. Havel's reframing of East and West is subsumed under the broader conviction that modern humanity is in the throes of a spiritual crisis, and to appreciate Havel's characterization of this crisis – both the causes of it and the ways to resolve it – will require us to reconsider who we were prior to 1989 and who we therefore are in the post-1989 world. The final thread that binds together Havel's various incarnations is a constant focus on restoring an experience of the transcendent in the modern world. How this plays out across Havel's oeuvre, and particularly with regard to the very language that Havel used in creating that oeuvre, will be a major concern of this book.

Figuring prominently in all four of these discussions (and binding them together) will be an emphasis on Havel's literary and political engagement as forms of appeal. I use the word "appeal" here in the special sense of Czech theatre of the appeal (*divadlo apelu*), which is a term associated with Havel's dramatic style. The renowned Czech writer, playwright, actor, director, and teacher Ivan Vyskočil, who was Havel's early theatrical mentor, defined *divadlo apelu* as a kind of theatre that aims "to engage the intellect and the imagination of the spectator in order to force him to agree, disagree, compare, and view a subject matter from various angles" (cited in Trensky 1978: 105). *Divadlo apelu* is absurdist theatre of a special type, in which the techniques associated with absurdism are deployed to provoke – and thereby "activate" (Grossman 1999: 71) – the audience by creating within the play an empty space for audience self-reflection; spectators (or "spect-actors") in the theatre co-create the meaning of the work as they fill in its empty space. In making an effort to internalize and personalize the message of the play, "the viewer's being [becomes] more fully embedded in [its] meaning" (Pontuso 2004: 75). The meaning of an appeal-oriented play is therefore less a function of the playwright's intentions than a matter of each audience member's existential "encounter" with the play, and this struggle to render the play meaningful can often prove uncomfortable or disturbing.

I will argue that the appeal component of Havel's thought is not limited to its dramatic incarnation. My goal is, in other words, to extend the concept of the appeal from a narrow application to Havel's absurdist plays to application to his oeuvre as a whole. The chapters in this book describe, each in its own particular way, various forms of Havelian appeal, and it will gradually become clear that the meaningfulness of Havel's engagement, both literary and political, arises from its anchoring in the appeal form. The principal way in which Havel structures his engagement thus becomes a crucial component of the intended message of his intellectual project.

In pursuing an integrative approach to reading Havel that highlights the importance of form for meaning and that raises the appeal to the level of a dominant principle in Havel's thinking, I will also present specific readings of themes and texts throughout Havel's works. Specific readings will be devoted to: Havel's typographic poetry (the *Anticodes*) from the 1960s; his 1966 essay "Anatomy of the Gag"; the trilogy of so-called Vaněk plays from the 1970s, as well as the 1975 play *The Beggar's Opera*; the essays "Dear Dr. Husák" (1975), "Power of the Powerless" (1978), "Politics and Conscience" (1984), and "Thriller" (1984); selected prison letters from *Letters to Olga* (1979–83); aspects of the late-1980s book *Disturbing the Peace*; key passages from the 1993 book *Summer Meditations*; and a variety of selected texts from Havel's post-1989 presidential period. In addition to their usefulness as readings of specific themes and texts in Havel's oeuvre, these analyses are also intended to enact the holistic and integrative approach to reading Havel that I propose in the book.

The holistic framework proposed here represents a radically different approach to reading Havel than exists in current scholarship. Existing approaches to reading Havel fall, broadly speaking, into three types: *biographizing* criticism, or reading him through the events of his own fairy-tale, dissident-to-president life; *historicizing* scholarship, or reading his works in relation to the historical context in which they were written; and *intellectualizing* criticism, or scholarship that situates Havel's thinking in its intellectual and cultural context. These three modes of reading Havel share a common feature. They all focus, each in its own way, on contextualizing Havel. In doing so, each also suggests a frame for reading him, and the reading that results is strongly influenced by the frame in question. More often than not, commentary within each of these frames tends to fragment Havel's incarnations. There is little sense that the various genres that Havel engaged in represent coherent parts of a larger intellectual project or related pieces in his life's mosaic.[8]

Biographizing, historicizing, and intellectualizing are ways of relating to Havel that have, moreover, a tendency to totalize or fix our reading of him. We appreciate (or we criticize) his writings and his political engagement, but we do so from an admiring and safe distance. Contextualizing commentary promotes the notion that Havel's life and work speak to a place and a time – to one particular sociopolitical and historical -ism – that has little to do with our twenty-first century world. It is as if the full meaning of Havel's works, both literary and political, can be reduced to the historical and cultural context in which they emerged; in these approaches, then, the appeal component of Havel's project is radically circumscribed, if not entirely absent. In reading Havel only or even primarily through a contextualizing filter, something essential about his message and his legacy is lost.

Discovering or recovering what has been lost in traditional approaches to reading Havel will also be a main theme of this book. This concern takes shape in two related questions: (1) If we adopt a biographizing or historicizing framework for reading Havel, do we contextualize him in a way that closes off interpretive possibilities as well as precludes readings that could, perhaps, lead to various forms of personal catharsis? (2) Does a safely contextualized Havel belong under glass in a museum display-case of some kind, or should we understand his legacy to be a living one?

It is for the most part true that historians – of a certain figure, of a particular era, or of an idea – necessarily think and write historically. If human history is imagined as a mosaic of past, present, and future eras or moments in time (or a mosaic of events, figures, and ideas), then historical writing tends to orient itself towards describing the individual pieces or the historical tesserae that comprise the mosaic as a whole. More often than not, the focus narrows onto the historical uniqueness of the individual tessera. Historical writing privileges contextualization. This, however, is not the only way to "read" the human mosaic. We could, for instance, ask how the pieces of the mosaic relate to one another. In this regard, we might specifically ask ourselves how past eras, moments, figures, events, and ideas relate to our own age, if not also to future ages. What is the message or meaning of these historical tesserae for us living in the here and now, and what is the value of the moral lessons that we may divine from them for future generations? In this approach, we transcend the historical moment and its context. We "read" history so that it speaks indirectly to us and about us, and the experience of doing so may even change how we understand ourselves.

When we read history in this way, it becomes a kind of present-day existential encounter with the past. To read ourselves through history, we need to break the glass in the museum display-case.[9]

Let me be perfectly clear that I am not dismissing the value of an approach to Havel (or an approach to human history) that focuses on contextualization in one form or another. It is indeed valuable to research and write the biography of a major historical and intellectual figure, and an English-language biography of Havel worthy of its subject still remains to be written. It is equally valuable to situate Havel and his works in his and their historical and intellectual context. These are necessary frames for reading Havel, but they are not in and of themselves sufficient. Each of these modes seeks, in its own way, to *explain* Havel, but this does not exhaust our possibilities for *understanding* him, and it is in our privileging of the former at the expense of the latter that we lose a connection to Havel's legacy as a living one.

We lose, in other words, an active connection to the appeal component of Havel's writing, because Havel's appeal cannot be adequately addressed in scholarship that privileges *explaining* over *understanding*. What is lost or dramatically underplayed in historicizing, biographizing, and intellectualizing are the ways in which Havel speaks directly to us and asks us, in the spirit of this introduction's epigraph, to rethink who we are. The argument that I will be making in this book is that this element of Havel's story is not an incidental part of his oeuvre, but rather the central thrust of his larger project. It is in this sense, then, that the approach to reading Havel proposed here proves complementary to existing scholarship.

A distinction between *explaining* and *understanding* is a key conceptual thread in Havel's thinking that I will explore in detail in the second chapter of this book. For the moment, however, we can capture the essence of the distinction through an analogy to music. Although it is certainly possible to historicize and intellectualize a musical composition – to write about the life of a composer and/or performer, to situate the music in its own rich historical context, to provide a critique of its style in relation to musical trends, influences, and theories – none of this sufficiently accounts for how and why the music may move us so deeply. Our "encounter" with music does not consist only, and perhaps not even primarily, in how we contextualize it and rationally investigate it. In other words, the meaning of music for us transcends our ability to *explain* it. It is even possible that too strong a focus on these aspects might undermine our personal encounter with the music in much the same way that a joke requiring explanation ends up being anything but funny. The full meaning of an artistic work – or, for that matter, of a human life – is not exhausted by contextualization of one kind or another. At the risk of overstating my case, it may even be more true to say that its primary meaning lies elsewhere, that is, in how we *understand* the piece through our own personal encounter with it. Does it move us? Does it change us, if only in some small way? If so, how does it move us to change who we are in ways that may not be amenable to rational explanatory analysis?

It is a small step from music to literature, and we might then ask what the value of great literature is, and how we might structure an approach to reading that does justice to it. In posing these questions, we thereby circle back to Havel. One source of inspiration for my approach to reading Havel is Mark Edmundson's 2004 book *Why Read?*, and it is worthwhile to explore briefly Edmundson's reflections on the reading (and teaching) of literature as a way of further clarifying the argument of this book.[10] Edmundson lists what he considers to be the core questions of the humanities: "Who am I? What might I become? What is this world in which I find myself and how might it be changed for the better?" (2004: 5). He writes: "We ought to value great writing preeminently because it enjoins us to ask and helps us to answer these questions, and others like them. It helps us to create and recreate ourselves, often against harsh odds" (2004: 5). Edmundson notes a crucial difference between how we read or analyse a work of great literature and how we might let that work read and analyse us: "We need to learn not simply to read books, but to allow ourselves to be read by them" (2004: 46).

Reading great literature can be a life-transforming experience. We do not, however, always relate to reading in this way, nor do we, as Edmundson also argues, typically teach it as such. Teaching great literature involves, more often than not, a focus on various forms of contextualization. We may touch upon the literature's potential application to "real life" here and there, but the primary message that we convey to our students is that the work "really has nothing to do with the present except as an artful curiosity" (2004: 15). Rilke's exhortation cited in the epigraph to this introduction, Edmundson contends, goes unheard.

Literature that matters transcends the limits of explanatory frames, and that is why we read it, and struggle with it, in the first place (1995: 232). If the essence of humanities criticism lies in dialogue and in the fostering of a continuing conversation, then attempts at contextualization often become, perhaps in spite of the critic's best intentions, ways of ending the conversation. The British playwright Tom Stoppard has metaphorically imagined the way in which criticism tends to end conversation by noting:

> Critics draw relatively crude rectangles or increasingly complex polygons that the curving lines of art inevitably elude. Something always gets left out because none of us – including the author – ever succeeds in squaring the circle. (Stoppard 1997: 10)

Stoppard's inspiration for this metaphor is the literary critic, philosopher, and writer George Steiner, who noted that critical reaction to a work of art is often an attempt to use straight lines to approximate the inimitable roundness of the work itself (Steiner 1989: 174–5).

Even when contextualizing criticism does not wholly square the circle and end the dialogue, it still often manages to neutralize the emotive force that arises from our personal encounter with the work. Edmundson calls this neutralizing process the "philosophical disenfranchisement of art," and he specifically notes that a heavy emphasis on historicizing a work gives the impression that it is merely a "symptom of its moment" (1995: 16). In countering this approach, Edmundson advocates in favour of an Emersonian approach to reading that emphasizes use and value (1995: 131ff.). What can we do with the work? Does the work give us a better language to talk to ourselves (and others) about ourselves, to understand the world and our particular place in it in perhaps a better way than we did before our encounter with it? This is, then, the essence of what I mean in suggesting that Havel provides us with conceptual tools for reading ourselves, and the approach to reading Havel proposed in this book has been formulated within just such an Emersonian framework.

A second source of inspiration for this book derives from my own experience in teaching a monograph course on Havel's writings.[11] The course is not aimed at specialists in Czech literature (or even at students whose major academic interest is literature), but is taught as a lower-level literature-in-translation class for undergraduates from across the academic spectrum. Enrolment is usually under twenty students, and I teach the class as a discussion seminar. At the start of the semester, students in my Havel course typically know little to nothing about Havel's cultural, historical, and intellectual context, and the course focuses much less on contextualizing Havel – although we necessarily do some of that – than on fostering a dialogue with Havel's ideas.

The course is, then, a literature-in-translation course in two senses of the term "translation," which parallel the two senses of reading that I discussed earlier. In the direct sense, we read Havel's works in English translation. In the second sense, we analyse the ideas in those works by attempting to "translate" them into contemporary American terms. We cultivate a personal encounter with the writings in Edmundson's sense of Emersonian use and value. Even as we read Havel, we allow ourselves to be read by him.

In a decade of regularly teaching the Havel course, I have been astounded at the extent to which Havel's ideas have resonated with largely naive American student-readers. It is not, of course, only my students who speak to Havel's ability to resonate with naive readers or with non-specialists in Czech(oslovak) literature and history. Even a cursory search of Havel-related sites on the internet illustrates just how much his life and work have transcended the limits of his specific historical and intellectual context. Research on Havel has yet to confront the phenomenon of Havel's resonance directly. We have superb close readings of specific texts (especially the plays), and an abundance of scholarship that contextualizes Havel's life and works. There exists, however, little to no critical reflection that examines Havel's oeuvre as an integrated whole and asks how we can apply Havel's ideas to our own lives, what lessons we may take from reading him, and how his writings and experiences may change our sense of who we are as individuals and how we understand our relationship to the larger world in which we live. Alongside critical commentary focusing on contextualizing Havel, there ought to be room for reading him in a way that takes the phenomenon of his resonance – that is, Havel's appeal – seriously.[12]

Towards the end of one semester, a student in my Havel course summed up her reaction to reading him across many of his genres by saying that he offers "a kind of manifesto of truth and responsibility to his readers" and "a set of tools for understanding our own world." My goal in this book is to expand upon this student's insight by detailing those tools that make up Havel's "manifesto" and the strategies that he offers to us as we navigate the often-turbulent waters of human identity in the modern age. In doing so, I hope to refrain from squaring the circle – from *explaining* Havel – and to try instead to suggest a way to *understand* the elusive roundness of his art. Only in this way can we take seriously the appeal component of Havel's project, and only by reading him from this perspective will we be able to do justice to his living legacy.

Outline of the chapters

The first chapter is devoted to the power of the mosaic image, which I explore through an attempt to make sense of Havel's remarkable cross-genre productivity. I start with a sketch of the nine literary genres (and the one non-literary "genre" of politics) that Havel engaged in during his lifetime. In mapping out the landscape of Havel's intellectual career, I situate each genre chronologically and describe each in terms of both content and form. I show that Havel was a remarkably consistent thinker across genres and time periods. He was concerned with the same general themes throughout his life, and he explored these themes using more or less the same small set of rhetorical or formal strategies. Throughout both his career as a writer and his time as president, Havel constantly emphasized the interrelationship of form and meaning: the medium is inseparable from the message; *how* and *what* go necessarily hand-in-hand. This tight interconnection of strategy and theme – of form and content – becomes clear only when the genres are juxtaposed with one another. At the end of this chapter on the interconnectedness of Havel's various "faces," I propose a general principle for reading Havel, the mosaic principle, that advocates in favour of cross-genre integration. I suggest not only that this principle is applicable to how we read Havel, but also that, in Havel's treatment, it becomes a strategy for making sense of modern human identity. It is, in other words, also a conceptual tool for how we might read ourselves.

For much of his life, Havel was known primarily as a playwright, and the second chapter emerges from the first by focusing on the theatrical genre and, more particularly, on Havel's own dramatic style. How might we read Havel's plays as enactments of truth? Havel was not a pedantic playwright, but his plays do teach us something about truth in a way that other genres (e.g., essays) cannot. In Havel's dramatic style, truth is reconceptualized as more of a process (a *how*) than a datum (a *what*). To make sense of the "weirdness" of Havel's plays requires us to rethink our own expectations about what truth is and how it can be meaningfully enacted through theatrical performance. Serving as an overarching framework for considering these matters will be the conceptual opposition between *explaining* and *understanding*, which represent two contrasting modes of discourse, thinking, and relating to the world. The *explaining / understanding* opposition runs throughout Havel's works and is a conceptual tool that can help us make sense not only of Havel's broader intellectual and political project but also, like the mosaic principle, of ourselves.

The main subject of chapter 3 is Havel's re-evaluation of the Cold War dichotomy between East and West, (post-)totalitarianism and (post-) democracy, communism and capitalism. I argue that Havel's reframing of East and West is not an incidental thread in the overall weave of Havel's project. If this particular thread is pulled out in an attempt to isolate it, then the fabric as a whole begins to unravel. Havel's restructuring of the Cold War dichotomy emerges from a larger hypothesis, an overarching hypothesis in the background of Havel's thinking that has received little attention in the critical literature. Throughout his life, Havel believed that the twentieth century marked the start of a transitional era in human history. The Modern Age (*novověk* in Czech), an age dominated by implicit faith in rationality and science, was ending. Humanity entered a period in which we began a search for a new self-understanding. Within the framework of this overarching hypothesis, East and West are understood not to be in opposition to one another, but are seen instead as two sides of the same modern coin. It follows from this that the scope of relevance of Havel's project – his literary endeavours as well as his political ones – comes to include West as well as East. Havel's intent in highlighting these related hypotheses is to explore the existential crisis that confronts the modern world. In light of this, it would not be an exaggeration to suggest that how we visualize the history of the Cold War has a direct bearing not only on our approach to reading Havel but also on the possibility of letting ourselves by read by him.

The focus of the book's final chapter is on Havel's language with specific regard to four keywords that act as intellectual touchstones around which many of his larger ideas coalesce and take shape: *(ne)klid* ("[un] rest, [dis]quiet"), *domov* ("home"), *svědomí* ("conscience"), and *duchovní* ("spiritual"). A paradox associated with Havel lies in that fact that he wrote in Czech but achieved world renown, and gained a global audience, through the translation of his writings into English (and other languages). A question that follows from this paradox is whether Havel's keywords carry the same burden of meaning in English as they do in the original Czech. This question becomes especially important when we consider that many English-language commentators on Havel have not been speakers or readers of Czech: they have read Havel only in translation. I subject these Havelian keywords to comparative ethnolinguistic analysis to discover what aspects of meaning might be lost in translation. I propose that Havel's treatment of these words enacts his larger concern with the need for "metaphysical reconstruction" in the face of humanity's spiritual crisis at the end of the twentieth and the beginning of the twenty-first centuries.

In the book's conclusion, I examine in more depth the centrality to Havel's project of the appeal. *Výzva*, the Czech word for "appeal," is itself a keyword in Havel's writings as well as a problematic term with regard to its translation into English. I reflect on possible paths for its translation, and these reflections serve as a vehicle both for summing up the main themes of my approach to reading Havel and also for considering his legacy.

I have no desire to play, with regard to Havel, the role of the Speaker in Eugène Ionesco's absurdist play *The Chairs*, and my approach to reading Havel therefore also takes, in its own way, the form of an appeal.[13] My goal in this book is not, in other words, to offer a totalizing account of the meaning of Havel's project. The framework that I offer is decidedly more focused on the *how* than on the *what*; its focus is on understanding Havel, not explaining him, which is, as I have already suggested, an entirely fitting framework for its subject. While I do propose readings of specific Havelian themes and texts along the way, one of my primary ambitions in writing this book has been to craft an appeal to its readers to return to Havel's writings with my understanding-oriented approach in mind. For those who have already read Havel across different genres, it is an appeal to reevaluate what you may think you already know about him. For those who have yet to read Havel to any great extent, it is an appeal to read him more widely. For both kinds of readers, this book also serves as a challenge to be open to being changed by Havel's words, which is the main reason that we read great literature in the first place.

1 The "restlessness of transcendence": Havel's Genres

Life rebels against all uniformity and leveling; its aim is not sameness, but variety, the restlessness of transcendence, the adventure of novelty and rebellion against the status quo...

– Václav Havel, *Dear Dr. Husák*[1]

Writing a book (an email, a letter, a memo) necessarily involves a search for the right form. The way we write strongly influences the message or meaning of that which is being written. Indeed, it often happens that we do not begin to understand what we mean until we try to put our ideas into words. We give shape to our thoughts by realizing them in a definite form, which is one reason that writing often proves useful as a kind of therapy. In artistic writing, a poet may choose to pound a poem into various forms representing contrasting voices for an image or idea, and a crucial stage in the writing process then turns on selecting the most appropriate vehicle (the best poetic form or voice) for that particular poem. *How* we write is in large measure *what* we write; style and technique shape the content.

This should not be surprising. We should think not about the relationship between form and content in writing, but rather about the primacy of form in more physical domains. In a physical domain, the *how* and the *what* are even more closely intertwined. For example, the meaning or message of a shot in tennis – where the ball ultimately lands and what it does upon landing – is almost entirely a function of how the ball has been struck, the technique of the stroke, the force and spin given to the ball as the shot is made. Form and meaning (to the extent that a forehand or backhand has a meaning) become physically inseparable.

The technical, formal outlines of the stroke shape the force, trajectory, and torque of the shot.

The same relationship generally holds true in less-physical, more conceptual instances in that the form or style of our expression places constraints on what can be expressed. The "medium is the message" is another way of suggesting that form becomes inevitably embedded in meaning, and the dramatic changes in communication technology over the last few decades illustrate this point as well. We should consider, however, that while selecting a certain medium does impose a constraint on the message by forcing us to think or act within pre-established formal grooves, like water from a downpour flowing into and along an existing riverbed, this interrelationship between medium and message can also be a creative or generative process. As a poet reflecting on her craft has said, "Patterned form comes from the premise that form is the *outside* of experience. My premise is that form is the *inside* of the experience, as a skeleton, not a cage" (Peacock 2010: 193).

Reflecting on the relationship between form (the *how*) and content (the *what* or the *who*) may seem a more appropriate starting point for an entirely different book, but it is actually not a bad way at all to begin a book on Václav Havel, particularly when the first chapter of that book presents an overview of Havel's literary genres. After all, one of the main characteristics of his writing was an obsession with formal experimentation, which can be taken as indicative of a particularly heightened awareness on his part of the form/meaning nexus. As Carol Rocamora has put it, "Havel clearly loved to 'exercise' his ideas in a variety of genres" (Rocamora 2004: 141). This chapter is devoted to a tour of those genres, literary and non-literary, in which Havel engaged throughout his life. In presenting an overview of these various "faces" or incarnations of Havel's persona as a politically engaged writer and intellectual, I will suggest why it proves productive to inquire into what was and still may be the significance of his cross-genre experimental "exercising."

If form is simultaneously cage and skeleton, and if Havel felt a need to express his ideas across a variety of forms (to vocalize, like a poet, more or less the same ideas in different voices), then this raises a series of questions that we will need to keep in the back of our minds, and that I will return to in due course, as we undertake a tour of Havel's genres. What, generally speaking, might Havel's cross-genre productivity tell us about him as a thinker? How might the cross-genre nature of Havel's creativity impinge upon how we read him? To what extent do we see continuity among the various genres in which he engaged? Is there a formal and thematic coherence in Havel's genres that spans 1989, the fateful year of the Velvet Revolution that brought an end to the communist regime in Czechoslovakia and propelled Havel from intellectual "dissidence" to the presidency, or should we posit a disjuncture between Havel's pre- and post-1989 faces? Would it be productive to view Havel's political engagement as a kind of non-literary, real-life genre that is continuous with, or an outgrowth of, his literary genres? And last but certainly not least, to what extent do Havel's own "exercises" in genre-crossing, read non-incidentally as an enactment of a restless search for meaning in the modern world, also suggest a way of reading ourselves?

Havel's cross-genre profile as an engaged intellectual represents the continuation of a Czech tradition. It has been noted that Havel himself once wrote a critical study of another Czech cultural figure with the same genre-crossing tendencies (Pistorius 1997). Josef Čapek was a painter, prose writer, playwright, stage designer, art critic and theorist; like Havel, he was also a leading actor in the cultural life of his time. In his study, Havel argued that Čapek had been, somewhat paradoxically, undervalued as an artist precisely because of his artistic versatility (*mnohostrannost*). Given the great variety of his endeavours, critics had proven incapable of a holistic evaluation of his artistic personality. Havel wrote: "'Josef Čapek is more than just the creator of this or that painting or the author of this or that book; his oeuvre is more than just the sum total of his individual works …'"; in Havel's estimation, Čapek's individual works acquire their true meaning [*pravý obsah*] only through their relation to one another (cited in Pistorius 1997: 105–6).[2]

If we, along with Putna (2012: 120), take Havel's reflections on Čapek as equally applicable to his own artistic persona, then the question of Havel's cross-genre productivity goes to the heart of how we read and understand him. If we fragment Havel's oeuvre by treating his various faces or incarnations more or less separately from one another, then we fail to do justice to his remarkable *mnohostrannost*. Despite occasional nods to the contrary, the fragmentation of Havel's genres has, in fact, been the approach undertaken by the great majority of Havel's English-language commentators during his lifetime: Havel-the-playwright is considered separately from Havel-the-essayist, and Havel-the politician is typically put in a different category altogether.[3] There is an obvious thematic continuity throughout his work; the theme of human identity in the modern world, as Havel himself noted on more than one occasion, looms quite large in each and every one of Havel's various styles. Even given this continuity of content, commentators on Havel have tended to reduce Havel's general versatility to a mere formal and personal "exercise" when they take it into account at all.

In providing an overview of Havel's genre-versatility, I argue for an integrative, cross-genre reading. This integrative focus is captured in my proposal for reading Havel's works in terms of a mosaic. The individual units or tesserae that comprise a mosaic are equivalent to the various genres in which Havel exercised his ideas. Just as a mosaic is more than the sum of its parts, the "true meaning" of Havel's intellectual and political project emerges from the relationship among the parts. The *what* behind Havel's project cannot be understood without reference to the *how*. The very process of genre-crossing, the fabric of Havel's mosaic, is therefore central not only to Havel's own engagement but also to how we should read him. His exercising of the same ideas in various forms becomes, in this view, a technical expression (a rhetorical and intellectual enactment) of a certain existential attitude that could be characterized, citing Havel himself, as a kind of *neklid transcendence* ("restlessness of transcendence"). The import of this attitude can then be extended not only to how we read and understand Havel, but also to how Havel suggests that we might read and understand ourselves.

A tour of the genres

Havel engaged in, arguably, nine written genres during his lifetime. A few of these genres are well known to non-Czech audiences or non-specialists in Havel, others much less so. Many of Havel's works, particularly those from his early period, are inaccessible to readers who come to him without knowledge of Czech. These tesserae in Havel's mosaic have consequently been ignored by commentators on Havel in the non-Czech-speaking scholarly community.

My goal is to provide a map of the landscape of Havel's genres.[4] I will situate them chronologically and then briefly describe each. My aim is not encyclopedic; my account is limited to those features of each genre that prove relevant to my larger argument. My ambition is not to present a totalizing account of Havel's genres, and one of my hopes is that this sketch may serve as inspiration for readers to explore more of Havel's artistic versatility on their own, since I cannot do full justice to it here. After the genre overview, I will discuss commonalities in form and emphasis across the genres, as well as argue that Havel's case represents not merely an example of cross-genre productivity but rather an almost obsessive need to redefine or rework the conventions of nearly all the genres in which he engaged. As we will see, then, Havel's restlessness of transcendence is rhetorically manifested in more than one way.

1. Literary-critical essays and art criticism (1950s and 1960s)

These are the least known of Havel's writings outside, perhaps, of the Czech context. The great majority of these works have not been translated into English, and they are, as a result, rarely cited by English-language scholars writing on Havel. They are a diverse collection of more than 80 essays that make up most of the third volume in Havel's seven-volume collected works (Havel 1999), and from the mid- to late 1960s they begin to overlap with or segue into the category of philosophical and dissident essays to be discussed below. These writings cover a small range of interrelated themes: philosophical reflections on art theory and modern art, criticism of both poetry and prose and the authors of both (this includes Czech writing as well as translations into Czech), theatre and film criticism. The study of Josef Čapek's artistic versatility that was mentioned above falls here, and we might arguably include here also the beginnings of Havel's writerly political engagement in the form of two speeches presented to members of the Czech Writers' Union (the first in 1965 and the second in 1967). In some measure, these early works represent stages in Havel's juvenilia, although at the same time it must be admitted that a good many of the essays from this period come across as intellectually sophisticated pieces regardless of how old he may have been when he wrote them.

If we think of Havel's literary mosaic as a multistorey building, then we might situate the early literary and art criticism on the ground floor. This is where the building as a whole begins, and these writings also constitute the foundation of the larger structure. Even those texts that fall squarely into Havel's juvenilia function to ground his later intellectual project. Indeed, Putna has noted that the motifs and themes from this early period of Havel's literary engagement anticipate his more mature writings. In commenting on several texts from the early 1950s, he writes: "To be sure, these are not the works of a great thinker but the texts of a seventeen-year-old adolescent. In them, however, one finds ideas and motifs that attest to Havel's continuity with inherited traditions – they also anticipate ideas and motifs characterizing his 'more mature' period" (2010: 360; see also Putna 2012: chapter 3). In agreeing with Putna and given a mosaic approach to Havel's genre-crossing, I would make the same point more forcefully: considered as a whole, Havel's early writings are foundational to his later development. They anticipate key themes and motifs that he will pursue relentlessly in his later writings, and they reveal Havel as a process-oriented and philosophically pragmatic thinker, one of whose main concerns (and this will prove true of Havel across all of his incarnations) was with the relationship between form and meaning.

Perhaps the best-known essay that can be counted as thematically and stylistically representative of this early genre is the 1966 "Anatomy of the Gag" (Havel 1984 and 1999, 3: 589–609), which was written late in this period of Havel's writing and after he had already begun writing in other genres. The essay was translated into English by Michal Schonberg in 1984, and appeared in the journal *Modern Drama*. In this essay, Havel is concerned with the larger philosophical and artistic meaning of the cinematic gag, a device deployed by Charlie Chaplin and Buster Keaton, among others, and one that is strongly associated with an early era in the history of cinema.

As might be expected given the title, Havel uses the essay to explore a definition of the cinematic gag, and he cites examples from Chaplin's and Keaton's films as the ground for his theoretical analysis. One of the examples that Havel cites comes from Chaplin's 1931 film *City Lights*, in which a Statue to Prosperity is being unveiled at a public gathering of wealthy and politically powerful personages:

> The unveiling of the Statue of Prosperity is not a gag. Chaplin asleep [hidden under the draping over the statue] is not a gag. But when upon the unveiling of the Statue of Prosperity it is suddenly discovered that the beggar Chaplin is sleeping in the arms of the statue – that is indeed a gag. (Havel 1984: 13)

Another example that Havel cites in developing his definition is the opening scene of the 1936 film *Modern Times*, in which Chaplin is hard at work on a factory production line but causes the whole line to be shut down so that he can brush a bug away from his face and scratch his ear:

> When Chaplin works at the assembly line – that is not yet a gag, although it might be funny. When Chaplin scratches his ear, that is not a gag either, although it is undoubtedly funny. But when Chaplin, while working at the assembly line, scratches his ear, and the parts which he is supposed to

> assemble elude him, thus causing a calamity all along the line – that is a gag. (Havel 1984: 13)

At the core of Havel's definition of a gag, then, and as both of these examples illustrate, is a two-stage process. The first stage, which Havel calls the stage of a "dehumanizing automatism" (the predictable ritual of the statue's formal unveiling, a factory worker mechanically engaged in line production), is juxtaposed with a second stage representing a "humanizing automatism" (a homeless man finding a comfortable and concealed place to sleep, the human need to brush away bugs and scratch an itch).

Havel draws on the theory of Russian Formalism in suggesting that this two-stage process underlying the gag represents a special kind of defamiliarization, a literary-critical term which is, in the original Russian, *ostranenie* (literally, "making things strange" or "enstrangement") and in Havel's Czech *ozvláštnění* (making things *zvláštní* or "strange in a provocative and interesting way").[5] Formalists like Viktor Shklovsky, who coined the term in his 1925 essay "Art as Device" (Shklovsky 1990), understood *ostranenie* as a poetic device that forces us to see the familiar in an unfamiliar or strange way. Poetic defamiliarization undermines a conventional or "automatized" understanding of a given phenomenon and compels us, through a new and provocative formal presentation of the seemingly ordinary, to reconsider or reframe the meaning of things. Shklovsky explained this artistic process in terms of an opposition between merely "recognizing" (automatized perception) and actively "seeing" (artistic perception that leads to heightened awareness): "And so, in order to return sensation to our limbs, in order to make us feel objects, to make a stone feel stony, man has been given the tool of art. The purpose of art, then, is to lead us to knowledge of a thing through the organ of sight instead of recognition. By 'enstranging' objects and complicating form, the device of art makes perception long and 'laborious'" (Shklovsky 1990: 6).

In Havel's analysis, the cinematic gag, along with the defamiliarizing process that underlies it, ceases to be a mere artistic "device" and is transformed into an artistic agent with the potential to exert unexpected influence over the minds of its audience. The title of the essay "Anatomy of ..." strongly hints at this, as only living entities – not textual "devices" – can be literally said to have "anatomy." Havel, not incidentally, also uses this title template in a number of later texts in which he analyses various conceptual phenomena (e.g., "reticence" and "hate") as if they were living entities. Indeed, it would be fair to say that many of his later writings not explicitly entitled "Anatomy of ..." could have justifiably been given that title. Endowing seemingly inert ideas and phenomena with potentially agentive status is an intellectual strategy characteristic of much of Havel's thinking and writing.

In teaching this challenging essay in my monograph course on Havel over the years, more than a few students, who often identify themselves as committed fans of Charlie Chaplin, have reacted to it with disappointment. They complain that Havel has ruined the humour of the gag for us by analysing it to death. Why can't, asked one student plaintively, a gag just be a gag? It is true that there are few things less funny than a joke that has to be explained (an observation to which we will return in chapter 2), and Havel is not content merely with appreciating the humour of the gag. His definition is more ambitious and aims to lay bare the full conceptual mechanism behind the gag. It is, in other words, oriented towards dissecting the form of the gag (the *how* of the gag) in order to render its meaning more clearly.

It is the meaning of the gag – the philosophical or existential implications of it as a popular cinematic "device" – that Havel is primarily concerned with in the later stages of the essay. Why did artists like Chaplin and Keaton structure their films around gags? If the artistic form known as the gag has a meaning or message for the viewer, then what is it? Here Havel dramatically breaks down the wall between art and everyday life by claiming that the gag represents a form of modern-day aesthetic and existential catharsis. Chaplin and Keaton make us laugh at our modern-day predicaments, and the humanizing automatism that triggers the defamiliarization in the gag's second stage, which is the prompt for our laughter, seemingly becomes an agent of spiritual cleansing.

As in all of his essays from this early genre, Havel is not engaging in art criticism for art criticism's sake. His criticism always speaks to a broader concern with the role that art plays in the formation of human identity and in society. In his analysis, Havel transverses and transcends the formal boundaries of the artistic space. The gag is not just a "device" used in film, but a cultural phenomenon with a meaning in its own right that has implications for how we understand who we are in the modern world. In this approach to art and to life, seemingly incidental or self-contained phenomena have meanings that may and should prompt deeper philosophical reflection. The gag is not just a gag, and our laughter at it is tinged with a sense of unease and discomfort. Put another way, Havel adopts a philosophically pragmatic approach to the meaning of art. It is not understood as an ideational superstructure or decorative overlay on the material structure of individual and social consciousness, but rather it is an active agent in the formation of that consciousness. This is a theme to which Havel returns in several of his major philosophical essays from the 1970s, and it is a theme that I will return to in later chapters of this book.

"Anatomy of the Gag" is a sophisticated example of Havel's early genre of art criticism. Few of the essays from this period offer the same depth of intellectual engagement with their subjects. The essay is, however, representative of the genre as a whole in its concern with the form/meaning nexus and, more particularly, through its focus on the procedural and relational dimensions of meaning: the *how* of meaning, Havel seems to be suggesting, may well be its very essence. Also representative is Havel's understanding of defamiliarization less as a poetic device than as a general conceptual strategy that might be deemed crucial for critical thinking; we remain satisfied with conventionally automatized "recognition" of things to our own detriment. In interpreting defamiliarization in this way, Havel arguably goes beyond Russian Formalist notions of art, profiling not so much art's uniqueness but rather its coherence with more prosaic modes of relating to the world and of being in the world. In these senses, then, "Anatomy of the Gag" exemplifies well one genre in Havel's larger literary mosaic, a genre that ought to be viewed as foundational for Havel's later development.

2. Visual poetry of the *Anticodes* (1960s)

The *Anticodes* are Havel's playful typographic poems that were originally written to amuse himself and friends (Rocamora 2004: 57). He typed hundreds of them, and they comprise roughly half of the first volume of Havel's collected works (Havel 1999).[6] Havel was first exposed to typogrammy by Jiří Kolář, a renowned Czech poet and visual artist who was an early and influential mentor. This visual poetry, in which form is inseparable from meaning, represented "an attempt to release poetry from its traditional form" that was also "consistent with a search for new forms" (Rocamora 2004: 57). Given that Havel had them published as a separate book in 1993 (Havel 1993a), Peter Steiner has argued that he likely did not consider these playful poetic efforts "episodic or unimportant" (Steiner 2008: 209).

The *Anticodes* mix highbrow themes with playful form, and partly in response to this juxtaposition, a critic has referred to them as "engaged articulations of absurdity" (Hiršal 1993: 5). The predominant themes found in these poems are language and meaning; the discourse of politics; human individuality, dignity, and freedom; modern-day bureaucratization (and quantification) of human identity; poetics; philosophical commentary; cultural and historical commentary; human relationships and routines; social automatisms; life and death; war and peace; love and truth. The overall thematic thrust of the *Anticodes* could be summed up with the question: who are we in the modern world and how do we understand (or, perhaps more often, misunderstand) ourselves? To a great extent, then, these typographic poems represent a strategic application of the themes and strategies in Havel's literary-critical essays, even if the formal presentation of these themes and strategies is completely different. At the same time, and in certain key respects, the *Anticodes* prefigure Havel's plays. Many of the poems exhibit latent dramatic tension, and they might easily be reworked as visual performances or mini-dramas.[7]

The *Anticodes* are easier to exemplify than to describe in words, and the examples below, which are followed by some discussion, give a feel for this genre.[8]

In example (1), Havel negates the idea of progress by the circular organization of the slogan "Forward" (Steiner 2008: 216). The poem is applicable in obvious ways to the realm of political discourse (and not only in Havel's Czechoslovakia), but at the same time its application is not limited to this particular domain. The second and third examples are taken from a series of anticodes that Havel wrote using the word *člověk*

Figure 1. "VPŘED" / "FORWARD"

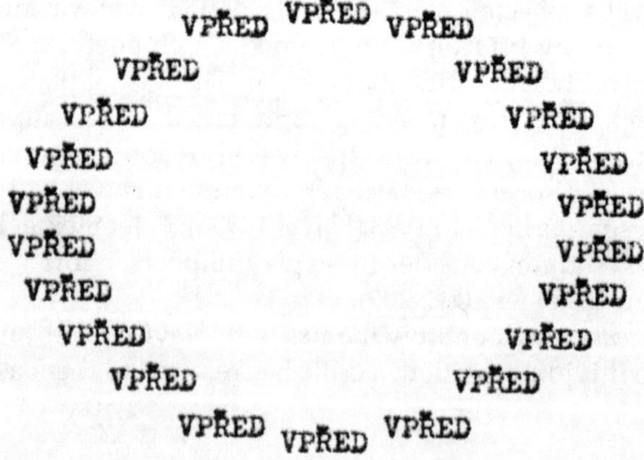

Figure 2. "Člověk" / "Person/Man"

```
9%864901§58300%%750%011§32§64%93019%42095§3%20§164§
107%6§4329%01923%4329%0110§548%648§§328901O%7681003
%8536§0        0%547%§0198%54301789%54320§§98%76%0§861
9§4103%   č   16943%0§90754319%1109%§53877308%05219%4
816%%52        08659%0§§43219§432%98016%72214 44%21006§
3%2%%0§045743%0§7397%07540110%90764l§§1%8532        17
10§3379%29           89%0065§§63%32015§42399913405    k  2%
%48763%0§1    l    §0158%75308%68%139%7§53201883        55
6§699%3015           80%970%§10%8497%01144 8%§§3%23901%0§2
6649%01§§57%52182           77%3890§%§876%4300%9219%4321%
5%947890§23611 79%    o    2122§69%08§6419%32%08884J§710
037§097%654320%81          1%3200§§%5337%011069%5320§§1%
§750%950§9870%3210 19§4829%0110%80§432%2938§8539%015
01773%63§§5%87063%08441 9§3%2%%§420%860%1§7413200005%
79%§4209 1%§589%270%70§730%53003 2%1%1§1173 90%4661 9§3
88%§05290%478235§           %40%830%169%§2§693%60%200§111
1759%32100§7§§481    v    1689%32%0§45           9%32§0%7418§
3321 0%5§4%%321§60           054987%5301%    ě    01%84%0§%752
%1159%6320%§85§432 10%754§39%329916            1§5390893-§§
010188§3%8530%§655§3.%590%1%489%0§0963%210%70%42301
7%640§%9321%654%21007 59%3%%§5201§§5289359%743%019§2%
49%201%6430§§42109%759%3§0%7520%110%%59%3§7%4760105
```

Figure 3. "Člověk" / "Person/Man"

lověk
lověk
lověk
lověk
lověk
lověk
lověk
lověk
lověk
lověk
lověk
lověk
lověk
lověk
lověk

("person" or "man" in a generic sense). In the first of these here, Havel decomposes the word into its constituent letters and graphs (or cages) them in a chart of numbers and mathematical symbols. Individual identity is iconically fragmented, bureaucratized, quantified, and fixed. To what domain of human experience does this anticode refer? Is it applicable only to East, or to the modern world in its entirety? The poem itself, and this is true of the great majority of the anticodes, does not definitively answer these questions.

Example (3) depicts the word *člověk* with its lead letter *č-* lopped off. The fragment *-lověk* is repeated a number of times in a perfectly organized column, and a collection of the severed head letters is caged off in a box below the column. There is any number of valid interpretations of what this visual poem might mean, and the most obvious would suggest figurative death by the severing of the head letter. We might also notice the way in which the individual *-lověk* fragments are lined up so neatly one below the other, and we might inwardly shudder at the rigidity and predictably of the alignment. Are they representative of mindless individuals conforming to an imposed structure and arrangement, or perhaps decapitated bodies lined up in a neat row? In reaction to this anticode, a student once noticed the odd fact that there are far more "heads" (*č-*) than "bodies" (*-lověk*), and suggested that each of the "people" in the poem is not reducible to one "head," to one persona, to one definitive interpretation. Regardless of how exactly we read the *how* of this anticode in an attempt to tease out its message, it must be admitted that human identity is more fluid than the arrangement presented in the typogram. Identity is much less like a geometrical formula and much more like a story or a more traditionally lyrical poem.

On the whole, the anticodes are purposefully ambiguous with regard to their scope of interpretation. The vast majority of them are schematic in nature. They suggest a template that has multiple applications to real-world experience, both personal and social, and their meaning is therefore not reducible to a single "correct" interpretation. This schematic quality renders ambiguous both their specific domain of application (does "FORWARD" apply only to political discourse?) and their range of applicability (is Havel thinking only in terms of one sociopolitical -ism?). In the latter case, it would be a clear mistake to limit interpretation of the anticodes to Havel's sociopolitical context, and in this respect we see a certain thematic continuity with the literary-critical essays and art criticism.

With the *Anticodes*, Havel invites us to reflect directly upon the form/content relationship as well as the way in which modern "forms" or ways of being influence how we understand our own selves. In much the same way that Chaplin defamiliarizes through his use of the gag, Havel triggers a playful re-evaluation of phenomena that may seem familiar to us, a reconsideration of things that we have become accustomed to recognizing but that we do not actually see. These poems embody the maxim that the medium is the message, and many do so through an imagistic representation that is maximally memorable or one that can, in the words of a critic, easily "dig into the mind" (Hiršal 1993: 8).

A student once wrote that Havel's anticodes are like ingenious doodles that function as secret messages. They say something profound without actually *saying* it. Havel appeals directly to his readers/viewers to make sense of the poems for themselves, to figure out what in fact is being "said." Sometimes this appeal culminates in a confrontation with the poem's form that we then rebel against (can identity really be quantified and graphed?), while at other times the form acts as more of a skeleton than a cage, generative of any number of possible messages and meanings.

3. Plays (1960s through the 1980s and 2007)

For much of Havel's adult life prior to 1989, it would have been natural to assume that his main professional incarnation was that of a playwright and that his primary genre was the theatre.[9] His pre-1989 role as a "dissident" was not, in other words, his most important day-job. Given Havel's engagement in later genres, the plays have now taken on the status of yet another genre in which he "exercised" his ideas or another piece in Havel's larger literary-professional mosaic. The dramatic genre, however, must be understood as key to Havel's thinking and his oeuvre for a number of good reasons, one being that theatre was the first genre to bring Havel widespread critical fame and worldwide attention. In chapter 2 of this book, I will offer a more substantive account of why theatrical performance ought still to be considered a key Havelian genre.

Havel wrote nearly twenty plays of varying lengths during his lifetime, beginning in the early 1960s when he began working in Prague's small-form Divadlo Na zábradlí (Theatre on the Balustrade).[10] Havel's early theatrical mentor at this theatre was the renowned Czech writer, playwright, actor, director, and teacher Ivan Vyskočil, and Havel also worked at the Balustrade in close cooperation with the Czech theatre director and critic Jan Grossman. By the end of the 1960s, Havel had established himself as a leading playwright not only in the Czech context, but increasingly abroad as well.

He introduced to the Czech scene a special kind of absurdist drama. Not long after the Soviet invasion of Czechoslovakia in August 1968, and because of Havel's public engagement in the cultural events of Prague Spring that led up to the invasion, the post-1968 "normalized" regime banned publication of Havel's writing and performances of his plays.[11] Havel nonetheless continued writing plays throughout the 1970s and 1980s, some of which were performed in private or semi-public settings, and many of which were circulated in print through samizdat networks.[12] Many of these plays also became popular abroad and were staged in European and American theatres.[13] During his presidency (1989–2003), Havel wrote no plays, and his final dramatic work, *Leaving* (Havel 2012b, 2007b), was written several years after the end of his last term as Czech president.

Thematically, the plays overlap significantly with Havel's concerns in the first two genres. The overarching theme in the plays is human identity in the modern age, or the relationship between *how* we live and *who* we are. Related sub-themes include language and, in particular, language as a source of miscommunication and obfuscation, the discourse of politics and dissidentism, the bureaucratization of human being, alienation and the undermining of human dignity, and reflections on truth and responsibility. Havel's plays have something else in common with both his literary-critical writings and his visual poetry: they do not promote art for art's sake, but rather make use of aesthetic strategies in order to engage with the world. Havel understood theatre as a "seismograph" of its time and place, which is one way of metaphorically imagining the larger cultural role that he assigned to it: "Theatre is always a sensitive seismograph of an era, perhaps the most sensitive one there is; it's a sponge that quickly soaks up important ingredients in the atmosphere around it. These movements in the theatre have to be seen against the wider background of the general climate of those times" (Havel 1991b: 51 and Havel 1990: 47).

Much has been written about Havel as a playwright, and I will not attempt even a succinct summary of the critical literature here. I will instead first characterize the theatrical genre as Havel himself understood it, and then illustrate these reflections by describing a trilogy of Havel's plays from the mid-1970s. My description of the three one-act Vaněk plays may also give readers unfamiliar with Havel's drama a feel for him as a playwright, and we will revisit the character (or rather the dramatic principle) that is Vaněk at later stages in the book.

In the first place, and somewhat surprisingly, Havel stated on several different occasions that he became involved in the theatre partly through a bit of luck and not because he was absolutely destined to do so. He was not, in other words, a born playwright or theatre-person (*divadelník*), but the theatrical form did seem to provide him with a vehicle appropriate to his needs. If another genre had offered him more fertile ground for the cultivation of his ideas, he would have taken it up (Havel 1983a and 1983b: letter 102). In other words, he chose the dramatic genre as his main calling in the 1960s as a by-product of his keen awareness of the form/meaning nexus and as a result of his search for a form (a *how*) that could most fully represent the meaning (the *what*) that he wished to convey. The meaning of Havel's plays is inseparable from the form in which they are created.

This was true for Havel-the-playwright on both a small and large scale. At the level of a single play, the structural devices that typically come to mind when one thinks of Havel's dramatic style – repetition and circularity, highly rational and often mechanistic patterning of dialogue, tightly choreographed entrances and exits and gestures (both verbal and physical) – are not deployed as ends in themselves, but rather as means that are appropriate for exploring the larger questions that his plays are designed to raise (Havel 1983a and 1983b: letter 80). On a much larger scale, Havel understood the potential of theatre as a genre in ambitious terms: the dramatic form makes it possible to "uncover something like the structure of Being [*odkrýt cosi jako kostru bytí*], to display in vivid terms its internal weave, its hidden structure, and its real articulation" (Havel 2007a: 277 and Havel 2006: 193). A play is like "a concentrated picture of the structure of Being, the world, life" in which "everything is related to everything else" (Havel 2007a: 286 and Havel 2006: 199). For Havel, to attend a performance of one of his plays ideally meant to participate in an "existential encounter" that would certainly prove to be entertaining but at the same time also *zneklidňující* ("disturbing"). His plays were not intended to instruct pedantically or provide easy answers as much as they were designed to provoke the audience to introspection and self-reflection (Havel 1983a and 1983b: letters 103 and 104).

Although his plays have been characterized as absurdist in the tradition of French theatre of the absurd (Esslin 2001), Havel himself was not particularly interested in this formulation (Havel 1983a and 1983b:

letter 116). He did, however, recognize a shared agenda with French absurdism, and acknowledged that the absurdist form facilitated the kind of discussion that he wanted to have: "Absurd theatre, in its particular (and easily describable) way, makes the fundamental questions of the modern human dimension of Being its themes" (Havel 1991b: 54 and Havel 1990: 50). A more fitting characterization of Havel's style would be theatre of the appeal (*divadlo apelu*), which Ivan Vyskočil defined as theatre that aims "to engage the intellect and the imagination of the spectator in order to force him to agree, disagree, compare, and view a subject matter from various angles" (cited in Trensky 1978: 105).[14] *Divadlo apelu* is absurdist theatre of a special kind, in which the formal techniques associated with absurdism are deployed to provoke the audience by creating within the play an empty space for audience self-reflection. In Jan Grossman's definition, theatre of the appeal is a performance that "calls into being [*vyzývá*] – and leaves open – a space for conjecture and inference" (Grossman 1999: 90). We could think of the "empty space" (Grossman 1999: 71) of an appeal-oriented play as functionally equivalent to the ambiguous schematicity of an anticode, because both the audience of the play and the readers/viewers of the visual poem co-create the meaning of the work. In the former case, the theatre audience attempts to account for the empty space of the play while, in the latter case, the readers of an anticode reify, to their own satisfaction, the schematic template of the poem.

In other words, the appeal-oriented form of the works forces the audience to exert an effort to make sense of them. Without this effort on the part of the audience, the plays will suffer from a certain meaninglessness. In making an effort to internalize and personalize the message of the play, "the viewer's being [becomes] more fully embedded in [its] meaning" (Pontuso 2004: 75). The meaning of an appeal-oriented play is therefore less a function of the playwright's intentions and authority than a matter of each audience member's "encounter" with the play, and it is this struggle to render the play meaningful that can often prove uncomfortable or disturbing. Like the cinematic gag, then, the formal elements of theatre of the appeal have "anatomy." They energetically act upon the audience, provoking and inviting – or at least providing the necessary space for – some kind of personal catharsis with extrapersonal implications. As we will see, the notion of the "appeal," which is an essential component of Havel's dramatic style, resonates in his thinking well beyond the plays. It will ultimately become for him an intellectual and spiritual touchstone, a concept that he returns to again and again throughout the rest of his life.

A sketch of several of Havel's plays, the trilogy of one-act Vaněk plays from the mid-1970s, will help concretize the above abstract description of his dramatic style. The Vaněk plays – *Audience* and *Unveiling*, both written in 1975, and *Protest*, written in 1978 – are among the most performed and perhaps also the "most accessible" (Pontuso 2004: 76) of Havel's works.[15] In these plays, we observe the same main character, a writer and an intellectual "dissident" by the name of Ferdinand Vaněk, in three different situations. In the first play, Vaněk has found work in a brewery and is called to the brewery foreman's office for a conversation while, in the second, he is at a dinner party with a married couple, Michael and Vera, who are apparently old friends; the third play finds Vaněk in conversation with another writer and intellectual whose name, Staněk, rhymes with his own. Each play has absurdist elements (e.g., in *Audience* the foreman drinks more than a dozen beers over the course of the single act) that contribute to the entertainment value of the play, but each also represents a kernel of a believable or real situation that is then absurdly defamiliarized in one way or another.[16]

Thematically, the Vaněk plays are concerned with how private individuals confront, or fail to confront, the society or the "system" in which they live. More particularly, the plays demonstrate the extent to which the "system" itself has become embodied (and is enacted) in the identities of the individuals as well as in their everyday relationships to other people and the world. In *Audience*, the foreman has been asked by "them" (and we assume that "they" in the Czechoslovakia of the time are the secret police) to write reports on the dissident Vaněk's life. The foreman's dilemma lies in the fact that he has no idea what to say in these reports, and the foreman's situation is further complicated by the fact that one of "them" is a friend who has done him certain favours in the past. To resolve the situation, the foreman offers Vaněk a cushy job in exchange for Vaněk's promise to write the reports and to therefore inform, paradoxically and absurdly, on himself. In *Unveiling*, Michael and Vera are "the perfect post-modern couple" (Pontuso 2004: 86) who just want to lead "normal" lives, but to do so requires that they selfishly retreat into their own private world and actively avoid civic or political engagement. As the play progresses, it becomes increasingly clear that they are desperate for Vaněk to approve of how they have chosen to live and of their choice to adapt to the "system" in this way. In *Protest*, Staněk, who has made a decision to cooperate with the regime in order to be able to continue his career, has asked Vaněk to begin circulating a letter of protest that urges the release from prison of a recently arrested musician. Staněk has a personal interest in seeking the release: the musician is the boyfriend of Staněk's daughter, who has just found out that she is pregnant. It turns out that Vaněk has already written just such a letter and has begun collecting signatures for it. Staněk's dilemma then becomes whether to add his own name to the letter and thereby risk his professional career.

As a whole, then, the trilogy explores the responses of three groups (workers, the middle class, intellectuals) to the "system" (Pontuso 2004: 91). The foreman, Michael and Vera, and Staněk all have good reasons for adapting to the demands of the system, that is, for not coming into direct conflict with it in the way that Vaněk has. Each play problematizes the characters' relationship with Vaněk, and one way in which Havel appeals to the audience is by suggesting that there is no correct way to resolve the dilemmas that the characters face. A natural instinct may be to take Vaněk's side as the underdog, especially since he is often bullied by his interlocutors in the plays, most particularly by Michael and Vera. Audience identification with or sympathy for Vaněk may in fact be emphasized by the director in the physical staging of the play. Vaněk may have his back slightly, but not fully, towards the audience, which invites us to inhabit his character. By the end of each play, however, we realize, along with Vaněk himself, that it is a mistake – an unfair and uncharitable oversimplification –not to feel for, and not to come to inhabit the skin of, the foreman, Michael and Vera, and Staněk as well.

All three of these plays have "speaking" titles, and our struggle with what each title means parallels the discomfort that we feel in trying to determine where our sympathies should lie. Is the word "audience" chosen to evoke a meeting between a powerful personage and a subject or subordinate (e.g., an "audience" with the pope) and, if so, who in the play, Vaněk or the foreman, occupies which position in the hierarchy? Or does the title refer to the theatre-goers who watch the play, or perhaps even more generally to any observers of a public spectacle?[17] *Protest* suggests similar ambiguity: Is it a concrete reference to the petition that Vaněk is circulating, or to the philosophical and existential stance taken by Vaněk but not, ultimately, by Staněk? What does the very word mean, and what role, the title further seems to suggest, does protest play in the formation of our identity? The original Czech title of *Unveiling – Vernisáž* from French *vernissage* – presents the most complicated and interesting case of a speaking title. The French term derives from a verb meaning "to varnish, to cover with a veneer," and a French *vernissage*, as well as a Czech *vernisáž*, refers to the pre-opening of an art exhibition, which can be public but is more often than not a private affair for valued (and moneyed) clients of the gallery.[18] The tradition was for artists to apply a varnish to their paintings before they were put up for sale at the gallery, perhaps to make them more superficially attractive (glossy and shiny) to potential buyers. Havel's title highlights the performative aspects of the married couple's "exhibition" for Vaněk, a performance that goes well beyond the ostensible purpose for the dinner party, which is to preview or "unveil" the new decorative scheme in the couple's apartment. More philosophically, the title may prompt us to ask ourselves to what degree, in what situations, and to what ends we "varnish" and perform aspects of our lives for other people. To what extent are we perhaps more like Michael and Vera than we are like Vaněk?

All three of the one-acts also have surprise endings that defy our expectations and prompt a sudden re-evaluation of what has taken place in the play. Each ending makes us question what we thought we already knew and understood, namely, that Vaněk is the "hero" of each play. Havel instead turns that intuition upside-down at the last possible moment and leaves us wondering how to make sense of each unexpected twist. In *Audience*, the play seems to end when the foreman, falling asleep from having consumed too much beer, lays his head on his desk in mid-conversation and begins to snore loudly. Vaněk stands up, leaves the foreman's office, and closes the door – only to return unexpectedly, knock on the door, and re-enter the office after the foreman wakes up and tells him to come in. This "ending" models the start of the play, and it thus begins anew. While the circularity of this ending is itself an unexpected development, there is yet a further twist in that Vaněk also adopts the foreman's perspective: upon re-entering, he rapidly downs a beer and uncharacteristically delivers one of the foreman's recurring lines.[19] *Unveiling* has a similar ending. Vaněk quietly begins to back out of the apartment, but Vera becomes hysterical at the idea that Vaněk might leave. He sits back down, just as quietly, and the play begins again. The audience is left to ponder why Vaněk came back. Finally, in *Protest*, the surprise twist lies in the fact that the musician ends up being released not because of Vaněk's open-letter petition (a form of protest that publicly confronts the regime in an attempt to change the system itself) but rather through Staněk's quiet back-door efforts (a form of protest from within that leaves the system unchanged).

Havel crafts a theatrical appeal through the way in which he problematizes our relationship to the characters, as well as through his use of speaking titles and surprise endings, but the crux of the appeal orientation of the Vaněk trilogy centers around Vaněk himself. Vaněk is a new kind of dramatic character, or rather he is not a character in any traditional sense, but instead a kind of dramatic principle. Havel himself offered the following *ex post facto* explanation of Vaněk:

> Vaněk is really not so much a concrete person as something of a "dramatic principle": he does not do or say much, but his mere existence, his presence on stage, and his being what he is make his environment expose itself one way or another. He does not admonish anyone in particular; indeed, he demands hardly anything of anyone. And in spite of this, his environment perceives him as an invocation somehow to declare and justify itself. He is, then, a kind of "key," opening certain – always different – vistas onto the world in which he lives; a kind of catalyst, a gleam, if you will, in whose light we view a landscape. And although without it we should scarcely be able to see anything at all, it is not the gleam that matters but the landscape. The Vaněk plays, therefore, are essentially not plays about Vaněk, but plays about the world as it reveals itself when confronted with Vaněk. (Havel 1987: 239)

A scholar of Havel's drama has suggested, in a related metaphor, that Vaněk "somehow takes on the quality of the quiet eye of a hurricane where things remain how they were and where there is shelter from the roaring and shifting turmoil all around" (Goetz-Stankiewicz 1987: xxi). As we might expect given these assessments, to play Vaněk on stage presents a peculiar challenge to the actor. His function as a "light on a landscape" combined with his eye-of-the-storm calmness (in Czech, his *klid*) demand a subtle and restrained performance, a kind of non-active acting or even non-acting (*neherectví*).[20]

There are other ways to understand Vaněk as a dramatic principle oriented towards appeal. We could note that the character acts as an empty space in the play onto which we in the audience, along with Vaněk's interlocutors on stage, project our own emotions and insecurities. We directly embed ourselves, through Vaněk, in the performance. We could also understand the Vaněk character as a witness to the troubled lives of his fellow characters whose words (as they "unveil" or reveal their consciences and souls to him) then function as a kind of moral testimony. The plays appeal to us by inviting us both to witness along with Vaněk as well as to take the part of the characters who unburden themselves to him. We in the audience are simultaneously both members of the jury and co-defendants in the case.

Havel's aim in the Vaněk trilogy, as in all of his plays, is not to provide definitive answers to the questions that he raises; Havel is not a pedantic playwright, and his plays are not, in this regard, morally instructive. The whole thrust of theatre of the appeal as instantiated in these plays is to suggest that perhaps definitive answers do not exist to life questions that cut to the core of our rich and nuanced human experience in and of the world. To make the plays meaningful, members of the audience themselves need to struggle with the questions, and part of that struggle revolves around trying to make sense of Vaněk. We struggle to define who Vaněk is and to understand what motivates him (why does he come back?) and how he might have been changed by each situation, and the struggle to understand Vaněk also becomes a struggle to understand ourselves.

A focus on the appeal orientation of Havel's dramatic style raises the question of Havel's audience. To whom exactly is Havel appealing? If a dramatic work is in fact a "sensitive seismograph" of an era, then what are the spatial and temporal boundaries of the era to which Havel's plays respond? I would not be the first to suggest that his dramatic work, like work from the first two genres, represents an appeal on two levels. At what we could call the domestic level, they can be read as quasi-absurdist case studies of life in a "normalized" Czechoslovakia. We understand Vaněk as a dissident intellectual in that society, and the trilogy as a whole can be said to defamiliarize or problematize certain conventional ideas about political power and the role of dissidents under the "normalized" system. It would be a mistake, however, to limit the appeal component of Havel's plays only to this domestic level. In the Vaněk trilogy, Havel clearly took pains to open up possibilities for interpretation beyond his own sociopolitical context, and the success of the plays abroad, in the West as well as the East, suggests that the appeal functions on multiple levels. As Pontuso claims (2004: 79), the Vaněk plays are about both "normalized" Czechoslovakia as well as the general crisis of human identity in the postmodern era, a crisis that includes both East and West. In relation to the latter, we might speak then of an existential level of interpretation that encompasses the domestic level but is not limited to it. This multi-level approach to interpretation holds true for Havel's other dramatic works as well, and it is a notion to which I will return at later stages in this book.

4. Philosophical and "dissident" essays (1960s through the 1980s)

The word "essay" derives from French *essai*, which is itself derived from the French verb *essayer*, meaning "to try or attempt." An essay is, in broad terms, an "attempt" to put thoughts into words. There is no precise formal definition of an essay. Formally and thematically, essays include a broad range of writing, and Havel's pre-1989 essays are no exception to this. In more specific terms, we might say that an essay typically represents, in formal terms, prose that is characterized by systematic and propositional discourse on a topic. An essayist is usually expected to rely on evidence and data, rational argumentation, and logical analysis to present certain views or beliefs.

In reflecting on the formal aspects of the essay as a genre, Aldous Huxley, the great English writer who was himself a master essayist, wrote that the essay is "a literary device for saying almost everything about almost anything" (Huxley 1959). He defined a "three-poled frame of reference" for classifying kinds of essays. The first kind of "pole" is the personal or autobiographical essay, in which the author uses "fragments of reflective autobiography" to view the world "through the keyhole of anecdote and description." The second pole is the objective or factual essay, in which the authors "do not speak of themselves but turn their attention outward to some literary or scientific or political theme"; the writer of this kind of essay lays forth relevant data for consideration, draws general conclusions from that data, and then passes judgment. Huxley's final pole is the "abstract-universal" essay that is maximally impersonal and devoid of facts; as such, it is an essay that deals in generalizations and inhabits "the world of high abstractions." Huxley himself considered that "the most richly satisfying essays are those which make the best use not of one, not of two, but of all the three worlds in which it is possible for the essay to exist," and the author of this kind of essay moves "from the personal to the universal, from the abstract back to the concrete, from the objective datum to the inner experience" in the course of the work. Although Havel's main "pole" may well be Huxley's second, he often wrote hybrid essays of the personal-autobiographical and objective-factual variety, and he was not averse to writing the "most satisfying" kind of essay, one that mixes in a good dose of the abstract-universal.

Along with the plays, the pre-1989 essays are, generally speaking, the best known of Havel's writings. He wrote over one hundred of these mostly philosophical and so-called dissident works, and they comprise the majority of volume four of his collected writings (Havel 1999). Many essays from this period remain untranslated, although all of the major (and longer) philosophical-political essays – "Dear Dr. Husák" (1975), "Power of the Powerless" (1978), "Politics and Conscience" (1984), and "Anatomy of a Reticence" (1985) – appear alongside a dozen or so shorter pieces in the English-language collection

Open Letters (Havel 1991a). Havel wrote essays of varying lengths and varying styles or tones – classic examples of rational discourse and logical argumentation side by side with works that read more like lyrical meditations.

Thematically, his concerns are similar to what is present in the other genres, and the essays from this period represent, in this respect, a thematic broadening of the literary-critical essays of the 1950s and 1960s. Although it would be difficult to place the essays into neatly defined thematic/stylistic categories, we could fairly say that most would fall into one or more of the following kinds: philosophical essays in the classical sense, open letters, intellectual polemics, literary-critical pieces, commentary to his own plays, responses to interview questionnaires, reports on dissident activities or events related to these, and reflections on the deaths of cultural figures. Perhaps it would be helpful to think of the essay genre as a mosaic in its own right within the larger mosaic of Havel's literary engagement. The mixed stylistic and thematic variations on the essay form are the tiles that compose, in their interconnectedness, the larger whole of the genre.[21]

Although much could be said with regard to Havel's essays considered as a genre, I will limit my discussion here to three specific points. I will then illustrate this genre by sketching the main features of what is arguably Havel's most famous and most influential essay, "Power of the Powerless."

The first point to be made with regard to the essays, or at least the major philosophical-political essays like "Power of the Powerless" and "Politics and Conscience," is that they could, on one level, be read as *explications du texte* for his plays (Rocamora 2004: 376). Havel arguably worked his ideas out first in dramatic form (and perhaps also in literary-critical and visually poetic form), and then gave a more logically systematic and rational expression to them in the essays. As I will argue in the next chapter, the plays privilege an *understanding* orientation to Havel's ideas while the essays are for the most part concerned with *explaining* them. The opposition between *understanding* and *explaining* is a thread that runs through Havel's thinking as well as a distinction that will prove to be crucial for making sense of his genre-crossing.

A second point concerns the political nature of the essays from this period, many of which are traditionally and primarily read in this light. Havel is, in other words, taken to be an anti-totalitarian dissident, a leading figure in a nascent political opposition, who keenly analyses the structure of power under a totalitarian regime. While not entirely untrue, this generalization ignores the fact that Havel defamiliarizes and undermines conventional understandings of "politics" and "political power" even in the most overtly political essays. He seeks, that is, to subvert the very notion of "politicalness." It also ignores the fact that by no means all of the essays from this period are political, even in the traditional sense of the word. An example of the latter is the 1984 essay "Thriller," which takes its title from Michael Jackson's song and video of the same name. "Thriller" is a lyrical meditation on modern human identity that opens with a collage of modern news reports. Havel uses this informational collage as ground for a meditation on what humanity in the Age of Science and Rationality – the age of hyperrational framing of identity, a great age in human history that is approaching its end – has lost, and the consequences for us of that loss. In "Thriller," Havel is concerned with the wider sociohistorical and cultural frame against which modern politics, in both East and West, plays out, but the same could also be said of his treatment of politics and power in the more traditionally "political" essays like "Power of the Powerless" and "Politics and Conscience." In the essays as a whole, Havel portrays political (and economic) matters as phenomena secondary to cultural and moral questions. The latter define the frame against which the former acquire their concrete form and meaning.

A final point concerns Havel's own apparent discomfort with the "cage" of the essay form. Although he was indisputably a master of this form, there are indications in the essays that he may have felt constrained by the rational, systematic exposition that is characteristic of the form. Some of the most rhetorically deft and memorable moments in the essays embody strategies that can be read as attempts to transcend (or escape) a prototypically essayistic mode. Bolton, for example, has noted Havel's extensive use of "multiplier metaphors" in his "Dear Dr. Husák" – culture as a nutrient necessary for society's survival and also as a mesh net that ravels when a single thread is cut – that bolster Havel's broader argument that "cultural factors exert a deep, invisible, and lasting influence" on the development of society (Bolton 2012: 111). Indeed, systematic use of metaphor, a rhetorical figure often considered to be more typical of poetry than prose, is one way that Havel tries to free himself from the propositional cage of the essay. Another strategy found in many of the essays and that also runs counter to the prototypically essayistic discourse is Havel's tendency to embody his main line of argument in a central image. It is this image that we often vividly recall after we have read the essay; like the visual form of the anticodes, images from the essays easily "dig into our minds." Thus, in "Politics and Conscience," we have the image of the factory smokestack with which Havel opens the essay, and "Power of the Powerless" features the image of the greengrocer's propagandistic sign ("Workers of the world, unite!") that he hangs in the window of his shop.

"Power of the Powerless" is, in fact, this genre's masterwork, and it is worthwhile to spend some time considering how these general reflections on Havel-the-essayist concretely play out in it.[22] The longest of Havel's essays, this densely argued piece is Havel's "attempt" to put into words his ideas on power and "dissent" in the Central/Eastern European sociopolitical context of the 1970s. He begins the essay by parodying the opening words of the preamble to the Communist Manifesto: "A specter is haunting Eastern Europe: the specter of what in the West is called 'dissent'."[23] Havel puts the word "dissent" (along with "dissident") in scare quotes throughout the whole original Czech version of the essay because he is sceptical of the phenomenon in its commonplace definition, and the rest of the essay will prove to be "nothing if not a sustained polemic with the word and the idea" (Bolton 2012: 2).[24] At the outset of the essay, then, Havel sets the stage for problematizing dissent, and the reader is uncertain if Havel is intending to write a manifesto of dissent or if he will show us that dissent as it is usually understood is really "just a phantom" (Bolton 2012: 1). Or perhaps Havel intends to do both of those things at once – he intends, that is, to exorcise the "specter" of dissent as it is conventionally understood by writing a manifesto of the phenomenon that simultaneously presents and represents a radical reconsideration of its meaning.

In this regard, Havel might have called this essay "Anatomy of Power and Dissent," given that the similarities to his approach to the cinematic gag in "Anatomy of the Gag" are palpable. In the latter, Havel showed us that the gag is not, in fact, just a gag; he defamiliarized this cinematic "device" by demonstrating how its form comes to serve as a vehicle for modern-day existential catharsis. In "Power of the Powerless," he analyses the mechanics of "dissent" and "power" in Central/Eastern Europe of the time, reframing their conventional definitions in order to reveal their true meanings. In other words, "dissent" and "power" in Central/Eastern Europe of the 1970s are not what they appear to be at first glance. Their true meanings transcend conventional definitions, and only by becoming aware of them can Central/Eastern Europeans be set on a path towards personal, and perhaps ultimately political, catharsis.[25]

Havel's master essay is a product of its era, and it can and should be read in terms of its historical, intellectual, and cultural context. We could, for example, understand it as Havel's manifesto for the newly formed "dissident" organization Charter 77 and thereby read it as Havel's contribution to the debates surrounding the meaning of Charter (and its future development) that were taking place at the time among Havel's friends and "dissident" colleagues. Bolton 2012 has a thorough discussion of the essay along these lines, and he concludes in part that "Power of the Powerless" emerged from a crisis that Charter was undergoing not long after its founding (Bolton 2012: 225ff.).

The essay can also be read in relation to Havel's other texts both before and after it, and to a limited extent Bolton does this, suggesting that "Power of the Powerless" acts as a follow-up to Havel's 1975 open letter to Gustáv Husák, the "normalizing" leader of Czechoslovakia. By 1978, Bolton argues, Havel had shifted his attention from the rulers to the ruled and began looking at how power functions differently under this kind of system (Bolton 2012: 220). In reading "Power of the Powerless" as a piece in Havel's larger literary project, we may wish to go farther than merely situating it in the genre-mosaic of Havel's essays. Contextualizing it in relation to the other essays is a necessary but not sufficient step, and it could also be read more broadly through a cross-genre framework as one work in one genre of Havel's larger intellectual mosaic.

In fact, I have already touched upon one of Havel's conclusions about power in this essay – that power in a "normalized" system is diffused, that people "are brought to participate in their own subjection" (Bolton 2012: 220) – in my earlier discussion of the Vaněk trilogy. In this respect, we can read "Power of the Powerless" as a kind of *explication du texte* for the Vaněk plays (if not also for Havel's other plays written before and during 1978). The essay is a more or less rational, sentence-by-sentence exposition of the ideas that Havel had begun working out in dramatic form. If we are to do justice to Havel's ideas about "dissent" and "power" in "Power of the Powerless," however, we would need to consider not only its relationship to the plays but also to other genres as well, and some of the genres that help illuminate this essay appear neither prior to nor simultaneous with but rather after 1978.

Although we can and should read the essay in its cultural context, it is also frequently read, in Bolton's words, "as a timeless and definitive statement of dissident morality" (2012: 220). I would prefer to state this in somewhat different terms: just as we saw for Havel's plays and anticodes, there are, in "Power of the Powerless," two levels or layers to Havel's analysis. The first analytic layer relates to the domestic level of mid-1970s "normalized" Czechoslovakia, while the second concerns what we might call the broad existential level of a modern world in civilizational and moral crisis. In terms of the first, the essay provides an in-depth analysis of how power actually works in the totalitarian system, and its function differs so much from our expectations of totalitarian power that Havel feels obliged to coin a new term, "post-totalitarian," to describe the system.[26] Havel's reconsideration of the power structure of the "post-totalitarian" system leads to its own localized catharsis at the domestic level. If true power does not reside in the hands of a few individuals at the top of the supposed power hierarchy (i.e., Husák and his fellow communist bureaucrats) and if the people in large measure are the system, then the "powerless" become, at least potentially, powerful. No less important, however, is the second analytical layer embedded in the essay, and here Havel suggest that the post-totalitarian system represents one form or aspect of a whole world in moral or existential crisis. The system is best understood, in this respect, as part and parcel of a "global attack on man." In this analytic layer, Havel's argument is not tied exclusively to one cultural or historical context or to one particular modern-day -ism.

If we read "Power of the Powerless" only in terms of the domestic level of analysis, we limit its scope of application – its appeal – to the post-totalitarian East, and we engage in a closed reading of the text. If we read it at the broader existential level, then we place East and West on a continuum and open the possibilities for interpretation. Havel clearly believed that these two levels of analysis were related, and that the second necessarily encompasses the first, although this is a point that many commentators on Havel have failed to appreciate fully.

Before summing up this brief sketch of Havel's master essay, I will mention one more of its characteristics that will be examined in greater detail in the next chapter. It seems clear from a careful study of the essay's style and from reflecting on Havel's cross-genre experimentation with form that Havel did not feel entirely comfortable within the propositional cage of the essay structure, and that he sought ways to escape this cage in the course of his writing. Not all meanings, and often not the most crucial ones, can be expressed through rational argumentation, sentence by logical sentence. On one hand, and as discussed earlier, one way to transcend the propositional mode is through metaphor, and Havel makes ample use of this strategy in "Power of the Powerless," most particularly in his treatment of the key role played by ideology in the post-totalitarian power structure.[27] A second way is to embody the essence of a logical argument in an image, and the central image in the essay is, as I previously noted, the greengrocer's sign, which is symbolic of the greengrocer's larger story.[28] The story of the greengrocer – who, at our first introduction to his character, does not even bother to think about whether to hang the propagandistic sign in his shop window but who later, as Havel develops the story, comes to realize that signs like his both represent and reinforce ideological conformity and adaptation to the system – becomes Havel's shorthand for his whole argument. The image of the sign and the story that goes along with it provide avenues to escape the rational confines of the essay form because images and narratives appeal to human experience and meaning-making in a way that transcends the level of the logical and abstract proposition. Havel does not merely bring real-world evidence to bear on the development of his argument, but he embeds that evidence in a narrative vehicle that allows readers to inhabit the argument. Readers come to make sense of Havel's argument through the experience of seeing signs like the greengrocer's in shop windows, as well as by adopting the perspective of the grocer as he gradually becomes aware of the "power" of his sign. Through these formal strategies, then, Havel's appeal in the essay is neither wholly logical nor abstractly theoretical; the message of "Power of the Powerless" also takes on experiential and lyrical shapes.

Escaping the essay's propositional cage shifts the emphasis in the argument from an *explaining* to an *understanding* mode, and this point brings us back to Huxley's three "poles" of essayistic prose. Havel's use of metaphor as well as his use of a central image and a story, all of which "dig into our mind" and linger there after we have finished reading the essay, could be considered elements of Huxley's first "pole," not in the sense that they represent personalized fragments of reflective autobiography, but rather as forms of personal appeal to general human experience. Given that Huxley's other two poles – the objective/factual and the abstract/universal – are also amply represented in the essay, we have to conclude that "Power of the Powerless" falls squarely into Huxley's "most richly satisfying" kind of essay, a powerful mixing of all three essayistic modes, and this may also be one of the reasons that it counts as Havel's masterwork in this genre.

5. Letters from prison (1979–1983)

In the aftermath of the regime's aggressive reaction to the establishment of Charter 77, Havel and other "dissidents" active in the organization were put on trial and sentenced – their guilt was pre-determined – to prison terms of varying lengths. Havel was sentenced to a term of four and a half years, and was imprisoned from May 1979 until February 1983.[29] His literary production during this time consisted of hundreds of short letters written ostensibly to his first wife, Olga. The selected letters were edited and eventually published in one volume titled *Letters to Olga*.[30] These letters from prison are the first genre in Havel's larger literary mosaic represented by only one work. This genre, like the philosophical essays, may also be taken as a mosaic unto itself. The letters are thematically and coherently intertwined, building upon each other; the meaning of the collection is greater than the mere sum of the individual letters.

These letters, though ostensibly written to Olga, were meant for a broader audience. Havel was permitted to write only to members of his immediate family, but eventually he began to use the letters to Olga to conduct a philosophical dialogue with other dissident intellectuals, chief among whom were his brother, Ivan Havel, a computer scientist and theorist; the biologist and philosopher Zdeněk Neubauer; and the philosopher and educator Radim Palouš.[31] As Havel noted in the introduction to Balabán (2009: 11), the letters were his only opportunities to be creative while in prison, and they had a deep spiritual meaning for him as such. In another context, Havel emphasized their personal value:

> By the very nature of things in prison, you're forced to think a little more about yourself, about the meaning of your actions, about questions pertaining to your own Being. The letters gave me a chance to develop a new way of looking at myself and examining my attitudes to the fundamental things in life. I became more and more wrapped up in them: I came to depend on them to the point where almost nothing else mattered. All week long I would develop my essays in my head – at work, during exercises, before going to bed – and then on Saturday, amid constant interruption, I would write them out in a kind of wild trance. (Havel 1990: 131 and 1991b: 150)

Putna describes Havel's letters from prison as "one of the most important works in his creative trajectory" (2012: 181).[32]

As part of an intellectual dialogue, the letters contain a core philosophical vocabulary: Being, faith, conscience, responsibility, spirituality, and the absolute horizon.[33] They also contain Havel's most extensive meditations on the nature and meaning of theatre, or rather of his own particular dramatic style. Havel's philosophizing in the letters is neither systematic nor scholarly. He is purposefully ecumenical and non-sectarian in a conscious effort to "open up" his ideas to everyone (Balabán 2009: 22). It is a kind of "private philosophising" (Neubauer 2010: 78) grounded in Havel's personal experience, but at the same time transcendent of his particular circumstances (Neubauer 2010: 64). The letters focus on understanding the dilemma of life in the modern age, with the prison experience as an especially concentrated variant of the human existential dilemma. The value of the letters as philosophical discourse may well lie in their informal or non-professional presentation: "And so we should listen very carefully indeed: that to which we are witnesses, is a true *ortus philosophiae – an emergence*, the sprouting of love towards wisdom" (Neubauer 2010: 66). Pontuso notes that Havel's philosophizing is not philosophy in the traditional sense: it is "confused, inconsistent, and poetic rather than rigorous and rational" (Pontuso 2004: 15); his search for himself is nevertheless "surely more penetrating than any 'systematic' philosophic text" (2004: 16).

We might conclude, then, that these letters are philosophical, but in a special Havelian sense, which could be said of nearly all of Havel's writings. Ivan Dubský has described Havel's presidential speeches as philosophical not in the sense of philosophy for philosophy's sake (not as a technical exercise in philosophical theorizing), but instead as expressions of practical concern for how to care for the world; in this respect, the speeches represent philosophy as "a caring look around oneself" (Dubský 1997: 10). The letters – despite their often odd stylings, a measure required to guarantee passage by the prison censor – read similarly.

The letters are not, of course, all philosophy all the time. Many begin and end with prosaic references to, among other things, Havel's physical health and comfort while in prison, with requests to Olga to write him more often, with advice to Olga on legal questions and practical matters related to her everyday life, with lists of items to include in prison care-packages, with detailed plans for and then reactions to Olga and Ivan's regular prison visits. The letters themselves are in this regard a decided mix of styles, reminiscent of those frequent moments in Havel's plays where petty pre-occupations – like eating, brushing one's hair, going out for groceries, smoking – always and inexplicably seem to interrupt ostensibly much grander goings-on. Mundane references to everyday human existence provide a frame for the philosophical meditations and give them value as personally meaningful expressions of

Havel's spiritual search. In this regard, Marketa Goetz-Stankiewicz has characterized the prison letters in the following way:

> Havel's *Letters to Olga* ... are eloquent documents of a thinking man's attempt to formulate and to try to answer – under very difficult physical and spiritual circumstances – some of the most private but also the most general questions of human life, from the salutary results of tea-drinking to the nature of human identity; from the quality of a man's moods to the essence of truth. (Goetz-Stankiewicz 1987: xvi)

Havel himself noted that it is a tribute to the editor of the prison letters that these non-philosophical references were left in: "The existential background of [the philosophical] meditations is uncovered and made present, and it may well give the book life and drama, if it can have such qualities at all" (Havel 1991b: 152 and 1990: 133). The mundanely human level of our lives, Havel seems to be suggesting, is inseparable from our philosophical and spiritual nature. The meaning or message of human existence cannot be divorced from the medium of day-to-day human concerns.

While in prison, Havel wrote neither plays nor essays because he was limited by circumstance to letters, but his imprisonment was both preceded and followed by extremely productive periods in these first two genres. This raises a question: if the essays function as *explications du texte* for the plays, then how might we characterize the prison letters in regard to the plays and the essays, if not also in relation to Havel's other writings? In one sense, the letters can be read as miniature philosophical essays unto themselves. Given that many of them were written as Havel's voice in a philosophical conversation with other intellectuals outside of prison, they are also mini-essays that have, somewhat like plays, a performative side. Read as a thematically coherent collection of mini-essays, the letters would count as prime examples, in an admittedly different form than "Power of the Powerless," of Huxley's "most richly satisfying" hybrid category. Havel mixes elements of autobiography with objective analysis, and the combination of these two modes then leads to abstract and philosophical reflection on human being in the world.

More broadly speaking, however, the prison letters function as *explications du texte* for all the rest of Havel's writings. They are a metaversion of his other texts, the underlying code for the more concrete and context- or genre-specific manifestations of his thinking. We might, for example, try to understand the relationship between the essays and the plays by using the meditations in *Letters to Olga* as a mediating frame or grid, a philosophically schematized reduction of Havel's understanding of human identity.

In the prison letters, Havel once again makes frequent use of central images that encapsulate the dominant messages in this or that letter. Some of the more memorable images from these works include the tree outside the prison wall, the view of which provides Havel with a privileged poetic moment and a momentary feeling of total harmony with the universe (Havel 1983a and 1983b: letter 91); the TV weatherwoman, caught unaware when the sound cuts off during a national broadcast, who must stand, helplessly and wordlessly, in front of the national television audience and for whose embarrassment Havel experiences a pained empathy (letters 130ff.); the junkyard left by astronauts who landed on the Moon and threw their trash outside their rocket's landing site (letter 134); and the empty night tram that triggers an introspective reflection on whether one should pay the fare or not (letter 137).

6. Collaborative autobiography (1986/1990)

The second of the genres to be represented by only one work, *Disturbing the Peace*, appeared in samizdat in 1986 and was also officially published in Czechoslovakia in 1990, soon after Havel became president, as a way of introducing him to the larger public. The original Czech title of the book is the playful *Dálkový výslech* (literally, a long-distance interrogation), and the title chosen for the translation makes reference to a criminal code that the regime used as a legal excuse to arrest and prosecute many "dissidents."[34]

The book was written in collaboration with Czech journalist and writer Karel Hvížďala. In the mid-1980s, Hvížďala, who was living in exile in Bonn, sent Havel written questions on a wide range of topics – personal, political, polemical, artistic, philosophical – and Havel answered these questions, or many of them, to produce a book-length collaborative interview that reads more like an autobiographical essay and intellectual/spiritual (self-)portrait. Themes from Havel's essays, his letters from prison, and his plays are taken up in a different form: the tone is purposefully conversational, even though the questions were submitted and answered by Havel in written form. In this respect, *Disturbing the Peace* represents an entirely new kind of autobiography, that is, a hybrid autobiography that contains elements of interview, essay, and performance. As a kind of partly collaborative collage, its form is echoed in Havel's later political memoir, *Prosím stručně* (*To the Castle and Back*), which also has a playful title in the original Czech (to be discussed shortly).

7. Personal political testament (1991)

Summer Meditations (a literal translation of the original Czech *Letní přemítání*) is another of Havel's one-work genres.[35] The book was written in the summer of 1991, and Havel frames his writing of it as necessary given that he was about to declare his candidacy for another presidential term. In this regard, it could be read as the product of a political campaign or rather the branding strategy for just such a campaign. It is simultaneously a meditation on the transformation of the Czechoslovak state after the 1989 Velvet Revolution as well as a platform for Havel's thoughts on the politics and policies of that ongoing process. Indeed, Havel's primary concern in *Summer Meditations* is process, and he makes a strong case for the inseparability of political means from political ends. This is also one of the focal moments of the book's strong and purposeful appeal: clearly one of the aims of Havel's personal political testament is to galvanize direct public support for his vision.

In Huxley's terms, the book is a long essay, or set of interrelated essays, that represents a mix of the first and second poles with only a few moments characteristic of the third "abstract-universal" pole. This makes it somewhat atypical for Havel's writing in that it is focused on technical policy measures, and its scope of application is therefore mostly limited to the Czechoslovak "domestic" context. At the same time, as Putna notes (2012: 283), Havel's musings on sociohistorical specifics are framed by a broader philosophical and ethical vision. While Havel explicitly tries to discuss policy in a brief manner (i.e., *stručně*, a term which resurfaces in Havel's later memoir), he makes it clear that policy specifics must be contextualized against the much larger background of human moral responsibility in the modern world. Political considerations in Czechoslovakia cannot be truly and adequately assessed at the domestic level alone. *Summer Meditations* is thus a political testament, but a somewhat non-traditional one in that it frames policy in terms of values and vision. Havel endows politics with a moral or spiritual component that both encompasses and transcends the specifics of the Czechoslovak context.

If we try to read *Summer Meditations* beyond the domestic level, we might say that Havel offers, as he does with the anticodes, a template or schematic vision not just for the future of the Czechoslovak state, but also perhaps for the future of humanity as a whole. This universally applicable moral and political vision is facilitated at certain moments in the text by the semantic ambiguity of the Czech word *země*, which can refer to either an individual state (i.e., the "country" or "state" of Czechoslovakia) or the whole "planet" (the future of politics on the Earth as a whole). Havel also makes use of a central (metaphorical) image in the book, which he introduces early in the text to prefigure his discussion of the Czechoslovak "national principle." I am referring here to his well-known discussion of the circles or layers of "home" (in Czech, *kruhy* or *vrstvy domova*) that provide a frame for human identity in the modern world (1993b: 30ff. and Havel 1999, 6: 409ff.). In Putna's words, Havel depicts *domov* as an "existential experience" (Putna 2012: 283), and it is a concept at the core of Havel's personal philosophical vocabulary, a key thread in the fabric of Havel's thinking, and one to which we will return in later chapters.

8. Presidential speeches and other texts (1990–2003)

In late 1989, with the culmination of the Velvet Revolution, Havel went from persecuted "dissident" to his country's president. Havel's election, by a cadre of communist deputies in the Czechoslovak parliament who could see the writing on the wall, was the result of negotiations between the regime and leading members of the Civic Forum, an umbrella organization of anti-regime activists.[36] Havel remained president of Czechoslovakia until his resignation in 1992 over objections to the political process leading to the 1993 dissolution of Czechoslovakia into its two component states, an event also known as the Velvet Divorce.[37] Havel then served as president of the newly created Czech Republic for another 10 years, from 1993 until 2003.

As president, Havel wrote all of his more than 300 speeches. These speeches, along with written texts that appeared in the news media, as well as interviews, comprise his post-1989 presidential texts.[38] The speeches can be divided into those given in and for a domestic setting and those given abroad as Havel travelled the world to speak before parliaments, at universities, and to other gatherings where he was an honoured guest. Generally speaking, these two kinds of speeches differ in content. Many of the domestic speeches tend to be, like Havel's *Summer Meditations*, policy-oriented and, not surprisingly, aimed at Czech "domestic" politics; this is, however, not true across the board, and even his domestic speeches often invoke and rely upon, also like *Summer*

Meditations, a transcendent or universally human level of analysis. This existential level of analysis is profiled in Havel's international speeches, in which he tries to understand the post-1989 human condition and the existential or civilizational crisis of the modern world. While all of the international speeches have been translated into English, most of the domestic speeches remain untranslated.[39]

The speeches are obviously another mosaic-like genre in their own right. Havel developed his themes from speech to speech, and they read like a coherent collection of thematically interwoven texts, with each speech highlighting a somewhat different facet of the whole. In his post-presidential memoir, Havel himself pointed out the coherence of the speeches, while at the same time lamenting the fact that this coherence had not been adequately appreciated:

> Anyone who reads them through will notice that they were not occasional shouts provoked by a particular situation and that together they make up a single unified whole, continuing and developing my view of the world, of politics, of the position of our country, and so on. In fact, I deliberately tried to write my speeches that way: more than once I started one speech where the previous speech left off, without anyone's noticing. (Havel 2007a: 207 and 2006: 144)

The speeches should, moreover, be considered thematically coherent with Havel's pre-1989 essays in that they develop the same themes, but from the perspective of the post-1989 world. As a British scholar and friend of Havel wrote:

> Havel told me that he regards his presidential speeches as the intellectual continuation of the essays, lectures, and prison letters of the dissident years. "Then I wrote essays, now I write speeches," he said, suggesting that only the form of what he does with words has changed, not the essential content of the intellectual activity. (Garton Ash 1999: 62)

The speeches might also be thought of as a hybrid genre in that they are mini-essays while also being, to a certain extent, performative play-like pieces that were written for a specific audience and occasion (Ceplina 2009). Like the plays, the speeches have clear and deliberate dramatic *apel*. In this respect, James Wilson (2000) has argued that Havel's speeches offer a vision of how rhetorical practice can be used to create and foster civil society.

Like Havel's works in other genres, the speeches also often contain one memorable image that serves to define the message. One vivid example is from Havel's 1994 speech upon receipt of the Philadelphia Liberty Medal in which he asks us to think of postmodern human society – as he argues in the speech, the current "state of mind" of the globalized world – in the following terms: "a Bedouin mounted on a camel and clad in traditional robes under which he is wearing jeans, with a transistor radio in his hands and an ad for Coca-Cola on the camel's back." Like other genres, the speeches are thematically and stylistically mixed. Many, or parts of many, are explicitly devoted to political matters, but there are also speeches on philosophical and spiritual themes that are essentially extensions of his prison meditations as well as on the theatre, literature, self-doubt. As with the essays, this mixing of style and theme cannot be considered incidental.

One of Havel's main rhetorical strategies in the speeches is frame-shifting: he defamiliarizes an issue that is seemingly already quite familiar to us by framing the issue in a consciously unconventional way. With the shift in frame comes a shift in values and roles within the frame, and the issue presents itself to us in a new light. A frequent result of Havel's frame-shifting is that questions that may have previously seemed predominantly political or economic become reframed as fundamentally moral or spiritual. In probably his most famous speech, his first as president in the traditional New Year's Address to the Nation in 1990, Havel started with a dramatic frame-shift of just this type:

> For forty years you heard from my predecessors on this day different variations on the same theme: how our country was flourishing, how many million tons of steel we produced, how happy we all were, how we trusted our government, and what bright perspectives were unfolding in front of us. I assume you did not propose me for this office so that I, too, would lie to you.

Although frame-shifting of this sort is particularly evident in the presidential speeches, it is a rhetorical strategy characteristic, in one way or another, of many of Havel's genres.

9. Political memoir (2006)

Havel stepped down as Czech president in early 2003, and it was not until 2006 that he published his next major piece of writing, his non-traditional political memoir with the playful Czech title *Prosím stručně*

(Havel 2006). The Czech title translates into English as "Please be brief," and the title is an ironic comment on the behaviour of a particular public-affairs talk-show moderator who would always ask his guests to answer the questions, no matter how involved they might be, briefly (*stručně*). Havel noted:

> I ask myself, why did he invite them on the show? These people are on television perhaps for the first and last time in their lives; they may have traveled from the far ends of the country to tell the nation something about their life's work, or about some crucial experience they've had, and the moment they arrive they are silenced and told not to speak at any length because the moderator has to finish in time for some idiotic commercial break. Naturally, his guests panic and don't say anything at all. (Havel 2007a: 286 and 2006: 199)

The title of the English translation of Havel's political memoir is the rather uninspiring (but perhaps more marketable) *To the Castle and Back* (Havel 2007a).[40]

The memoir is the last of both Havel's one-work genres and literary genres overall. As a political memoir, it is traditional to the extent that he addresses expected aspects of his presidency and at the same time manages to settle a number of old political scores (chiefly with his rival, Václav Klaus, who became president after Havel). The overall effect of the memoir, however, is to force a radical reconsideration of what politics means and who a politician (in this case, Havel) is. The book grounds itself in a given form while transcending that form – frame-shifting away from that form – in order to make the point that conventional ways of relating to politics and politicians are not always adequate. The book becomes less a book about politics proper or Havel's presidency and more a book about the human condition (Rocamora 2004: 329).

The frame-shift derives from Havel's use of a conscious collage format to write the memoir, and the collage format proves generative – less a formal cage than a skeleton – of Havel's intended frame-shift. Havel notes in the book that he chose to write a literary collage because it represented "one of the ways to touch on [the] hidden fabric of life" in which "everything is related to everything else; anything from a particular period points to something from the period that preceded it or the period that followed; everything is linked together in all kinds of ways ..." (Havel 2007a: 286 and Havel 2006: 199). The collage technique allows for a focus on combining "things that, on the surface, are unrelated, in such a way that they ultimately tell us more about the connections between them and their real meaning than any mechanical chronology could, or any other ordering principle that suppresses accident" (Havel 2007a: 286 and Havel 2006: 199). Putna describes Havel's use of the collage technique as a special kind of synthesis through which he attempts to "capture unity through a caleidoscope of fragments" (2012: 317) and argues that the memoir is, after *Letters to Olga*, Havel's second most spiritual work (2012: 320). One reviewer of *Prosím stručně* noted that the collage form also exerts a certain "poetic charm" on the reader (Šlajchrt 2006: 22).[41]

There are three strips to Havel's literary collage, or three distinct voices in the political memoir, and these are interlaced throughout the book. The first strip comprises reminiscences written post-presidency, and the voice of these is lyrical, at times melancholic in tone, and deeply personal. The second strip consists of selected memoranda written by Havel to his presidential staff during his presidency, and these are mostly arranged in chronological order. As the book progresses, some of the more absurd memoranda (e.g., the need for a longer hose to use in the gardens of Prague Castle) become playfully repeated motifs. The final strip consists of analytical mini-essays written as answers to questions from Karel Hvížďala, the same journalist who interviewed Havel in his pre-presidential incarnation for *Disturbing the Peace*. With the return of Hvížďala, Havel's conscious use of collage transcends the book itself and suggests that the various periods of Havel's life – his pre-1989 dissident and his post-1989 presidential faces – ought perhaps to be interpreted also as a collage. This suggestion is reinforced by the Czech title of the book, the abbreviation of which establishes the book as a P.S. – a post-scriptum – on Havel's literary and political life.

The three strips that comprise the book represent a formal and stylistic mix that is characteristic of Havel's works in general. The mundane is juxtaposed, often playfully, with the grandiose, resulting in a dramatic tension among the parts of the book. One effect of this is to challenge our perceptions of the practice of politics or to force us to rethink our conventional framing. The interpretative process triggered by collage – the shift or displacement that the collage form causes – has much less to do with logical or rational thinking and much more to do with feeling (Taylor 2004: 105). In other words, interpretation of a collage is not computable or rationally systematizable. Making sense of a collage requires an appeal to personal experience that leads to conjecture or inference about the possible meaningful relationship among the strips of the work. Collage as an art form is thus anti-system and anti-mechanical: interpreting a collage is less a matter of explaining the relations among its parts than a matter of intuiting or feeling one's way into the potential for meaning implicit in, but not fully realized by, the work. In this respect, collage represents a kind of ordering that transcends order, and we must consider this an essential part of the memoir's – that is, of Havel's – meaning.

Much like his plays and other works, Havel's literary collage can also be read as an appeal, and this also relates to the way in which the book's formal skeleton (the book's *how*) comes to embody or enact its message. Resolving a collage requires active interpretation on the viewer's (or, in this case, reader's) part. The collage, like a puzzle, invites us to solve it, which is also the essence of the art of the theatrical appeal: the audience must participate in confronting and resolving the dramatic tension brought into being by the play because the play's "empty space" calls out to be filled with meaning. Like the presidential speeches, then, the memoir itself offers a rhetorical enactment of participatory engagement in civic or political life.

Havel's political engagement as a tenth "genre"

At this point we might pause to consider a more general question suggested by a number of the genres (in particular, *Summer Meditations*, the presidential speeches, and the political memoir), but also potentially relevant for all of Havel's writing. Are Havel's texts inherently political? On the one hand, this seems like an absurd question to ask, as the default assumption is that the essays and plays – and, it ought to go without saying, *Summer Meditations*, the political speeches, and the memoir – are naturally so. Questioning the "politicalness" of Havel's writing goes hand-in-hand with the question of how to integrate Havel's various faces throughout his life: a writer in many different genres as well as political "dissident" and post-1989 politician. This question may never be fully resolved, although some have definite opinions on the matter. For example, the Czech writer Ivan Klíma, in a conversation with Philip Roth in the late 1980s, said:

> Havel is mainly known to the world as an important dramatist, then an interesting essayist, and lastly as a dissident … But in this list of Havel's skills or professions there is one thing missing, and in my opinion it's the fundamental one … I used to say, half jokingly, that Havel became

> a dramatist simply because at the time the theater was the only platform from which political opinions could be expressed. Right from the beginning, when I got to know him, Havel was, for me, in the first place a politician, in the second place an essayist of genius, and only lastly a dramatist. I am not ordering the value of his achievements but rather the priority of interests, personal inclination, and enthusiasm. (Roth 1990: 126)

Havel's own strategy was to assert the primacy of his literary endeavours and to deny, repeatedly and on different occasions, any driving interest in politics for politics' sake. To the extent that he was political, as Havel would assert in various ways prior to 1989, he was so because he was sociable. His concern was not with politics in a professional sense of the word, but rather with questions related to the polis or the larger community and society in which he was living (see, for example, Havel 1983a and b: letter 103).

Taking a cue from Havel's pre-1989 self-assessment, I would suggest that the best approach to the question of Havel's politicalness does not involve ordering or ranking his professional incarnations in list form. Reflection leads to the conclusion that his various faces, both his literary and his political ones, are of a kind with one another; that is, there is no clear line between Havel's literary endeavours and his political ones, but rather that the former melds into the latter. Appreciating the relationship between Havel-the-writer and Havel-the-politician may require us to reframe our understanding of "political," and we can begin to do this by considering the seemingly obvious "politicalness" of Havel's texts. Reading the texts primarily as political statements in a traditional sense is problematic with regard to the essays, and it proves equally problematic for the plays and even, somewhat paradoxically, for the ostensibly "political" writings (the testament, the speeches, and the memoir).

In regard to the plays, Alena Štěrbová has argued that they are not political in the direct and traditional sense of the word; that is, they are not grounded in one political situation or in a specific set of political circumstances (Štěrbová 2002: 25). Havel had a strong interest in the "political aspects" of his reality (Štěrbová 2002: 25), but this is not the same thing as saying that the plays represent "tendentiously political" texts (Štěrbová 2002: 31). Havel was, in fact, clear that his plays did not relate specifically and only to the one sociopolitical -ism, that is, to socialist (post-)totalitarianism alone. They can be read as parodies of or commentaries on the context in which they were written, but this does not exhaust their interpretation. Havel's plays were written to resonate beyond the borders of the socialist bloc, and they did indeed enjoy (and often still do) wide popularity in the non-socialist world. Their themes and their form of presentation resonate with audiences who know little to nothing about life in a post-totalitarian society of this kind. In light of this, Štěrbová focuses on the plays' "openness" to various readings; Havel intended them to be "open" texts, and this is in fact their strength as dramatic works (Štěrbová 2002: 26).

In his 2009 study of "meta-temporal drama," Cole Crittenden makes a point similar to Štěrbová's, but one that has more general implications. While Havel's plays are typically read, and with good reason, as political satires on the "domestic" political scene, "none of [his] plays, even the ones written after 1968, are only political pieces, and the uncertainties he depicts have relevance beyond the borders of political art" (Crittenden 2009: 156). Critics have tended to overlook those aspects of Havel's plays that are not political, especially those that are not "tendentiously political." On a similar note, Pontuso points out that Havel's absurdist style finds a target that is beyond both politics proper as well as the Central European post-totalitarian context: "Bureaucratic absurdities, twisted meanings and sense, the loss of meaning and the dehumanization of life are things that are familiar to people the world over" (Pontuso 2008: 10). Goetz-Stankiewicz echoes these reflections on Havel as a playwright by questioning the very idea of "political" theatre: "Is not drama, dealing mostly with human conflicts and tensions, 'political' by its very nature?," to which she adds that "if Havel's theater is to be called 'political', then only in the broadest sense" (Goetz-Stankiewicz 1999: 229). A similar tone was also adopted by Přemysl Rut, a Czech musican, actor, director, writer, and theatre critic, who read *Largo Desolato*, one of Havel's plays written in the mid-1980s after his release from prison and ostensibly one of the more "political" of his dramatic works:

> Five years ago, when I read the manuscript of Havel's *Largo Desolato*, it made me disgusted, angry, regretful, doubtful, fascinated, grateful, and frightened. And I laughed. That's what we call a strong artistic experience. It isn't that easy to affect me so much. Most forbidden literature was egocentric and defensive, and was written only to solve pseudo-problems. But *Largo Desolato* was completely different. Havel not only depicts himself, but also he reflects on the human condition. Meaning that he also reflects me. He doesn't comment on how he is – rather, he asks how I am. (cited in Rocamora 2004: 298)

The main concern of the plays is not with politics proper, but with the human condition. They seek, via the techniques of absurdist theatre and theatre of the appeal, to prompt the theatre-goers to question their own self-perceptions. This questioning often includes a political component, but the message of each play is not limited to this one analytic layer.

In the plays, then, Havel is concerned with politics as one area (or one existential form) in which the human condition is given expression. Havel's plays prompt us to pursue a new understanding of what we mean by "political," and what proves true for the plays will be equally true for the other genres. This should not be surprising given Havel's own attempts to reframe, and thereby reclaim, the meaning of the words "politician" and "politics." Our new understanding must be one that encompasses multiple levels of analysis – both the narrowly political and the broadly existential, the domestic scene as well as modern society writ large – that are present in the great majority of the works. As I wrote earlier, Havel is concerned with the wider cultural (and, by implication, also personal) frame against which modern politics in both East and West plays out. We misread him if we interpret his works in a closed or narrowly tendentious political sense.

We might follow Jiřina Šiklová, a Czech sociologist and political activist as well as herself a former "dissident" and signatory of Charter 77, who understands Havel's literary endeavours as forms of "action" that were meant to engage a community of people (friends and fellow intellectuals, readers of the samizdat essays, theatre-goers) in purposeful reflection that could perhaps lead to more traditional forms of political involvement. The texts are, in this view, political, but in a pre-political sense. In regard to Havel, Šiklová writes: "All his life he needed not only to reflect, not only to write, but also to become directly involved in the goings-on around him [*přímo zasahovat do dění kolem sebe*], and he in fact always did as much from his adolescent years onward" (Šiklová 1997: 129). Literary reflection and civic involvement went hand-in-hand.

Martin Palouš (M. Palouš 1997), citing the great twentieth-century political philosopher Hannah Arendt, offers a reframing of Havel's "politicalness" in terms similar to Šiklová's. Arendt made a distinction between an instrumental and communicative understanding of politics and politicians:

> In the instrumental framework, political actors strive for the success of their own political agenda and their goal is the implementation of their political will *in opposition to* the will of their political opponents. In the communicative model, however, political activism is motivated by a need to achieve consensus among actors looking on the same political questions but from differing viewpoints. (M. Palouš 1997: 133)

A communicative politics is not teleological or end-focused. It is not tendentious "power" politics in a traditional sense, but a politics of process in which the very process itself is inseparable from the end-goal (M. Palouš 1997: 133). Palouš notes that Havel was suspicious of the instrumental model and, as a political thinker and politician, much closer to the communicative model. Havel understood, along with Arendt, that the latter is not a relic of the ancient past, but a key to confronting totalizing forms of modern-day political power in whatever particular -ism these forms may arise (M. Palouš 1997: 136).[42]

It seems that Havel was not, in his own words, "tendentiously political" but rather "authentically political" in all of his writings (Štěrbová 31), and we can perhaps best understand what is meant by Havel's phrase "authentically political" in Šiklova's and Palouš's terms. Reflection and writing are forms of "pre-political action" that are both grounded in and have as their ultimate goal a communicative, but not an instrumental, model of politics. We might further take Havel's focus on Arendtian communicative politics as the essence of his reframing of the phenomenon. What if the root of the crisis in modern politics lies in the very way in which we understand the phenomenon itself? The actual cause of our political crisis is systemic, but our attempts to address and "fix" it have dealt only with symptoms; unless we reorient our efforts to address the real problem – unless we move away from an instrumental conceptualization of politics towards a communicative one – the crisis will persist. It is not difficult to see how this reorientation could apply equally to both (post-)totalitarian East and (post-)democratic West, nor is it difficult to imagine how this approach might effect a reconciliation of Havel's literary face with his "political" one.

Even Havel's most overtly political texts ought to be read in light of these considerations. *Summer Meditations*, the presidential speeches, and the political memoir all strive, each in its own way, to redirect our attention to the systemic nature of our modern political crisis. By decoupling "politics" from a pursuit of power for power's sake, Havel seeks to humanize it. If we think of politics more as a *process* for fostering dialogue and developing consensus, then "politics" seems less like a special sphere of human activity and much more like an everyday human phenomenon. In *Summer Meditations*, Havel wrote (1993b: 6 and 1999, 6: 521):

> Genuine politics – politics worthy of the name, and the only politics I am willing to devote myself to – is simply a matter of serving those around us: serving the community, and serving those who will come after us. Its

> deepest roots are moral because it is a responsibility, expressed through action, to and for the whole.

Emphasizing the procedural nature of "authentic" politics, he added (1993b: 8 and 1999, 6: 523):

> [I]f there is to be any chance at all of [political] success, there is only one way to strive for decency, reason, responsibility, sincerity, civility, and tolerance, and that is decently, reasonably, responsibly, sincerely, civilly, and tolerantly. I'm aware that, in everyday politics, this is not seen as the most practical way of going about it.

In authentic and communicative politics, the end (the *what*) is enacted through the means (the *how*), and this represents a fundamental move away from traditional notions of party-driven power politics.

Given these reflections on the "politicalness" of Havel's literary endeavours, it would seem warranted to consider his political engagement as a tenth genre that is coherent with the literary genres and that could therefore be added to the list of genres in which Havel engaged during his lifetime. While political engagement is not traditionally understood as a "genre," there are good reasons for claiming that it was in Havel's case, and advantages to seeing it as such. First and foremost, it allows us to make coherent sense of the relationship between Havel-the-writer and Havel-the-politician without resorting to a hierarchical ranking of Havel's priorities and interests. Moreover, understanding Havel's political engagement in these terms helps to bridge the divide between Havel's pre-1989 "dissident" engagement and his post-1989 presidential engagement. Many commentators on and critics of Havel place his post-1989 political incarnation in an almost entire separate category from the other genres and also see it at odds with his "dissident" political engagement. In other words, it is frequently assumed, despite Havel's obsession with genre-crossing, that there is no relationship between Havel-the-"dissident" and Havel-the-president, or rather that the relationship has a negative character. There is, in this approach, an implied or assumed disjuncture between Havel's pre- and post-1989 faces.[43]

Havel himself did not consider his transition to the presidency a radical disjuncture with either his past or his literary endeavours. If we understand Havel's presidency as yet another genre on an already long list, and if we reflect on how and why genre-crossing defines Havel as a thinker, then Havel's political engagement in both time periods takes the form of a natural extension of his "pre-political" or "authentically political" literary endeavours. In other words, while Havel's propensity to "exercise" his ideas in a variety of genres went beyond the formal limitations of literary engagement, the roots of his politics lie in a morality or a spirituality that has more of an affinity with literature than with direct political action. In the final analysis, however, there is only so much that can be accomplished through writing, and it can be said that direct political engagement provided Havel with a formal skeleton (a new genre) that was coherent with his literary project while simultaneously being generative of its own kind of meaning.

Cross-genre commonalities

To the extent that critics have commented directly on Havel's cross-genre productivity, they have done so only matter-of-factly. Havel's proclivities in this regard are seen as rhetorical "exercises" that correspond to his personal preferences. The mapping of Havel's nine written genres along with the proposed tenth "genre" of political engagement demonstrates, however, that the genres are tightly integrated both thematically and rhetorically. His genre-crossing cannot, therefore, be viewed as incidental. The *how*, especially in Havel's intellectual world, is never separable from the *what* or the *who*. Havel's artistic and literary versatility as well as his role as a leading actor in the culture and society of his time, like Josef Čapek's before him, ought to have a direct bearing on how we read him. In order to make sense of Havel as a writer and thinker, as well as of Havel's legacy, we need a holistic evaluation that does not fragment but rather integrates his cross-genre engagement.

A clue to the value of genre-crossing for Havel is found in prison letter 62 in which he frames the modern crisis of human identity in terms of responsibility. Indeed, the relationship between identity and responsibility is a central theme of the prison letters as a whole. Havel concludes his musings in letter 62 by qualifying them. He asks that his readers not take him too literally because he is not a philosopher, and his ambition is not to build a systematic theory of meaning. He admits that he is, in fact, always contradicting himself and never manages to explain everything, or rather that he explains things – and this is the crux of the matter – in very different ways. We might take this as one way of understanding the import of Havel's genre-crossing: as an attempt, or even a compelling need, to explain the same things continually but in different terms and through different forms. All ten genres – Havel's political engagement included, since what is true for the first nine genres is equally true for the tenth – might best be seen in this light.

At the same time that the genres represent ways of "explaining things in different ways," there are cross-genre commonalities that reinforce an integrative approach to reading. First and foremost, Havel presents the same themes across all the genres, and these all fall under the general rubric of reflections on the crisis of human identity in the modern world. Moreover, throughout his intellectual career, he treats these themes, or this overarching theme, in a remarkably consistent way. From the earlier literary-critical Havel to his presidential incarnation in the speeches and beyond, Havel does not fundamentally alter his positions. He develops his ideas as circumstances change, but the development takes place consistently within the same broad intellectual framework. Havel, in other words, reimagines the same set of ideas in a series of different forms.

The underlying rhetorical strategies that Havel uses in his treatment of these ideas are also remarkably consistent, although their surface manifestations vary given the formal demands of each genre. The meaning of these rhetorical "devices" for Havel's larger project can only be appreciated when we consider how and why they are used across the genres. Havel understood that form is not just a cage, but also a skeleton. It is generative or productive of meaning because the very ways in which we think and write (as well as the ways in which we, as humans, live out our lives) shape, embody, and enact the meaningfulness of those activities. Given the discussion of the form/meaning nexus that opened this chapter, we can say that these rhetorical strategies represent threads in Havel's thinking that weave together medium (*how*) and message (*what* and *who*).

One strategy that we have noted across a number of Havel's genres, particularly in the *Anticodes* and the plays, is to provide a template or conceptual schema that has multiple applications to human experience. In Štěrbová's words, the texts are characterized by their interpretative "openness." The *Anticodes* and plays have no single "correct" interpretation, but are rather conceptual skeletons that can be fleshed out variously.

Another common strategy is Havel's use of a central image that becomes a vivid and memorable symbol or a condensed representation of the broader argument of a given work. The *Anticodes* represent this in its most reduced form, since the image is, to a great extent, also the argument. But central images also play a key role in many of the other texts – in the plays, the essays, and the prison letters, as well as in the presidential speeches. Imagery, along with metaphor and stories, is also one strategy that Havel uses to escape the rational or propositional cage typical of some of the genres.

Mixing of levels and styles is a third cross-genre strategy that must not be considered incidental but intentional. Broadly speaking, we saw that Havel often intentionally mixes together two analytical levels in his writing. A "domestic" layer becomes embedded in a larger "existential" layer or frame, and the viewer/reader is prompted to reflect upon their relationship. At a local level, mixing of levels and styles is manifested in a range of genres, including the plays and the prison letters. The political memoir, however, might be taken as the work in which this particular strategy reaches a culminating point. The strategy is pushed to one possible logical end in the explicit writing of a literary collage. Highbrow concerns (the need to write a new federal Constitution or the planning of state visits to foreign countries) are juxtaposed with expressions of personal melancholy and self-doubt as well as seemingly petty details related to practical administration (the length of the Castle's garden hose). A plaintive, lyrical tone is stylistically juxtaposed with analytical and rational argumentation characteristic of Havel-the-essayist.

All three of these strategies – schematizating, using central images, and mixing levels and styles – work together to create a strong appeal component in the great majority of Havel's texts. Normally associated only with the plays (as quintessential theatre of the appeal), this component is also present in the essays to the extent that their aim is to raise questions – frame-shifted questions that run counter to conventional understandings – rather than provide concrete answers in the form of policy proposals for effecting change. It is not accidental that two of Havel's earliest essays, the letter to Alexander Dubček (1969) and the letter to Gustáv Husák (1975), are, as nominal letters, direct appeals to individuals. Nor is it incidental that the later "Politics and Conscience" (1984) ends with a dramatic appeal in the form of a rhetorical question. Havel's aim was to "enstrange" the seemingly already familiar; he forces us to rethink what we already believe that we know. This was clearly true of Havel-the-writer (his first nine genres), but it was equally true of Havel-the-politician (his tenth genre).

There is a final rhetorical commonality cutting across all of Havel's genres, including his political engagement, that further clarifies Havel's "exercises" in genre-crossing. Havel did not merely cross from one genre to another, but he also tended to challenge the formal conventions or constraints of each of the genres in which he engaged, effectively redefining the contours of each in order to suit his own purposes.[44] The literary-critical writings are not examples of insular and self-contained art criticism, but approach artistic "devices" as a starting point for critical thinking about personal and social identity; the anticodes redefine poetic form to special effect; the "political" essays undermine traditional political notions; the "philosophical" letters from prison represent a particularly Havelian spirit of philosophizing; many of the presidential speeches are like no speeches that any other president would (or perhaps could) ever give;[45] and Havel's collaborative interview/autobiography with Hvížďala is a completely new genre unto itself.

Havel's political memoir is also a radical reworking of the traditional genre. It is, in the words of Havel's translator Paul Wilson, structurally unlike anything that a former head of state has ever written (Wilson 2006: 15). This was, of course, Havel's intent. By redefining the formal conventions of political memoir, he effectively reframes our understanding of politics. This may well have been what he was attempting to do also while serving as president and perhaps why the significance of his political engagement – as a challenge to the conventional framing of the genre – has yet to be adequately appreciated.

Havel, in other words, employed frame-shifting in his genres as both a localized strategy (in the details of this or that text) and as a global strategy (by reworking the conventions of the genres themselves). Havel's case is therefore not merely one of genre-crossing but of genre-transcending and genre-problematizing. This is not surprising, given that in his post-presidential memoir Havel admitted to being particularly taken with everything and anything "that escapes order and makes it problematic [*co se vymyká řádu a co ho problematizuje*]" (Havel 2007a: 335 and 2006: 239). Frame-shifting, along with the problematizing of conventional forms that often comes with it, becomes for Havel an almost necessary component of critical thinking.[46] Genre-crossing and genre-transcending do not represent ways that Havel exercises his ideas, but rather they strategically enact his search for authentic forms of meaning.

An authentic response to life's call requires both explaining things in different ways as well as realizing that true meaning emerges from the relationships among different forms. The confrontation of one form with another represents an *apel* or *výzva*, and the proper response requires not fragmentation or atomization, but integration. This principle is at work in and among Havel's nine literary genres and is equally active within and for the tenth genre of political engagement.

Havel's audio-collage and the "restlessness of transcendence"

By way of summing up a sketch of Havel's genre-crossing, we might consider yet another genre – a one-off bonus genre – that illustrates well the features and the relationships that we have been discussing. In 1968, Havel created an audio-collage for a contest that Czechoslovak radio held to mark the 50th anniversary of the founding of the first Czechoslovak Republic in 1918. Havel composed an audio-collage that included recorded excerpts of famous speeches from Czech politicians in the democratic tradition that included Tomáš Garrigue Masaryk, Edvard Beneš, and Alexander Dubček.[47] These recordings alternated with excerpts from Bedřich Smetana's opera *Libuše*, a symbol of Czech nationhood. But there is also a third sound layer on the recording, that of a man wordlessly having lunch. As Rocamora writes: "The sense is that of 'the common man' eating and drinking, oblivious to the speeches and their meaning. As the tape is played, the musical excerpts get shorter and shorter; the last speech to be heard is Dubček's on the futility of defending his country against foreign armies. Dubček is weeping" (Rocamora 2004: 100). Havel won the radio contest, but his audio-collage was not broadcast until after the Velvet Revolution.

Given the strategies that Havel typically employed in his other genres, we must see this work as quintessentially Havelian. It is not an odd one-off "exercise" but rather a particularly compacted or compressed form of the Havelian prototype. It has an explicit collage structure that mixes and juxtaposes high- and low-brow forms, and it has a strong image component (in this case, an audio-image) that is the thrust of the whole "argument" of the work. It is political, but in Havel's understanding of authentically communicative politics. In other words, the question raised by the collage is not one of a technical political response, but a matter of human identity and morality at a pre-political level. Havel's audio-collage does not appeal to reason as much as it evokes, in a dramatically tense but at the same time playful way, a powerful feeling that becomes the crux of its *apel*. Finally, the meaning of the audio-collage is fundamentally relational and derives from this appeal. It emerges and takes concrete form in the listener's mind from the interaction among the individual strips.

The feeling that is evoked by Havel's audio-collage as well as by many of Havel's works across the genres could be described via the

Czech word *neklid* ("restlessness"). Havel's is a special kind of *neklid*, a disturbing feeling that leads, through provocation and appeal, to transcendence beyond conventional ways of thinking, acting, and being in the world. This kind of *neklid* represents a running theme in Havel's prison letters (Havel 1983a and 1983b). In letter 141, for instance, Havel argues that a constant "restlessness" or "turbulence" of the soul is necessary for developing an authentic sense of self that leads to genuine responsibility:

> Something that might be called a constant, deepening turbulence of the mutual illumination, verification and augmentation of everything primordial, everything that has been achieved, everything intended and acted upon, spontaneously felt and worked out by the mind; a kind of unceasing dramatic confrontation between primordial vulnerability and achieved experience. (Havel 1983a and 1983b: letter 141)

In a 2002 presidential speech ("Gala Evening"), Havel also invokes "restlessness of the soul" as the driving force behind his "dissident" engagement prior to 1989 and an ongoing source of inspiration (and doubt) for him as president. A turbulence or restlessness of the soul is thus the starting point for Havel's understanding of dissidentism as well as arguably for "living in truth." Both are characterized by going beyond or transcending an existing conventional form or order, and both are oriented towards *neklid* as a process, not necessarily as an outcome.[48]

Havel's most famous use of the term *neklid* – in the phrase *neklid transcendence* or the "restlessness of transcendence" and cited as the epigraph to this chapter – occurs in his 1975 letter to Husák. In this open letter to the "normalizing" leader of Czechoslovakia, Havel contrasts the demands of life with the leveling conformity required by authoritarian systems:

> Life rebels against all uniformity and leveling; its aim is not sameness, but variety, the restlessness of transcendence, the adventure of novelty and rebellion against the status quo … On the other hand, the essence of authority … consists basically in a distrust of all variety, uniqueness, and transcendence; in an aversion to everything unknown, impalpable, and currently obscure; in a proclivity for the uniform, the identical, and the inert; in deep affection for the status quo. (Havel 1991a: 71 and 1999, 4: 93–4)

This passage comes towards the end of the letter where Havel is envisioning the dissolution of Husák's "normalized" regime by means of life itself. The language of the letter becomes more and more metaphorical as the essay progresses, and culminates in competing images of *klid* and *neklid*. Life, Havel asserts, is the restlessness of transcendence, and attempts by authoritarian systems to stifle life by imposing an artificial order upon it are ultimately doomed to failure. Life cannot be boxed up or forcibly shaped into preconceived ideological forms. Life transcends all of our attempts to systematize and "order" it.

As we have seen in regard to Havel's genres, restlessness manifests itself in more than one way at both local and global levels. His obsessive genre-crossing and genre-reworking – that is, his restlessness of transcendence as both writer and politician – is a metaform for his larger project.

The mosaic principle: Reading Havel and reading ourselves

On a recent trip on the Boston subway, I was struck by an advertisement. The ad depicted a decorative mosaic that had been shattered, and its constituent pieces were imagined as tiles of various colours. The image also implied a certain dynamism: broken away from the whole, the coloured tiles were re-joining, merging back into one coherent form, striving to recreate the original mosaic. The text accompanying the image read "Brokenness made beautiful."

Taking a cue both from this subway ad as well as from Havel, I will attempt to synthesize the various facets of the argument that I have presented in this chapter – the focus on a form/meaning nexus, the details of Havel's genres and their formal/thematic interrelationships, Havel's obsessive genre-crossing and genre-transcending, his privileging of a communicative "politicalness," his "restlessness of transcendence" – by proposing a principle for reading Havel that is embodied in the same central image, the image of a mosaic.

Associating the mosaic with Havel is fitting because it represents an image or form, like the collage, that was seemingly a deep part of Havel's personal and intellectual make-up. One Czech scholar's "intellectual portrait" of Havel, for example, emphasizes, in mosaic terms, the young Havel's analytic ability to discern a whole in a mass of "shattered details" (Putna 2012: 83).[49] A second Czech scholar even imagined Havel as a "carbon molecule" in large part because of his natural tendency to combine eclectically ideas from this or that thinker and discover in their combination a profound sense of unity, a transcendent whole greater than the sum of its mere parts (Hejdánek 2009).

Like a collage, a mosaic is oriented towards appeal. To make sense of it, we must actively interpret it because the meaning of each tile or tessera in the mosaic is incomplete without reference to its place in the larger composition. In other words, the meaning of the whole is realized through its parts and their relation to one another, and that meaning – the process of establishing relationships among the individual tesserae – serves as an appeal to the intepreter. A mosaic invites us to make sense of it, and as with collage, this is not merely a rational sense-making, but a feeling-oriented process. In the process of making sense of it, we project onto the mosaic aspects of our experience and our own expectations of meaningfulness, thereby inserting ourselves into the interpretative process in much the same way that the audience watching a Vaněk play inserts itself into the drama on stage. Like a collage, a mosaic is not so much a problem waiting to be solved as it is an appeal (*výzva*) to the spirit and mind of the individual interpreter.[50]

The traditional approach to reading Havel puts the focus on reading the individual genres, or individual works within a genre, without reference to the larger mosaic in which they participate. In reading Havel in this way, we fail to see each tessera's connection to Havel's project as a whole; we miss the forest for the individual trees. The mosaic principle for reading Havel suggests that his obsessive "exercises" in genre-crossing and genre-reworking call out for a synthesizing reading. This principle is active on small and large scales. Both individual works within multiwork genres (the speeches, the prison letters, the essays, the plays) as well as the genres themselves are understood to be in dialogue with one another. On the larger scale, the various genres – the nine literary ones as well as the tenth political genre – represent a polyphony of voices on the same themes. These diverse perspectives are shaped by the formal contours of each genre, the cage or skeleton of each form and the resultant form/meaning relationship that emerges. Different forms interact with each other to capture crucially different aspects of meaning.

A multiplicity of genres implies a search for the right form, which also implies a "communicative" focus on the very process of searching. The richness and complexity of human meaningfulness, Havel seems to be suggesting, cannot be reduced to one genre or one form; the whole is more than the mere sum of its individual parts. The conceptual thrust of his larger project, which is the "true meaning" of his works and perhaps also his legacy, consists in a holistic reading that strives to makes sense of the various ways that he tried to "explain things differently." If we fragment Havel, we misread him because the essence of his message lies in making sense of the interplay of the various tesserae in the larger mosaic through our own personal intellectual struggle. Havel's "restlessness of transcendence" models, in metaform, how we should read him.[51]

The mosaic image is a structure, a conceptual schema or template, that Havel himself often evoked in local contexts as well as in more globally meaningful ways. Mosaic images occur, explicitly and implicitly, throughout his writing. Havel, in other words, often filtered his own reading of the world through the mosaic principle. One local example is a letter from prison in which Havel exhorts his wife, Olga, to be more specific in her letters to him because it is the small, seemingly insignificant details of everyday life that matter: "[W]rite as concretely as possible, even about things that seem meaningless. It is only from a mosaic of apparently meaningless things that one can create an approximate picture of the situation and atmosphere around you outside; generalities don't say much" (Havel 1983a and 1983b: letter 31). A human life is, then, a kind of experiential mosaic.

In a more philosophical meditation from another letter, Havel also sees one person's life as participating in the larger mosaic of human (and cosmic) Being: "Human personality is a particular view of the world, an image of the world, an aspect of the world's Being, a challenge to the world [*výzva světu*]" (Havel 1983a and 1983b: letter 60). Here Havel applies the same structure operative in his writings – one genre (or work within a genre) relates to another strip in a collage or tessera in a mosaic – to the hermeneutics of human identity. He develops these thoughts on human identity in more detail:

> The point is that human existence ... is not just something that has simply happened; it is "an image of the world," "an aspect of the world's Being," a "challenge to the world," and as such – it seems to me – it necessarily forms a very special node [*zvláštní uzel*] in the tissue of Being.[52] It is not merely separate and individual, enclosed within itself and limited to itself, but it is, repeatedly, the whole world. It is as if it were a light constantly reilluminating the world; a crystal in which the world is constantly being reflected; a point upon which all of Being's lines of force constantly appear to converge, centripetally, as it were. Human existence, I would say, is not just a particular fact or datum, but a kind of gospel as well, pointing to the absolute and,

in a way that has no precedent, manifesting the mystery of the world and the question of its meaning. (Havel 1983a and 1983b: letter 60)

This is, according to Havel, a meditation on how modern man can understand the immortality of the soul. The great mosaic of Being becomes, via our participatory relationship to it, the background of all human meaning. He even suggests that this existential mosaic has, via the "memory of Being," a temporal or historical dimension: "Nothing that has once happened can un-happen; everything that once was, in whatever form still is – forever lodged in the 'memory of Being'" (Havel 1983a and 1983b: letter 60). The multidimensional mosaic of Being is understood as an existential matrix, and the node that we occupy in the matrix and the relationships that follow from this particular connection provide a ground for meaningfulness. We reflect the larger mosaic-like structure of Being even as we participate individually and locally in it.[53]

The mosaic principle becomes, given this perspective, not merely a strategy for reading Havel across genres, but also a way of modelling human identity. In other words, Havel's spirituality of "restlessness" is not just a feature of his thinking and writing, but it also provides a framework for understanding human meaning and meaningfulness writ large. A student in my monograph course on Havel once said that reading Havel and reflecting on his writings was like being granted access to a conceptual toolbox; she was able to make better sense of who she was by using the strategies and concepts that characterize Havel as a thinker and writer. The mosaic principle suggests a framework for an integrative reading of Havel across genres, but at the same time it suggests a way to read ourselves. What "genres" comprise our identity? How do the formal conventions of those genres shape us as actors in them? How do the various "faces" in each of our life genres interact with one another? If we want to realize ourselves fully as human beings, we ought not to limit ourselves to the confines of one formal cage. Genre-crossing and genre-reworking, as a personal restlessness of transcendence, come to model a certain way of being in the world.

Havel is, of course, not the only thinker to have proposed a mosaic approach to making sense of human meaning. For example, the American cognitive philosopher Mark Johnson has written eloquently in favour of an "aesthetics of human understanding" that has much in common with Havel's mosaic approach to Being:

> No isolated thing, percept, or quality has any meaning in itself ... Things, qualities, events, and symbols have meaning *for us* because of how they

> connect with other aspects of our actual or possible experience. Meaning is relational ... Aspects of our experience take on meaning, then, insofar as they activate for us their relations to other actual or possible aspects of our experience. (Johnson 2007: 268)

In a manner that directly evokes the mosaic principle as well as much of Havel's philosophizing in *Letters to Olga*, Johnson adds: "Things and events have meaning by virtue of the way they call up something beyond them to which they are connected" (Johnson 2007: 269).

Another example would be the Holocaust survivor and celebrated psychotherapist Viktor Frankl. Frankl wrote of the transcendent nature of an individual human life, and of the relationship between individuals and the society in which they live, in explicitly mosaic terms:

> For just as the uniqueness of the tessera has a value only in relation to the whole of the mosaic, so the uniqueness of the human personality finds its meaning entirely in its role in an integral whole. Thus the meaning of the human person as a personality points beyond its own limits, toward community; in being directed toward community the meaning of the individual transcends itself. (Frankl 1986: 70)

Frankl went on to note the essential way in which an individual's life also reflects the larger social mosaic by comparing societies that value individuality and those that promote mass conformism:

> If the relationship of the individual to the community may be compared with that of a tessera to a whole mosaic, then the relationship of the individual to the mass may be equated with that of a standardized paving-stone to uniform gray pavement: every stone is cut to the same size and shape and may be replaced by any other; none has qualitative importance for the whole. And the pavement itself is not really an integral whole, merely a magnitude. The uniform pavement also does not have the aesthetic value of a mosaic; it possesses only utilitarian value – just as the mass submerges the dignity and value of men and extracts only their utility. The meaning of individuality comes to fulfillment in the community. To this extent, then, the value of the individual is dependent upon the community. But if the community itself is to have meaning, it cannot dispense with the individuality of the individuals that make it up. In the mass, on the other hand, the single, unique existence is submerged, must be submerged because uniqueness would be a disrupting factor in any mass. (Frankl 1986: 70–1)

In Havel's (as well as Johnson's and Frankl's) meditations on the mosaic-like nature of human being, we begin to see the outlines of a civil society.

Indeed, the very nature of the mosaic principle as applied to human personal and social identity, not to mention its potential as a general framework for understanding human meaningfulness, does allow for, or may even require, integration of a political component. If society is a mosaic of individuals and an individual's life is a mosaic of experiences that both comprise and enact the larger whole(s) in which they participate, then "politicalness" becomes imbued with a kind of meaning that both explains and validates Havel's focus on authentic and communicative politics.

Conclusion

In this chapter, I have presented a sketch of Havel's genres with an eye towards exploring the implications of his focus on the relationship between form (the medium) and meaning (the message). By way of summarizing this chapter, we might return to the questions asked at its start and provide brief answers to them:

What might Havel's cross-genre productivity tell us about him as a thinker and how might the cross-genre nature of Havel's creativity influence how we read him? We have seen how Havel's so-called exercises in genre-crossing and genre-transcending enact a key thread in the fabric of his thought, and this has also suggested a principle for reading Havel integratively across the genres. Havel's creative obsession with the form/meaning nexus was neither accidental nor incidental, but rather representational of a core part of the meaning and message of his life's work.

To what extent do we see continuity among his various genres, and is there a coherence that spans 1989 or should we posit a disjuncture between Havel's pre- and post-1989 faces? I have argued unequivocally for coherence across both genres and time periods. The coherence is manifested, not surprisingly given a form/meaning nexus, both in the themes that Havel treats and the rhetorical strategies that underlie his treatments of them. *How* he explores these themes becomes inseparable from *what* he has to say about them.

Would it be productive to view Havel's political engagement as a kind of non-literary, real-life genre that is continuous with his literary genres? Havel's various faces, both literary and political, represent aspects of his larger project, and his politicalness must be understood as continuous with, if not emerging from, his literary endeavours. Havel's engaged artistic versatility, like Josef Čapek's before him, ought to be examined holistically in order for us to arrive at an understanding of its "true meaning."

Do Havel's own exercises in genre-crossing, read non-incidentally as an enactment of a search for meaning in the modern world, perhaps also hint at a way of reading ourselves? The mosaic principle is not only an approach to reading Havel, but also suggests a framework for understanding human meaningfulness. How Havel thinks and writes thus models both how we should read him and how we might choose to read ourselves.

Our reflections on the relationship between form and meaning do not end with this chapter. In chapter 2, I consider yet another central thread in the fabric of Havel's thinking that, like the mosaic principle, simultaneously represents a manifestation of meaning through form. Nor are we entirely finished with a discussion of Havel's genres. This second conceptual thread – Havel's profiling of an opposition between *explaining* and *understanding*, which we can take as two modes of thought or, more philosophically speaking, two ways of being – will help make sense of Havel as playwright and essayist. By juxtaposing these two particular faces of Havel, I will seek to clarify the implications of his intellectual project as a whole.

2 *Explaining* and *Understanding*: The "Weirdness" of Havel's Plays

Whether I want to or not, whether I plan it or not, one basic theme always gets into my plays, almost obsessively, and thus not by chance at all, but from the very essence of those aspects of the world that have chosen me as their interpreter – that is, the theme of human identity.

– Václav Havel,
Disturbing the Peace[1]

In 2003, I attended an English-language production of Havel's 1965 play *The Memorandum*.[2] One of his earliest dramatic works and a fine example of absurdist theatre combined with Czech theatre of the appeal, the play is concerned with mechanization and automatization of modern human identity. It is set in an unidentified office, and the characters appear to be office workers (although they seem to do very little real work). All of the characters are enmeshed in a bureaucratized system that they cannot control, and most are oblivious to the nature of their dilemma. The main intrigue of the play revolves around the introduction into the office of an artificial language called ptydepe. Ptydepe, as we are informed, has been created on the basis of scientific principles and designed to eliminate redundancy, and thereby maximize efficiency, in office communication. Bizarrely unaware that ptydepe has been adopted as the new medium of communication, the office director has received a memo in the language and spends nearly the whole play trying, mostly in vain, to find out what the memo says. By the end of the play, ptydepe has proven to be a disastrous failure, and another artificial language, which is based on scientific principles directly opposite to those underlying ptydepe, has been introduced. As with many of Havel's plays, *The Memorandum* ends by beginning all over again.

The performance that I saw was staged by students at a university theatre in the United States. I sat directly behind two (American) undergraduates, each holding a pen and a sheet of paper with numbered questions on it. Eavesdropping on their conversation before the play began, I learned that they were students in a communication arts course attending the production to complete a class assignment requiring them to take notes on certain aspects of the play's staging. I never learned exactly which aspects were of interest to them or if they managed to fulfil the assignment, but I did witness their general reaction to the performance. When the play ended and the applause had died down, one of the students turned to the other and said in an emphatic voice that invited no discussion: "That was so weird!"[3] The other student nodded wordlessly in agreement, and they quickly got up and left the theatre.

In evaluating these students' reaction to Havel's *The Memorandum*, we should keep in mind that Czech has two words that overlap in meaning with the English "weird": there is *divný*, which is strange, odd, or peculiar in a predominantly negative sense, but there is also *zvláštní*, which is strange or curious but in a (potentially) interesting and thought-provoking way. In this chapter, I will make sense of the "weirdness" of Havel's dramatic style in a way that will create an appreciation for his plays as *zvláštní* works of art – admittedly a bit weird, but in a positive and provocative sense of the word. They are works of art designed to provoke the audience to reflect more thoughtfully and productively about their meaning than my two communication undergraduates were seemingly either able or willing to do. In arguing in favour of Havel's *zvláštní* dramatic style, I also hope to clarify why Havel, who did engage in so many different genres, has often been thought of primarily as a playwright. To what extent would it have been true to say this of Havel at any stage in his professional life? This question calls out for an answer, especially because Havel did not consider himself to be a born playwright; theatre did not choose him, but rather he chose theatre.

How might we then understand the assertion that theatre was Havel's "primary" genre? If we consider a chronological list of his genres, the statement seems inaccurate. Plays are not, as we have seen, his first genre, nor do they represent the foundational genre of his literary oeuvre. If we imagine Havel's literary endeavours as a multistorey building, then the earlier literary and film criticism is the cornerstone of the larger structure of his work, and these writings could be understood as primary in a developmental sense of the word. Looking at the various genres in terms of renown and influence, it is still not possible to say – given Havel's whole life, including his post-1989 political incarnation – that the plays are primary. This statement would certainly not be true in terms of Havel's global reputation; internationally, the plays compete with the essays for primacy, if not also with the presidential speeches or the "genre" of politician.

Instead of relying on distinctions among the genres based on chronology or reputation, we need a conceptual definition of what being "primarily a playwright" might mean. A focus on the conceptual nature of what we intend by Havel's primary genre avoids a possibly ill-fated attempt to define Havel's various forms of engagement in relation to one another by hierarchically ranking them. The different genres provide different forms for realizing his ideas, and it is not a question of hierarchizing the genres vis-à-vis one another as much as it is a question of understanding the value of the form/meaning nexus that each genre embodies. Thus with regard to the conceptual primacy of the dramatic genre, we might ask why the formal skeleton of theatrical performance (and in particular of a dramatic style that mixes French absurdist techniques with Czech theatre of the appeal) so attracted Havel's interest. According to Jan Grossman (1999: 142), Havel approached everything through a dramatic lens: the ground of his thinking, from which he drew the means to express himself in all of his genres, was theatre. Drama offered Havel a form best-suited to capturing the meaning of what he wished to convey, and we must therefore refocus our question onto the form/meaning nexus as it is embodied in Havel's *zvláštní* dramatic style.

In developing my argument, I first consider theatre as a formal genre in contrast to other genres, and I juxtapose, for simplicity's sake, Havel's plays with his essays. The juxtaposition of genres leads us into a more general discussion of human meaning and meaningfulness: what is meaning and what counts as meaningful discourse? To explore this question, I will examine the opposition – between *explaining* and *understanding* – that runs throughout Havel's oeuvre and acts as a key thread in the fabric of his thinking. I will argue that the form/meaning nexus embodied in Havel's plays is oriented towards *understanding*, and will illustrate this point through a structural analysis of one of his plays, *The Beggar's Opera*. The analysis of this one play by Havel will suggest a general framework for reading his dramatic style. In concluding the chapter, I will propose that theatrical performance was Havel's primary genre, given the way in which his plays enact a kind of truth that opens up, like the cinematic gag, a space for existential catharsis.

Essays and plays

My course on Havel's writings is not structured chronologically. We read and discuss a selection of Havel's essays before we encounter the plays, and more than a few students over the years have embraced Havel-the-essayist but have found themselves, towards the middle of the semester, sorely disappointed with and rather confused by Havel-the-playwright. One student characterized the difference between the essays and plays by saying that the former were "objective" while the latter were "subjective." In the student's mind, the presumed objectivity of the essays seemed more meaningful and worthy of admiration, while the ostensible subjectivity of the plays made them seem less valid, more frivolous and arbitrary. The student's expectations of what counted as a meaningful form of discourse – that is, what type of form can serve as a vehicle to communicate a seriousness of meaning – interfered with his appreciation of Havel as a playwright.

A strong conceptual contrast emerges from a juxtaposition of the essayistic form with the dramatic form.[4] To examine this contrast, it will be productive to recall certain aspects of the contrast that I already noted in the first chapter, and to expand upon them. Essays typically profile rational analysis and logical argumentation, the main vehicle for which is the propositional statement. As a result, we read an essay sentence-by-sentence and parse the arguments systematically and linearly, usually alone in a quiet room. Although we may do the same with the text of a play, theatre-as-performance represents an entirely different experience. Rational analysis and systematic, linear argumentation are generally not highlighted, and we "read" the performance by experiencing it. Attending a performance of a Havel play means having a communal encounter that is, ideally speaking, as existentially disturbing as it is entertaining.

In emphasizing this particular contrast between reading an essay and experiencing a theatrical performance, we should mention an obvious point. After we finish reading an essay, we do not (at least not as a matter of course) applaud. We most certainly do not give the essay a standing ovation. The energy of and emotions stimulated by a live performance of a play, especially in the context of small-form theatre where we can vividly see the actors' expressions and movements, are entirely absent in how we process an essay. In comparison with attending a theatrical performance, reading an essay is a largely detached, impersonal, and abstract experience.

It is in this connection that we should recall Rocamora's statement that Havel's essays generally function as *explications du texte* for the plays; that is, conceptually, the plays are primary, with the essays serving as the rationalized explanations of the dramatic form. If the themes and ideas in each of the genres are largely the same, then the distinction between them falls on *how* those themes are presented, that is, on the contrasting ways in which the reader/viewer processes the ideas as such. Applauding (or not) is one example that illustrates the contrast, and another concrete example might be the essayistic observation, commonly repeated, that language in Havel's plays often takes control of the characters. For example, the language in *The Garden Party* or *The Memorandum* becomes the real "hero" of the play in the sense that it is the most prominent and active dramatic component. It is one thing, however, merely to note in essayistic mode that language in Havel's plays takes control of the characters, but quite another thing to experience this phenomenon happening on stage during a live performance.

Havel wrote complexly alliterative passages into the text of *The Garden Party* that are extremely difficult for an actor to perform (at least in part because they are semantically nonsensical). At the same time, the form of the text takes over the speech, and it becomes difficult for the actor to stop the monologue once it has begun, because the alliteration – the very sonic fabric of the text – propels the actor forward in his delivery. One such monologue from *The Garden Party* occurs in the midst of a verbal battle between the Director and Hugo (Havel 1994: 35 and 1999, 2: 80). The two combatants are arguing over the proper roles of the "inauguration office" and the "liquidation office" in inaugurating the liquidation of the former (and here we already begin to see, even in English translation, the challenging alliterative contours of the play's nonsensical language).

Hugo, a young upstart careerist, strikes a blow against the experienced Director in delivering the following monologue: "Another training will have to be organized. Inaugurationally trained liquidation officers training liquidationally trained inaugurators, and liquidationally trained inaugurators training inaugurationally trained liquidation officers."[5] The passage does have its own (absurd) logic, but Hugo gains a momentary advantage over the Director not through the logic of his argument – not, that is, propositionally – but rather by verbally outdoing (or actually outdueling) him. The complex sonic texture of Hugo's short speech is stunning, and its brilliance is perceived by both the Director as an on-stage character and the members of the off-stage audience. If the actor playing Hugo manages to get through this and other similar monologues flawlessly, the audience often erupts in spontaneous applause at the brilliance of the actor's performance. On more than one occasion, I have participated as a member of the audience in a spontaneous standing ovation at the end of just such a typically Havelian monologue.

In a 1975 play titled *The Beggar's Opera*, Havel takes this strategy to a new level by using a more subtle technique to engage as well as implicate the audience in the play's linguistic manipulation. Audience applause in this case is not elicited by the actor's flawless production of a phonetically difficult passage, but rather by the brilliantly deceptive content of the monologue itself. One of the main characters in *The Beggar's Opera* is a charismatic crime boss named Macheath. Macheath is young, handsome, and confident, and he is quite the ladies' man. Macheath has become romantically involved with two women, Lucy and Polly, and these romances are complicated by the fact that both women are supposed to feign love for him in order better to manipulate him. One of the girls is the daughter of the chief of the London police, Lockit, and the other is the daughter of Macheath's main rival in the criminal underworld, Peachum. Both romances become further complicated when Lucy and Polly actually fall in love with Macheath, and he marries both of them.[6]

The audience has, of course, known of this multilevel deceit all along and fully realizes, on a rational level, that Macheath is not to be trusted. The audience may even sympathize with Lucy and Polly who, despite their initial self-interested intentions with regard to Macheath, have genuinely fallen in love. Unlike the audience, however, the two women discover Macheath's polygamous deception only late in the play, and they angrily confront him during a joint visit to his jail cell. Macheath's exculpatory monologue is a kind of speech that Havel characterized as "balancing on a knife's edge," a monologue "in which pure truths are expressed with veracity and subtlety, truths which are pure lies from beginning to end" (Havel 1991b: 193–4 and 1990: 167–8). It is as deeply touching as it is rationally absurd, and it is worth citing at length. The polygamous Macheath pleads with his wives:

> "Girls! Girls! I respect your anger, and I understand your pain, because I know that seen from the outside, my behavior may indeed have invited

the kind of interpretation your agitated minds have placed on it. But precisely because I understand you, and even more because I know my own faults, I must defend myself where I stand wrongly accused, where your anger prevents you from seeing beneath the surface of my actions to the real, human substance that lies beneath them. In the first place, it is not true that I don't love you. I love you both sincerely, and I have never uttered a word to you that did not reflect my true feelings. Often, in fact, I felt more strongly about you than modesty and pride allowed me to admit. So what have I done to you? Was I wrong to have married you? But what else could I have done? After all, I loved you. Today, of course, such things are usually handled differently. Society finds it more acceptable, and men find it more convenient, to marry only one of the women they love, while – out of a dubious respect for his legitimate spouse's feelings – he banishes the other to second-class status as his mistress, as a slightly better class of prostitute whose duties are virtually those of a wife but whose rights are far inferior … At the same time, the wife is equally at a disadvantage. For, while the mistress knows of the wife and often – we may assume – talks about her at great length and in great detail with the husband, the wife must remain submerged in a slough of ignorance, and this quite naturally alienates her from her husband, since the husband is not compelled to hide anything from his mistress – as he must from his wife – so they develop a deeper understanding of each other and the final result is that he grows fonder of the mistress. Can you not see how unfair this arrangement is to both women? And was that the path I was supposed to follow? No, girls, to live up to my responsibilities to you in the fullest possible way, I could not follow other men, but had to go my own way, down a path that would allow both of you an equal degree of legitimacy and dignity ... Tomorrow, in all probability, I shall be hanged and that will end the matter ... When I am no longer here, your memories will be all that remain of me. Only one thing will brighten my final hours and assure that I go content to my death, and that is the hope that those memories will not be unpleasant. Therefore I beseech you, try to put yourselves in my place and understand the logic and morality of my behavior. Try to see that I have behaved – insofar as I could – honorably. And if you cannot find it in your hearts, even now, when the peace of my soul is at stake, to accept what I have done, then at least try to forgive me. This I beg of you in the name of all those beautiful moments we spent together, and all those fabulous plans that we had no time to bring to fruition." (Havel 2001: 60–1 and 1999, 2: 488–90)

Before the end of the speech, Lucy and Polly are sobbing, and at the end of it they "both fling themselves on Macheath, kissing him passionately and weeping hysterically" (Havel 2001: 61 and 1999, 2: 490). The speech is so beautifully written that it convinces the women to forgive him and embrace their unusual conjugal situation with tears of joy.

If Macheath delivers the speech as he should, the audience, which is perfectly aware that Macheath is a self-interested fraud, never fails to endorse the speech with a standing ovation. If anything, audience enthusiasm for Macheath's monologue in *The Beggar's Opera* is much greater than for Hugo's alliterative feats in *The Garden Party*. I have seen two different audiences award Macheath not only with an extended standing ovation, but one that was punctuated by multiple and repeated shouts of "Bravo!" In an essay, we might be warned that noble-sounding words can be deceptive and that we should be wary of empty flattery, but the Macheath speech shows us what it actually means to be controlled by language. Havel not only engages the theatre spectators (the "spect-actors") through the experience of the performance, but he also implicates them in the staged manipulation. By energetically appreciating Macheath's performance, the audience is made momentarily "inauthentic," forced to do reverence, along with the characters, to the power of empty, manipulative language.[7] In describing the intended effect of his "knife's-edge" speeches, Havel said, in decided understatement: "[T]he audience members identify with the truths expressed in them, yet they sense a scarcely perceptible tinge of mendacity, given the situation and context, and they become uneasy, wondering how it was all meant" (Havel 1991b: 194 and 1990: 168).

These examples from *The Garden Party* and *The Beggar's Opera* raise four interrelated points of contrast between essays and plays that were mentioned briefly before but that can now be examined in more depth: the inherent socialness or communal nature of theatrical performance; the appeal orientation of Havel's dramatic style; the conceptual limitations of the essayistic form; and the predominance in the plays of the broadly existential over the specifically domestic. I will discuss each of these in turn largely by citing Havel's own views on the meaning of theatre as an art form.[8]

Unlike reading an essay, attending a theatrical performance is, by its very nature and in multiple ways, a communal or social phenomenon as well as an existential encounter. Havel stated that this was one of the reasons that he took up theatre in the first place: "I am a sociable creature and the less solitary genres suit me more; and since I've already taken up something as solitary as writing, then at least I write plays, which bring me closer to the theater, a 'nonsolitary' institution [*nesamotářský žánr*]" (Havel 1983a and b: letter 56). All theatre presupposes engagement in a group activity (*skupinovost*), but not all theatre takes genuinely aesthetic advantage of this basic feature; in other words, if *skupinovost* is present superficially as a mere formality, then this is not, for Havel, theatre in an authentically social form (Havel 1983a and b: letter 103). Genuinely social theatre begins to emerge when those participating in it stop being merely a group and become a community (*pospolitost*):

> It is that special moment when their mutual presence becomes mutual participation; when their encounter in a single space and time becomes an existential encounter; when their common existence in this world is suddenly enveloped by a very specific and unrepeatable atmosphere; when a shared experience, mutually understood, evokes the wonderful elation that makes all the sacrifices worthwhile. It is a moment when a common participation in a particular adventure of the mind, the imagination and the sense of humor, and a common experience of truth or a flash of insight into the "life in truth" suddenly establishes new relationships between the participants. Halfhearted coexistence suddenly blossoms into a feeling of mutual solidarity or brotherhood, even of brotherly love, despite the fact that many of the participants may not have known or seen each other before. This electrifying atmosphere of "alliance" or "fellowship" is a central aspect of the "socialness" of the theatre I am talking about. It is hard to investigate its causes and consequences theoretically, because it is supremely difficult to investigate existential reality theoretically. (Havel 1983a and b: letter 103)

Havel asserts in this sense that plays were meant to be staged because only staging can give them authentically social meaning: "A play is written such that only performance can impart meaning to it. If plays were written to be read, they would be written differently" (Havel 1983a and b: letter 32).

The socialness of theatre has an inherent deeper layer in that the sense of community created by theatrical performance depends upon a particular kind of collective perception: "[I]n the theater the work we are watching is not finished, but instead is being born before our eyes, with our help, so that we are both witnesses to its birth and, in a small sense, its co-creators as well";[9] theatrical performance is not a dead thing created by a living person but rather a living phenomenon that therefore produces "an immediate existential bond ... between the work and we who perceive it" such that the work "can only come into being and take place as a social ('interpersonal') event; seeing it is more than just an act of perception, it is a form of human relationship" (Havel 1983a and b: letter 105). Cultivating a sense of theatrical performance as a human relationship is the job not only of the actors on the stage but also of the spectators themselves as they become engaged in the performance. Theatre, in this sense, is "not just another genre, one among many" but rather "the only genre in which, today and every day, now and always, living human beings address and speak to other human beings"; it is not just a venue for the performance of stories and tales, but "a place of human encounter, a space for authentic human existence, above all the kind of existence that transcends itself in order to give an account of the world" (World Theatre Day 1994).[10]

Even more abstractly, the performance of a play, in Havel's understanding, represents a ritual that acts as

> ... a kind of immediate and vivid enactment of the very mystery of human existence. The viewer remains himself, a living, thinking, consciously acting person, and yet at the same time ... he steps outside himself and ... he relinquishes his own identity and assumes that of another (the one being represented). It is this that points toward the real mystery of human existence and human identity, actualizes that mystery, brings it to the foreground of our awareness, opens it anew. (Havel 1983a and b: letter 105)

In another context, Havel described the inherent socialness of theatre as an "existential cord" that binds the public to the experience of the performance. Unlike an essay, then, a play derives an essential part of its meaning from its realization in performance. When we react to Macheath's monologue with shouts of "Bravo!," we simultaneously witness and co-create the performance, and we do so in existential fellowship with other members of the audience. The process of making theatre happen – the communal form that defines, at least partially, theatrical performance as a genre – thus enacts key features of its message or meaning.

Obviously not unrelated to Havel's emphasis on genuinely "social" theatre is his focus on the appeal or *apel*, another feature of his dramatic style. Previously we noted that Havel uses absurdist techniques to create an "empty space" for audience self-reflection. The empty space exists because the play has intentionally left things unsaid and undecided; it is crafted in such a way as to focus the audience's attention towards this unresolved space (Grossman 1999: 71). In order to make sense of the play, the audience must engage and struggle with it, becoming implicated or "embedded" in the performance, and theatre-goers thus come to experience the performance as a kind of existential encounter. It is not, of course, the only way that the viewer is drawn into the performance, and we noted some of the varied manifestations of the appeal in the first chapter's analytic sketch of the Vaněk plays. If, however, the viewers are unwilling to be drawn into the performance for whatever reason, and do not ultimately confront the play's empty space, then the play will not seem meaningful to them; it will seem "weird" merely in the negative sense of the word. This point may account for the initial reaction of my two communication undergraduates to *The Memorandum*. We expect a play to be entertaining, but our concept of entertainment does not normally include an expectation of being provoked into a personal intellectual and spiritual struggle with a play's "empty space."

Havel characterized the audience's intellectual and spiritual struggle with a genuinely social play in the same terms that he used in reference to the cinematic gag. The appeal-oriented play disturbs the viewer's perception through a special kind of defamiliarization that ideally triggers deep self-reflection:

> Instead of seeing and immediately recognizing life as they know and understand it and delighting in that, the audience becomes party to an unexpected and surprising "probe" beneath the surface of phenomena which, at the same time as it gives them a new insight into their own situation, does it in a way that is comprehensible, credible and convincing on its own terms. This kind of theatre allows us to see beneath the surface of phenomena, to see their inner coherences, the questions they raise, their hidden meaning, how they bear witness, in a "model" way, to man's general situation in the world. (Havel 1983a and b: letter 104)

Absurdist techniques are deployed in service of the play's defamiliarizing aesthetics.[11] Absurdity rids everyday phenomena of their conventionalized or automatized meanings and thereby opens up the question of their true meaning: "The absurdity of entities [acts] as an invitation to inquire after the nature of Being" (Havel 1983a and b: letter 52).

Using a different vocabulary than Havel but arriving at the same conclusions, Grossman described the theatre of the appeal as an art form designed to "activate" the audience. He also argued that audience activation was greatly facilitated by the rise of small-form theatres (Grossman 1999: 71). For Grossman, as for Havel, activation of the audience had a deeper significance than just a theatrical one. It engendered not merely a kind of theatre-specific energy and engagement, but created the existential ground for engagement in the broader communal space of society itself. In this regard, I am reminded of a statement by the Brazilian theatre director, writer, and politician Augusto Boal, founder of the Theatre of the Oppressed. According to Boal, the essence of theatre as empowerment "resides in the means by which the performance can be extrapolated to other realities" (Boal 1998).

Audience activation in the theatre of the appeal, though, is not pedantically instructive. In this regard, Havel himself stated in *Disturbing the Peace* that his "author's credo" – and not only as a playwright – could be summed up in two lines delivered by a character in one of his plays: "I don't give practical advice, and I don't make arrangements for anyone. At most, I occasionally goad into action" (Havel 1991b: 199–200 and 1990: 173).[12] Havel thus goads his audience to consider the ways in which the performance may be, to borrow Boal's phrasing, "extrapolated to other realities." The paths for such extrapolation are many, and depend on what each member of the audience takes from the encounter:

> This kind of theater neither instructs us, nor attempts to acquaint us with theories or interpretations of the world, but by "probing" beneath the surface, it somehow inspires us to participate in an adventurous journey towards a deeper understanding, or rather to a new and deeper questioning, of ourselves and the world. (Havel 1983a and b: letter 104)

Martin Esslin, in his seminal book on absurdist theatre, reached a similar conclusion in emphasizing that absurdism does not represent a solution-oriented appeal: "Instead of being provided with a *solution*, the spectator is challenged to formulate the *questions* that he will have to ask if he wants to approach the meaning of the play" (Esslin 2001: 416). When spectators give Macheath a standing ovation and, in doing so, experience a probing moment of personal inauthenticity, they have been goaded by Havel into questioning the meaning of that moment for their off-stage lives. While the spectators' encounter with Macheath does not resolve any concrete personal (or sociopolitical) dilemmas, it prompts them to reflect more deeply on what form those dilemmas might actually take.[13]

Coming into sharper focus now is an understanding of why Havel may not have felt wholly comfortable with the essay as a form. Despite being a master essayist himself, Havel recognized the conceptual limitations of the form, and he made efforts in his essays – through use of metaphor, images, and stories – to escape the confines of the form's propositional structure. Our experience of meaning, not to mention our sense of meaningfulness, is much greater and often considerably more nuanced and complex than what can be captured in logically propositional (or even verbal) form. We have all experienced moments in our lives when words have failed us; we all therefore recognize that words are sometimes inadequate for capturing how things are. Plays are able to get at forms of meaning that elude the propositional cage. A theatrical performance may succeed in conveying a rich complexity of meaning that an essay on the same theme simply fails to do. To borrow a phrase from Stoppard, the tendency to "square the circle" of human meaning is much stronger in an essay than a play.

The approach to the meaning of theatre as a genre that Havel outlines in the metatext of his prison letters has strong affinities with an account of meaning and meaningfulness presented by Johnson in his 2007 book *The Meaning of the Body: Aesthetics of Human Understanding*. Johnson's approach is inspired by the American philosopher John Dewey's book *Art as Experience* (Dewey 2005). Johnson's views on meaning shed light on the form/meaning relationship that underlies Havel's dramatic style, as well as on the essay/play contrast.[14]

Johnson writes, for example, about the irreducibility of our experience of meaning to the verbal proposition, and argues instead for an "embodied" view:

> Human meaning concerns the character and significance of a person's interactions with their environments. The meaning of a specific aspect or dimension of some ongoing experience is that aspect's connections to other parts of past, present, and future (possible) experiences. Meaning is relational. It is about how one thing relates to or connects with other things ... Sometimes our meanings are conceptually and propositionally coded, but that is merely the more conscious, selective dimension of a vast, continuous process of immanent meanings that involve structures, patterns, qualities, feelings, and emotions. An embodied view is naturalistic, insofar as it situates meaning within a flow of experience that cannot exist without a biological organism engaging its environment. Meanings emerge "from the bottom up" through increasingly complex levels of organic activity; they are not the constructions of a disembodied mind. (Johnson 2007: 10)

In an embodied theory of meaning, then, conceptualization is a process within the ongoing flow of experience; it is the interfusing of feeling and thought that goes into what Johnson, following Dewey, calls the mind-body (Johnson 2007: 279). Meaning-as-flow does not require formalization or systematization, and meaningfulness cannot be reduced to a propositional account, especially given that visual and kinetic properties of meaning cannot themselves be readily represented in propositional or verbal form. By fetishizing the rational and the verbal, we thus misconstrue human meaning: "[I]f we reduce meaning to words and sentences (to concepts and propositions), we miss or leave out where meaning really comes from. We end up intellectualizing human experience, understanding, and thinking, and we turn processes into static entities or properties" (Johnson 2007: 11). According to Johnson, most philosophical approaches to meaning "focus exclusively on the conceptual-propositional skeletal structures of meaning while entirely overlooking the emotional flesh and blood of actual human meaning" (2007: 53).

Directing these reflections back onto the contrast between essays and plays, we may say that an essay privileges "conceptual-propositional skeletal structures" while a theatrical performance in the style of the theatre of the appeal represents a procedural form of meaning-as-flow in which the viewer is engaged if not also implicated. If the essayist explains to us precisely how language may end up controlling us, the playwright simulates or models – performatively enacts – this same idea through an embodied experience. While the argumentative thread of an essay is not entirely divorced from the flow of experience, the essay presents its theme detached from the flow itself; an essayistic presentation simply cannot match the impact and phenomenal immediacy of a theatrical performance. A play as performance more deftly captures Dewey's "pervasive quality of a situation," that is, those qualities, feelings, images, and patterns of embodiment that Johnson argues are the ground of all meaning (2007: 72ff.).

Essays and plays, in other words, contrast in their respective realizations of the form/meaning nexus. While an essay is mostly *saying*, a theatrical performance is much more *experiencing* and *being*. In Havel's own words, plays create, unlike other genres, an autonomous world that is simultaneously tied to and disconnected from the phenomenal "order of things" that surrounds us. We are drawn into that world "by living people, who directly represent it to us and who are [themselves] both in it and not in it"; the play is therefore "literally a living fiction" (Havel

1983a and b: letter 114). Thus, the representation of meaningfulness via a theatrical performance emphasizes what we identified earlier as the existential level of interpretation. Havel himself noted that theatre is "an existential phenomenon par excellence" that is, by its very nature, "an 'intersubjective' event" as well as "an 'interexistential' (or perhaps more precisely, a 'superexistential') phenomenon"; the performance resides in the here and now, but at the same time transcends its concrete existential moment (Havel 1983a and b: letter 112).

A theatrical performance is existential to the extent that it can act as a form of therapeutic empowerment for the individual engaged in it. It is "intersubjective" and "interexistential" to the extent that it is a communal event that captures the "collective spirit" of the community in which it emerges; it is, in Havel's words, "naturally bound by [a] complex 'metabolic' system to its own age and society" (Havel 1983a and b: letter 112). A play is

> ... an organ in the larger organism of society and its time, necessarily influenced by everything that influences them. It is a confluence of their currents – be they ever so hidden. Like it or not, theater is always more or less connected to everything by which the "collective spirit" lives – to its hidden and open themes, its dilemmas, to the existential questions that manifest themselves to it or as it manifests them, to the sensibility, the emotivity of the age, its moods, its thought and expression, its gestures, its visual sensibilities, its life-style, fashion ... (Havel 1983a and b: letter 112)

Theatre is, then, "the point at which the intellectual and spiritual life of the human community crystallizes" (World Theatre Day 1994), and the bond between theatre and its historical context is symbiotic. Theatre "connects up with its age in one way or another; it reflects and cocreates it, analyses and alters it, parodies and negates it; all of that is always more present in theater than in anything else" (Havel 1983a and b: letter 112).

The existential level of interpretation is, at multiple levels, built into the very form of theatre. Theatre, however, existentially reflects something beyond the individual human being and human society. It also manages to convey something of the very "skeleton of Being." This deeper manifestation of the existential level derives from theatre's ancient foundation, side by side with spirituality and religion, in human awareness of the time-space continuum and of a compositional structure or order to human life. The deeper philosophical meaning of theatre is as a concentrated and performative enactment of human awareness of the "order of things," and this includes our sensitivity to deviations from and interruptions of that order and structure.[15]

According to Havel, theatre today is one of the many late cultural renderings of an absolutely fundamental human experience of the world and an experience of being human in the world. The stuff of theatre – a sense of relational time, a sense of spatial form, repetition and cycling, an awareness of connections or linkages (*souvislosti*) among phenomena – is the very fabric of human consciousness reduced to its existential building-blocks. Because of this, Havel could assert that theatre is nothing other than "an attempt to comprehend, in concentrated form, the world itself," an attempt that is moreover "mediated through our comprehension of the world's temporal and spatial logic." Drama is "a kind of special [*zvláštní*] attempt to comprehend ... the very logic of Being," and every play, even if it lasts for only two hours, "manifests, or wants to manifest, the whole world" itself.

Havel himself made clear that his personal and philosophical reflections on theatre do not apply to plays of all types. Indeed, we certainly have moved far beyond conventional American expectations of theatrical performance, which are oriented, for the most part, to its entertainment potential. Havel's reflections on theatre do give us much (and much-needed) insight into the ways in which his dramatic style enacts its meaning. We may recall our discussion in the first chapter of the Vaněk plays, and specifically of the effects that these plays have on the audience. The Vaněk plays do not offer solutions to the dilemma of human identity in the modern world as much as they prompt us to self-reflection. The plays invite us to engage in dialogue with ourselves and others about their meaning. They embed us, in various ways, into the dramatic tension enacted on stage, and they force us to take multiple perspectives as engaged witnesses to that tension. They create a longing for action, disruption, and change. They make us existentially uncomfortable by prompting us to self-reflect through questioning. What is valid for the Vaněk trilogy is also valid, in one form or another, for all of Havel's plays, and we could characterize the import of Havel's dramatic style in Vaněk terms as a kind of "catalyst" that opens up "certain vistas onto the world" in which we live; his plays as a whole represent a "gleam, if you will, in whose light we view" the larger landscape of our lives (Havel 1987: 239).

Through contrasting the essays with the plays and delving more deeply into Havel's views on the meaning of theatre, we better understand why theatrical performance is, conceptually speaking, Havel's primary genre. Theatrical performance generates meaning in a way that the essay, by its very nature, cannot. Plays do things to us and through us in ways that essays mostly cannot, just as music acts on us in a way that words cannot. In fact, in *Disturbing the Peace*, Havel used an analogy to music to describe his dramatic aesthetic. He specifically compared the deliberate formal arrangement of his plays to the structure of a musical composition:

> You will find that ... [the] interior structure [of my plays], the way they're put together, is not very cleverly disguised, nor do they appear to be a spontaneous, smooth-flowing, natural unfolding of life in a series of incidents. I'm the type of author who constructs his plays, and I admit it; I deliberately make their structures easy to grasp, I stress them, reveal them, and often give them geometrically direct and regular features – all in the hope that it will not be understood as a clumsy fault, or as something deliberately self-serving, but as something that has a certain meaning as well ... [I am not a musician and don't know much about music ...] but I still think that, because of this intensified emphasis on composition, something close to music and musical thought enters my plays. (Havel 1991b: 192 and 1990: 166)

Form is key to Havel's overall project, and the plays are conceptually primary because the form/meaning nexus embodied in a theatrical performance represents a kind of meaningfulness central to the project in both its literary and political realizations.

Thus, the plays provide the formal and conceptual skeleton most suited to conveying Havel's message. They are not one genre among many that we may comment on (or not) when discussing Havel's intellectual trajectory, but rather the embodiment, in concentrated form, of that trajectory's essential shape. In other words, the fact that we applaud both during and after a performance of one of Havel's plays is not incidental to the meaning of our encounter. Havel certainly engages us in the performance by entertaining us, but he also embeds and implicates us in the meaning of the play as an existential experience that is designed to change us in some deep way. According to Havel, the audience should be delighted with the play as theatre, but at the same time they should be disturbed or spiritually unsettled by the performance (Havel 1983a and b: letter 71).[16]

In spite of the key role that theatrical performance played in Havel's oeuvre, it would not be wrong to say that most English-language commentators on Havel – who are, for the most part, academics oriented towards the social sciences rather than the humanities – have given priority to Havel's essays over his plays.[17] The rational argumentation and propositional logic characteristic of the essayistic mode has taken pride of place over the experiential "flow" of meaning associated with theatrical performance. Our conventional expectations of the most meaningful form of discourse (i.e., what type of form can best serve as a vehicle to communicate seriousness of meaning) results in a misconstrual or misreading of Havel's project and, at the same time, interferes with our appreciation for Havel as a playwright.

We have now come full circle and returned to the comment made by one of my students, which praised the explanatory "objectivity" of the essays while bemoaning the unserious "subjectivity" of the plays. This student's attitude reflects much the same stance that follows from the scholarly tendency to prioritize the essays over the plays. The labels "objective" and "subjective" miss, however, their targets, and in the next section I will suggest an alternative approach to modelling the contrast between essays and plays that extends our reflections on human meaning and meaningfulness by taking advantage of a conceptual opposition that runs throughout Havel's oeuvre and acts, like the mosaic principle in the first chapter, as a key thread in the fabric of his thinking.

Explaining and *understanding*

Making sense of theatrical performance as central to Havel's project requires us to rethink conventional ideas about human meaningfulness. To take seriously the idea that Havel's essays serve as *explications du texte* for his plays means accepting that essay and play represent two contrasting modes of discourse or ways of conveying meaning. I will propose that we can account for the essay/play contrast as a token of a larger type of conceptual opposition that Havel often invoked, explicitly and implicitly, in his writing and thinking. The opposition between *explaining* and *understanding* – the respective Czech terms are *vysvětlení* and *chápání* – represents two divergent ways of thinking, two different perspectives on meaning and truth, two contrasting ways by which we understand ourselves and our relationship to the world around us. Havel did not theorize or intellectualize the *explaining/understanding* opposition, but the opposition does serve as a background assumption in much of his thought. Like the mosaic principle, it may also be taken as a conceptual tool for making sense of the world in which we live. It is a tool that we can use to read the world as well as to read ourselves.

As a first step in exploring this opposition, we should consider the etymology of each of the words involved in it, and I will amplify this step by investigating the etymology of the Czech as well as the English terms. The origin of English "explain" is clear: it derives from the Latin prefix *ex-* ("out") and the root *planus* ("flat"), which gives an original meaning of "to make level, flatten out."[18] While the etymology of English "understand" is less clear, the original meaning was spatial and probably meant something like "to stand in the midst of": *under* + *standan* ("to stand"), although *under* not in its usual meaning of "beneath" but derived from Proto-Indo-European **nter-* "between, among" (cf. Latin *inter*). Etymological dictionaries indicate that the ultimate sense may have been "to be close to," and in this respect "understand" is semantically similar to Greek *epistamai* ("I know how, I know") with the literal meaning "to stand upon."

The English etymologies hint at the broad contours of the opposition between *explaining* and *understanding* as Havel made use of it. The former implies an impersonal and mechanical experience of the phenomenon under consideration, a "flattening out" of the phenomenon in order, perhaps, to facilitate manipulation of it. The latter establishes, in contrast, a personal and dynamic relationship between subject and object: we ourselves are "in the midst of" (or "close to") that which is being confronted. We might think of this in terms of the vantage-point implied by each etymology: *explaining* places us outside of the phenomenon and seemingly in detached control of it, while *understanding* represents an experiential view from nearby or perhaps even from the inside. In the former case, we are removed from meaning, but in the latter we are in the midst of it.

Also relevant here is the etymological origin of *chápání*, the Czech word for "understanding." The literal meaning of the root *chap-* or *chop-* in Czech is "grasping" or "seizing." In this regard, it is exactly like English "comprehend," which derives from the Latin prefix *com-* ("completely") and the verbal root *prehendere* ("to catch hold of, seize"). Both words imply a dynamic relationship between the human subject and the object that she or he is trying to "take hold of" mentally. While the semantic thrust of *explaining* is to remove the dynamism from the object under consideration by leveling it away, the etymology of *chápání* suggests active human involvement in the procedural flow of meaning. Understanding as *chápání* implies being engaged in a struggle – a grappling or wrestling – with meaning and for meaningfulness.

The same object or phenomenon can of course be construed with respect to *explaining*, on the one hand, and *understanding*, on the other, but our respective construals will differ in fundamental ways. An example of this might be our reaction to the telling of a joke. To be funny, a joke must be *understood* or spontaneously "grasped" as a dynamic or holistic experience; the listener is a participant in the flow of the humour. There is, however, nothing less funny than a joke that needs to be *explained*. Explaining a joke tells us something (or everything) about the mechanics of its humour, but at the same time it deflates the joke's very essence.

In teaching the *explaining/understanding* opposition in the context of my course on Havel, I have often told my students about my first time flying. I was in the fifth grade, and a relative took me to Disneyworld in Florida. I missed several days of school because of the trip, and my teacher was willing to give me permission to go only if I would promise to report back to the class about my experience. Flying was much less common in the 1970s than it is now, and I may well have been the first student in my fifth-grade class to fly. Knowing this, my teacher gave me a specific assignment. I was to find out as much as I could about the plane and the flight: what kind of plane it was, how many seats it had, how fast it flew, how many miles the trip from Baltimore to Florida entailed, and how long the journey took. As I tell my students, my teacher's assignment was wholly oriented towards the *explaining* mode. What seemed to matter most to my teacher was the technical or mechanical aspects of the flight, and the experience of flying for the first time was reduced to these. Yet most of us can recall our first experience flying, and it is doubtful that the statistical particulars of the trip are what first come to mind.

My teacher did not, that is, ask me to write a story, a poem, or a play about what it felt like to take off into the air, and she did not want me to report back to the class on my emotions and impressions as I saw the ground below me (through clouds!) for the first time in my life. In the modern world, flying has become routine, and we tend to equate the "meaning" of a flight with a speedy and safe delivery to our destination. But to flatten out the meaning of flying as a human experience, especially the meaning of a child's first time on an airplane, is to miss something essential about that experience. We can fly in a plane because we have been able to *explain* the mechanics of flight, but *understanding* flying as an experience – how it changes our perspective on the world, how it may change us as human beings – is not reducible to a scientific accounting.

As might be expected, *explaining* is characteristic of the modern scientific world view, and this is a key point that we will examine in the next chapter. *Explaining* deals in facts, statistics, and formulae. It is a mode privileging analysis, which is from Greek *ana-lusis*: "un-loosening" or "unfastening," breaking things down into their component parts. *Explaining* is largely about knowledge as information; we know through discrete quantification and incremental measurement. Through the *explaining* mode, we view phenomena in the world as problems to be "solved" through technical means. In contrast to *explaining*, *understanding* is a mode of relating to the world that is more art than science. It deals in stories, myths, and emotion. An *understanding* construal always has some form of "human content" (*lidský obsah*), and this is a favourite Havelian phrase that occurs in many of his presidential speeches. If *explaining* is impersonal and "objective," *understanding* privileges the personal and "subjective" contours of human experience.[19] In construal via *understanding*, there is appreciation for the value of insight through human intuition and not just through "objective" forms of measurement.[20]

If we bring the *explaining/understanding* opposition to bear on themes from the first chapter of this book, we can say that traditional ways of reading Havel are attempts to *explain* him, and that these attempts circumscribe the appeal component of Havel's writings. They do facilitate a certain reading of Havel, but at the same time they may make it more difficult for us to read ourselves through him. In this regard, the *explaining* mode could be thought of as equivalent to Stoppard's "squaring the circle": explanations may launch related trails of inquiry, but they tend to shut down the local conversation by "resolving" the ambiguity and mystery surrounding a given phenomenon. If we apply the *explaining/understanding* opposition back to the mosaic principle, then we could say that *understanding* is about making connections between phenomena, putting pieces of the mosaic together to create a sense of the bigger picture. *Understanding* is about "brokenness made beautiful," intact, and whole again. The only way to *understand* Havel, then, is through an integrative approach to his various faces. Fragmentation of the genres is merely an expedient for *explaining* him, which often results in reinventing him in the reader's own image or preconceptions.

Havel's invocation of the opposition

With a general account of the *explaining/understanding* opposition behind us, we are in a position to consider specific examples of the ways in which Havel invoked the opposition in his writings. These examples will, in turn, shed more light on the opposition itself. As a conceptual thread woven into his overall intellectual project, Havel frequently invoked the opposition implicitly rather than explicitly, and we have already seen one case of this. In reflecting on the communal nature of theatre earlier in this chapter, we noted the key distinction that Havel made between theatre as *skupinovost* and theatre as *pospolitost*, the former being a kind of mechanical definition of theatre's social nature (theatre as a project that necessarily involves a group of people) and the latter being an *understanding*-level reading of theatre's communality (theatre that results in the creation of an existential bond or an authentic community). In theatre as *skupinovost*, the experience is the mere sum of its parts; in theatre as *pospolitost*, the parts call out a larger whole that renders the experience meaningful. This example also hints at the notion that *explaining* is conceptually more narrow than *understanding*: theatre as an experience of genuine community presupposes theatre as a group of people engaged in a common project, but the former transcends and transforms the latter. *Explaining* and *understanding* represent a conceptual opposition, but not a dichotomous one.

Unlike *skupinovost*, *pospolitost* has "human content," and Havel frequently emphasized the personal or human content of the *understanding* mode. For example, in an address at the University of Michigan in 2000 upon acceptance of an honorary degree, Havel reflected on the meaning of truth and, more specifically, on the difference between truth and information. He begins by pointing out the obvious fact that the modern age is also the age of information:

> We now live in the age of an information revolution when hundreds of thousands – or millions or even billions – of pieces of information crisscross the globe every second at a frantic speed, covering the whole surface of the planet with one continuous communication network. This is undoubtedly a marvelous achievement to which I have no objection whatsoever.[21]

He then takes note of a paradox arising from this: "However, it seems to me that it is of paramount importance – and especially given the global information revolution – to understand the subtle difference between information and truth." Havel addresses the difference directly:

> To put it briefly and simply, I believe that truth is also information but, at the same time, it is something more. Truth is obviously information that, like any other kind of information, has been clearly demonstrated or

> affirmed or verified within a certain paradigmatic system of coordinates, or information that is simply convincing. It is also, however, information that has been vouched for by a human being with his or her whole existence, with his or her reputation and honor, with his or her name.

In Havel's account, truth is information that does not merely have "human content," but is defined by having it. Truth is not impersonal and abstract, but rather something that we are willing, and perhaps even compelled, to vouch for or guarantee with our very being. While we can remain comfortably detached from information as a form of *explaining*, truth can only be grasped or *understood* as such from the inside.

In insisting on a distinction between *explaining*-oriented information and *understanding*-oriented truth, Havel is suggesting that a relationship to the world mediated through information alone does not and cannot do justice to the meaningfulness of human experience. We might say that *explaining* deprives us of an aesthetic and ethical relationship to the phenomenon being considered, in much the same way that my teacher's assignment, focused on the technical facts of air travel, undermined the meaningfulness of a childhood experience of flying. In privileging *explaining* over *understanding*, we distance ourselves from the world, but this stance comes at a price.

Havel described the price paid for fetishizing the *explaining* mode in a memorable passage from one of his letters from prison. His specific theme in the letter was, of all things, cows:

> Not long ago, while watching a report on cows on the television news, I realized that the cow is no longer an animal: it is a machine that has an "input" (grain feeds) and an "output" (milk). It has its own production plans and its own operator whose job is the same job of the entire economy today: to increase output while decreasing input. The cow serves us quite efficiently, really, but at the cost of no longer being a cow ... [M]an has grasped the world in a way that has caused him, de facto, to lose it; he has subdued it by destroying it ... [B]y robbing the cow of the last remnants of her autonomy as a cow, man has, at the same time, robbed himself of his human identity. (Havel 1983a and b: letter 118)

Havel's larger theme here is the modern crisis of human identity, and he uses the cow example to illustrate his broader point. Modern society treats cows (and not only cows) as resources to be controlled and exploited for human benefit. Cows have become machines for producing milk and other products like leather and meat. However, in cultivating a relationship to cows (and, more broadly speaking, to the world as a whole) that maximizes the *explaining* mode, we not only deprive the cow of its inherent cow-ness, but we unintentionally deprive ourselves of our human-ness. At a certain point in the letter, Havel predicts the death of modern human civilization unless we fundamentally change our relationship to the world in which we live. In other words, recovery or rediscovery of an *understanding* orientation through transcending modern society's obsession with *explaining* will prove key to the survival of humanity.

Havel offered a more philosophical account of the *explaining/understanding* opposition, one that both reinforces and extends the points made above, in a 1992 speech to the French Academy of Humanities and Political Sciences. In this philosophical account, Havel explicitly uses the terms that define the opposition. The main theme of the speech is existential waiting.[22] Havel argues that the world as a whole ought to learn what he calls a "dissident's kind of waiting," which is a waiting that is

> ... based on the knowledge that it made sense to resist on principle by speaking the truth simply because it was the right thing to do, without speculating whether it would lead somewhere tomorrow, or the day after, or ever. This kind of waiting grew out of the faith that repeating this defiant truth made sense in itself, regardless of whether it was ever appreciated ... [A] seed once sown would one day take root and send forth a shoot. No one knew when. But it would happen someday, perhaps for future generations.

A dissident's approach to waiting is a kind of "cultivated patience" or waiting "as a state of hope." Dissidents learned to wait, in other words, "in a way that has meaning."

Havel juxtaposed this kind of waiting to the waiting embodied by Godot, a character from Samuel Beckett's (in)famous play *Waiting for Godot*, a classic of French absurdist theatre. In Havel's view, Godot-like waiting is

> ... a meaningless form of self-deception and therefore a waste of time ... To wait until good seeds sprout is not the same as waiting for Godot. Waiting for Godot means waiting for lilies – ones that we have never planted – to begin to grow.

To the extent that Godot embodies the idea of universal salvation, then, Godot-like waiting – Havel calls this an "extreme position" – characterized many in the post-totalitarian world who had lost the sense that there was a way out of their existential dilemma. People lost the will to resist and they lost hope, but they did not lose the need for hope "because without hope a meaningful life is impossible." As a result, they

> ... waited for Godot. Because they did not carry hope within them, they expected it to arrive as some kind of salvation from without. But Godot ... will not come because he simply does not exist. He only represents hope. He is not hope itself, he is an illusion. He is a product of our own helplessness, a patch over a hole in the spirit.

Havel then generalizes Godot-like waiting from the Central/Eastern European sociopolitical context to the modern world as a whole by asserting that it is akin to "the destructive impatience of contemporary technocratic civilization" that "grows out of a vain ratiocentrism and assumes erroneously that the world is nothing but a crossword puzzle to be solved [and] that there is only one correct way – the so-called objective way – to solve it."

Havel's "vain ratiocentrism" is the modern world's obsession with *explaining*. In the culminating passage of the speech, Havel asserts:

> The world cannot be brought under total control because it is not a machine. And it cannot be rebuilt from the ground up merely on the basis of a technological idea. Utopians who believe this sow even greater suffering. If reason is disengaged from the unique human spirit and becomes the main guide to political action, it can only lead to the use of force, to violence. The world will resist an order forced upon it by a brain that has forgotten that it is itself merely a modest aspect of the world's infinitely rich morphology. And the more systematically and impatiently the world is crammed into rational categories, the more explosions of irrationality there are to astonish us.

Immediately following this, he invokes the *explaining/understanding* opposition in explicit terms:

> Yes, even I – the sarcastic critic of all those who vainly try to explain the world [*kritik všech pyšných vysvětlovačů světa*] – had to remind myself that the world

> cannot just be explained [*svět nelze jen vysvětlovat*], it must be grasped and understood as well [*je třeba ho i chápat*]. It is not enough to impose one's own words on it, but one must also listen to the polyphony of often-contradictory messages that the world sends out and try to penetrate their meaning. It is not enough to describe, in scientific terms, the mechanics of things and events; their spirit must be personally perceived and experienced.

Explaining, Havel suggests, is a degenerate form of true human *understanding*. Disembodied reason lacks a spirit, the aesthetic and ethical core underlying human meaningfulness.

It is the *explaining* mode's lack of a spirit, along with the necessity of a spiritual component for human meaningfulness, that proves crucial to how Havel deploys the *explaining/understanding* opposition in his literary and political writings. In the presidential speeches, Havel exploits the opposition to reframe the meaning of a diverse series of modern cultural phenomena. Should the law be meaningful to us merely as a technical code, or does the spirit of the law provide a necessary conceptual foundation for the meaning of its letter?[23] What does it mean to be European, what is the import of the European Union, and does European identity have a spiritual or moral component?[24] Is democracy best conceived of as a set of institutional mechanisms or as a form of identity, a way of relating to one's fellow citizens that both encourages and embodies a democratic way of being? We might also best read Havel's broader political project along these same lines as a conscious attempt to reframe the meaning of politics itself away from an *explaining* orientation (politics as a mechanism for acquiring and keeping power) and towards an *understanding* mode that incorporates "human content."

Context-specific invocations of the *explaining/understanding* opposition in the presidential speeches represent echoes of its realization in Havel's pre-1989 works. As we have already noted, the opposition appears in the philosophical letters from prison, and it also plays a central conceptual role in many of the so-called dissident essays. His 1984 essay "Politics and Conscience," for example, could be productively read through the filter of the *explaining/understanding* opposition. Havel begins the essay by describing his boyhood impressions of a factory smokestack, an emblem of the modern *explaining* mindset, that he would see in the distance on his walk to school:

> As a boy, I lived for some time in the country and I clearly remember an experience from those days: I used to walk to school in a nearby village

> along a cart track through the fields and, on the way, see on the horizon a huge smokestack of some hurriedly built factory, in all likelihood in the service of war. It spewed dense brown smoke and scattered it across the sky. Each time I saw it, I had an intense sense of something profoundly wrong, of humans soiling the heavens. I have no idea whether there was something like a science of ecology in those days; if there was, I certainly knew nothing of it. Still that "soiling of the heavens" offended me spontaneously. It seemed to me that, in it, humans are guilty of something, that they destroy something important, arbitrarily disrupting the natural order of things, and that such things cannot go unpunished ... If a medieval man were to see something like that suddenly on the horizon – say, while out hunting – he would probably think it the work of the Devil and would fall on his knees and pray that he and his kin be saved. (Havel 1991a: 249–50 and 1999, 4: 418–19)

Havel defamiliarizes the smokestack by describing it first through the eyes of a child and then from the hypothetical perspective of pre-industrial man. He argues that the child and the medieval man have something in common in that they "have not yet grown alienated from the world of their actual personal experience" and both remain "far more intensely rooted in what some philosophers call 'the natural world' ... than most modern adults" (Havel 1991a: 250 and 1999, 4: 419). In modern industrial society, a factory smokestack is accepted as a normal part of our everyday landscape, and we only come to question the meaning of the smokestack – to object to the dense brown smoke spewing forth from it – if the stench of that smoke penetrates the windows of our own home (Havel 1991a: 252 and 1999, 4: 421–2).

The smokestack in "Politics and Conscience" represents a central image embodying the larger argument of the essay, which explores the ramifications for modern man of the *explaining/understanding* opposition. Havel does not see the smokestack merely as "a regrettable lapse of a technology that failed to include 'the ecological factor' in its calculation, one which can be easily corrected with the appropriate filter," but rather as "the symbol of an age which seeks to transcend the boundaries of the natural world and its norms" (Havel 1991a: 251 and 1999, 4: 420). The smokestack is

> ... the symbol of an epoch which denies the binding importance of personal experience – including the experience of mystery and of the absolute – and displaces the personally experienced absolute as the measure

of the world with a new, man-made absolute, devoid of mystery, free of the "whims" of subjectivity and, as such, impersonal and inhuman. It is the absolute of so-called objectivity: the objective, rational cognition of the scientific model of the world. (Havel 1991a: 251–2 and 1999, 4: 420–1)

To modern science, the natural world appears "as no more than an unfortunate leftover from our backward ancestors, a fantasy of their childish immaturity," and it is a world that we – through science or through an *explaining* mode of being – systematically leave behind, deny, degrade, and defame (Havel 1991a: 252 and 1999, 4: 421). Havel clearly states that he is not proposing a nostalgic return to a pre-industrial way of life, but rather that he wishes to "consider, in a most general and admittedly schematic outline, the spiritual framework of modern civilization and the source of its present crisis" (Havel 1991a: 253 and 1999, 4: 422).

It should be clear that the argument in "Politics and Conscience" represents a much more developed treatment of the cow theme from the prison letter that Havel had written two years prior. In the essay, Havel is concerned with the loss of our human-ness in an epoch dominated by the *explaining* mode of being. His goal is not to abolish a scientific mindset in the modern world, but rather to direct attention to the loss of meaning that occurs when we blindly promote *explaining* at the expense of *understanding*. He suggests that recovery or rediscovery of our "human-ness" will necessitate a shift away from the former in favour of the latter.[25]

A companion piece to "Politics and Conscience," which was written less than a year later, is the short and lyrical essay "Thriller." "Thriller" is problematic, and therefore virtually ignored by commentators on Havel, because it does not fit into the usual politicized reading of the "dissident" essays. Titled after Michael Jackson's song and video of the same name, "Thriller" is a densely lyrical meditation on modern human identity that examines the loss of meaning that necessarily follows from an obsession with *explaining*. The opening paragraph is dramatic:

Before me lies the famous *Occult Philosophy* of Heinrich Cornelius Agrippa von Nettesheim, where I read that the ingestion of the living (and if possible still beating) heart of a hoopoe, a swallow, a weasel, or a mole will bestow upon one the gift of prophecy. It is nine o'clock in the evening and I turn on the radio. The announcer, a woman, is reading the news in a dry, matter-of-fact voice: Mrs. Indira Gandhi has been shot by two

> Sikhs in her personal bodyguard. The corpse of Father Popiełuszko, kidnapped by officers of the Polish police, has been fished out of the Vistula River. International aid is being organized for Ethiopia, where a famine is threatening the lives of millions, while the Ethiopian regime is spending almost a quarter of a billion dollars to celebrate its tenth anniversary. American scientists have developed plans for a permanent observatory on the Moon and for a manned expedition to Mars. In California, a little girl has received a heart transplanted from a baboon; various animal welfare societies have protested. (Havel 1991a: 285 and 1999, 4: 506)

In the juxtaposition of the events from the newscast with Agrippa's *Occult Philosophy*, Havel sees "a sophisticated collage that takes on the dimensions of a symbol, an emblem, a code," and although he does not know "what message is hidden in that unintentional artifact, which might be called 'Thriller,' after Michael Jackson's famous song," he feels "that chance – a great poet – is stammering an indistinct message about the desperate state of the modern world" (Havel 1991a: 289 and 1999, 4: 510–11).

The remainder of the essay is devoted to exploring the message of the collage in terms of the *explaining/understanding* opposition. Modern human civilization "has put its full weight behind cold, descriptive Cartesian reason and recognizes only thinking in concepts"; it is a civilization that believes that "everything can be 'rationally explained'" and that nothing is obscure (Havel 1991a: 286 and 1999, 4: 507–8). The modern age treats the heart merely as a mechanical pump, and modern man has, as a result, become a "methodical civil servant in the great bureaucracy of the world" (Havel 1991a: 290 and 1999, 4: 512). Havel calls this stance "a grand self-delusion of the modern spirit" (Havel 1991a: 287 and 1999, 4: 508), and asks how, in a completely rational age where everything can be *explained* and nothing is obscure, we can even hope to *understand* Hitler's crimes, committed at least partly in the name of a pseudo-scientific theory of race, or the cruel transformation of positivistic Marxism, which promulgated scientific knowledge of the laws of human history, into totalitarianism? Modern reason has jettisoned "human content" – a grounding in myth and a spirituality that transcends the reductive dictates of cold, abstract reason – and has substituted for it a kind of "natural" order that has often proven "erroneous, false, and disastrous, because it is always in some way deceitful, artificial, rootless, lacking in both ontology and morality" (Havel 1991a: 288 and 1999, 4: 509). A deeply dangerous irrationality hides "behind sober reason and a belief that the inexorable march of history demands the sacrifice of millions to assure a happy future for billions" (Havel 1991a: 288 and 1999, 4: 510). In a world where *explaining* has been elevated to the status of a cult, morality has taken "diffident refuge in the final asylum" to which it has been driven, the privatized asylum known as human conscience (Havel 1991a: 288 and 1999, 4: 510).

In Havel's account, modern human history is "pure medieval history," but the historical actors are scientists "possessing an allegedly scientific worldview" (Havel 1991a: 288–9 and 1999, 4: 510–11). Reason is the modern shroud that conceals dark things in human nature: "The demons have been turned loose and go about, grotesquely pretending to be honorable twentieth-century men who do not believe in evil spirits" (Havel 1991a: 289 and 1999, 4: 511). Towards the end of the essay, Havel recalls the collage of news items from the essay's dramatic opening and writes that while modern man has a human heart, we also have something of a baboon within us, and when we treat the heart only as a pump and deny the presence of the baboon, then "this officially nonexistent baboon, unobserved, goes on the rampage" (Havel 1991a: 290 1999, 4: 512).

Before beginning an in-class discussion of the essay, I often ask my students to briefly summarize "Thriller" in their own words by completing, as succinctly as possible, the sentence "'Thriller' is about ..." One student once wrote that the essay is about "the transition of human culture from the world of myths to the world of science," and another said that it is concerned with "a civilization in transition" that reminded her of "emergence from childhood into adulthood." Still another suggested that the main theme is a "loss of meaning in the modern world." All of these descriptions capture something about both the message of "Thriller" and the import of Havel's reliance on the opposition between *explaining* and *understanding*. "Thriller" is an essay that does not fit into traditional accounts of the politics of dissent because it is concerned instead with the wider sociohistorical and cultural frame against which modern politics in both East and West plays out. In Havel's essay, we are shown that it is not just that the modern age reduces the meaning of things, like flying, to *explaining*, but also that we have been systematically trained to disattend the *understanding* level. The price that we pay for such disattendance may be much greater than a mere inability to appreciate the poetry of flight.

Realizations of the opposition beyond Havel

Although the opposition between *explaining* and *understanding* represents an organizing principle in Havel's thinking, it is not an opposition that Havel originated, nor is it unique to his thought. In teaching Havel and having as a result become sensitive to the *explaining / understanding* contrast, I have encountered the same idea realized in a diversity of contexts and forms. A few examples will be instructive in that they should help make better sense of the opposition and, therefore, of its focal role in Havel's thought.

In considering Havel's fascination with the *explaining / understanding* opposition, I am reminded of a particularly evocative passage from the writings of the American pragmatic philosopher and semiotician Charles S. Peirce, in which a similar opposition is described:

> Take a corpse: dissect it, more perfectly than it ever was dissected. Take out the whole system of blood vessels entire, as we see them figured in the books. Treat the whole systems of spinal and sympathetic nerves, the alimentary canal ..., the muscular system, the osseous system, in the same way. Hang these all in a cabinet so that from a certain point of view each appears superposed over the others in its proper place. That would be a singularly instructive specimen. But to call it a man would be what nobody would for an instant do or dream. Now the best definition that ever was framed is, at best, but a similar dissection ... It will enable us to see how the thing works, in so far as it shows the efficient causation. The final causation ... it leaves out of account. (Peirce 1931, 1: 220)[26]

In relation to Peirce's description, we can say that *explaining* is the "instructive specimen" resulting from the idealized dissection as well as the verbal definition of a concept, both being for Peirce representations of "efficient causation" whereby "the parts compose the whole" (Peirce 1931, 1: 220). Opposed to this is a form of *understanding* represented by a living person or the concept as it is enacted; the phenomenon is understood with regard, in Peirce's terms, to final causation, or the "kind whereby the whole calls out its parts" (Peirce 1931, 1: 220). This example gives us perhaps a clearer appreciation of what is lost through an *explaining* focus, and of how and why we might consider *explaining* to be a degenerate form of *understanding*. A corporeal dissection is indeed a grossly inadequate stand-in for the living person.

The domains of spirituality and religion also yield realizations of the *explaining/understanding* opposition. Karen Armstrong begins her 2009 book *The Case for God* by discussing the contrast between two "ways of thinking, speaking, and acquiring knowledge" that were recognized in most pre-modern cultures (Armstrong 2009: xi). The ancient Greeks, she notes, called them *logos* and *mythos*, and they were both considered essential and complementary: "Each had its own sphere of competence, and it was considered unwise to mix the two" (Armstrong 2009: xi). *Logos* ("reason" or, in Havel's terms, *explaining*) was a pragmatic mode of thought that enabled people to function effectively in the world (e.g., to make an efficient weapon or plan an expedition); *logos* was aimed at control of one's environment, improvement of old insights, invention (Armstrong 2009: xi). While essential to survival, *logos* had its limitations: "it could not assuage human grief or find ultimate meaning in life's struggles," and for that people turned to *mythos*.[27]

In later parts of her book, Armstrong notes that modern interpretations of religion and spirituality have become couched in terms of *logos*: we "have become used to thinking that religion should provide us with information" (Armstrong 2009: 318). In Havel's terms, the *explaining* mindset has encroached upon the domains of religion and spirituality, which are usually considered (and truly ought to be considered) as emerging from and oriented towards *understanding*. Much of the argument of Armstrong's book focuses on the modern spiritual hunger for *mythos*, a deep-seated desire to make sense of the world in terms that restore *understanding* to its proper place. While the *logos/mythos* opposition may not present a perfect parallel with Havel, Armstrong's discussion of the crisis of modern spirituality is strongly reminiscent of Havel's contrast between *explaining* and *understanding* with regard to human or spiritual content, the distinction between information and truth, and the loss of meaningfulness that follows from a *logos*-centred world.

Two additional writers and thinkers provide us with realizations of the *explaining/understanding* opposition, and we have already encountered both of these thinkers. Both are, unlike Peirce and Armstrong, close to Havel in one respect or another. The first of these writers predates Havel and very probably influenced his thinking, while the second is Havel's contemporary, and his treatment of the opposition between *explaining* and *understanding* arguably emerges directly from a thoughtful reading of Havel's own texts. The first is Arendt, and I will consider her treatment of, on the one hand, totalitarianism (Arendt 1968) and, on the other, the "banality of evil" as embodied in the figure of Adolf Eichmann (Arendt 2006). The second writer is Stoppard, whose 2006 play *Rock 'n' Roll*, directly inspired by Havel's pre-presidential writings, highlights the dramatic tension and human dimensions of the dilemma inherent in the *explaining/understanding* opposition.

Hannah Arendt on totalitarianism and the Eichmann trial

According to Bernard Bergen, an opposition between *explaining* and *understanding* is an Arendtian theme that "we confront ... at virtually every point in her work" (Bergen 1998: 28). For Arendt, *understanding* "was not a term equivalent to *explanation*, but contrary to it," and her seminal work that coined the term "totalitarianism" in reference to both Nazism and Stalinism (Arendt 1968) was aimed at *understanding* the phenomenon and was not intended to define it as a problem to be *explained*. In Arendt's thinking as in Havel's, explanatory knowing is primarily about control of events, and it provides a framework for accounting for events. Explanation, in this light, is a kind of objective knowledge that deals in causes (Bergen 1998: 29). Explanatory knowledge does not, however, provide a foundation for *understanding*, which is not reducible to causal explanation; *understanding* deals in reasons rather than in causes. *Understanding*, then, "flows toward events from a self-understanding that precedes the claims of objective knowledge," or, put another way and in terms that cohere with what we have seen in Havel, true *understanding* makes knowledge somehow meaningful (Bergen 1998: 29–30).

How then can the human experience of totalitarianism become meaningful to us in Arendt's sense? Not through limiting ourselves to an explanation of totalitarianism that derives from its place in a typology of political systems: "The idea that unprecedented totalitarian regimes pose a challenge to us to make them meaningful has been lost to the idea that they challenge us to explain them as variations of class of political regimes" (Bergen 1998: 30). In light of this, we might read Arendt's analysis of totalitarianism, as Elisabeth Young Bruehl (2006) does, as a kind of "field manual" for totalitarianism as an existential phenomenon active in the modern world. Totalitarianism does of course represent a type of historically delimited political system, but this is one specific sociopolitical realization – and not the sum total – of its potential meaning. Arendt *understood* the meaning of totalitarianism in a different light:

> Totalitarianism, [Arendt] argued, is the disappearance of politics: a form of government that destroys politics, methodically eliminating speaking

> and acting human beings and attacking the very humanity of first a selected group and then all groups. In this way, totalitarianism makes people superfluous as human beings. This is its radical evil. (Young-Bruehl 2006: 39)

To *understand* totalitarianism in Central/Eastern Europe and to render it meaningful, we need to focus on its "radical evil," or the multiple ways in which it systematically and efficiently rendered people superfluous as human beings. At the same time, we also need to admit that this particular "evil" has not been eliminated from the world with the collapse of the Soviet Union and its satellite regimes. There is, after all, more than one way of rendering people superfluous and causing politics, in Arendt's communicative sense of the word, to disappear. To understand totalitarianism (and Havel's "post-totalitarianism"), then, we need to place it, as Havel himself does, within the larger context of a world in moral and existential crisis.[28]

Arendt's controversial account of the Eichmann trial, written more than a decade after *Origins of Totalitarianism*, clarifies her views on *explaining* and *understanding*, and thereby helps to elucidate her treatment of totalitarianism. Adolf Eichmann was a logistics officer in Hitler's SS, responsible for organizing and managing the mass deportation of Jews to ghettoes and concentration camps in Nazi-held parts of Central and Eastern Europe. After the war, he fled to Argentina and lived under a false identity until 1960, when he was captured by the Israeli secret service and taken to Israel to face trial for, among other things, crimes against humanity. He was found guilty and executed in 1962. Arendt covered the trial for *The New Yorker* magazine, and her reporting eventually appeared as a book titled *Eichmann in Jerusalem: A Report on the Banality of Evil* (Arendt 2006).

While Eichmann's crimes could be easily *explained* and his guilt was obvious, Arendt observed that it was Eichmann's seeming normality – he was certified as psychologically "normal" by seven Israeli psychologists – that was difficult for anyone, including the judges, to *understand*: "This simple truth of the matter created a dilemma for the judges which they could neither resolve nor escape" (Arendt 2006: 27). Young-Bruehl summarizes Arendt's conclusions:

> After listening to Eichmann at his trial and reading the pretrial interviews with him, she concluded that he had no criminal motives but only motives – not criminal in themselves – related to his own advancement in the Nazi hierarchy. He was neither a man who did not know what he was doing nor

> a man who intended to do harm; he was a man who, conforming to the prevailing norms and his Führer's will, failed altogether to grasp the meaning of what he was doing. He was not diabolical, he was thoughtless, which [was] the word Arendt used for a mental condition reflecting remoteness from reality, inability to grasp a reality that stares you in the face – a failure of imagination and judgment ... No deep-rooted or radical evil was necessary to make the trains of Auschwitz run on time. (2006: 107–8)

Arendt's study does not seek to *explain* Eichmann's actions legalistically, as his guilt was already predetermined, but rather it attempts to *understand* his horrifying complicity in genocide as the act of a seemingly normal person: "[F]or Arendt, Eichmann's past acts had convicted and sentenced him before the trial began, but what the trial opened to question was the person who had committed those acts" (Bergen 1998: 40).

In her attempt to *understand* Eichmann as a person, Arendt coined the phrase "banality of evil" to describe the deeply disturbing notion that a psychologically "normal" individual could knowingly commit unthinkable crimes and, at the same time, insist that he was not guilty of these crimes in the technical sense of the indictment. The phrase ignited a controversy that followed Arendt for the rest of her life, and one that she addressed directly in a later edition of the book:

> I also can well imagine that an authentic controversy might have arisen over the subtitle of the book; for when I speak of the banality of evil, I do so only on the strictly factual level, pointing to a phenomenon which stared one in the face at the trial. Eichmann was not Iago and not Macbeth, and nothing would have been farther from his mind than to determine with Richard III "to prove a villain." Except for an extraordinary diligence in looking out for his personal advancement, he had no motives at all. And this diligence in itself was in no way criminal ... He *merely*, to put the matter colloquially, *never realized what he was doing*. It was precisely this lack of imagination which enabled him to sit for months on end facing a German Jew who was conducting the police interrogation, pouring out his heart to the man and explaining again and again how it was that he reached only the rank of lieutenant colonel in the S.S. and that it had not been his fault that he was not promoted ... He was not stupid. It was sheer thoughtlessness – something by no means identical with stupidity – that predisposed him to become one of the greatest criminals of that period. And if this is "banal" and even funny, if with the best will in the world one cannot extract any diabolical or demonic profundity from Eichmann,

> that is still far from calling it commonplace ... That such remoteness from reality and such thoughtlessness can wreak more havoc than all the evil instincts taken together which, perhaps, are inherent in man – that was, in fact, the lesson one could learn in Jerusalem. But it was a lesson, neither an explanation of the phenomenon nor a theory about it. (Arendt 2006: 287–8)

Understanding Eichmann's "normality," then, yields a moral lesson about modern humanity in general. Eichmann's case becomes disturbingly meaningful to us as it warns us of the dangers arising from myopic dissociation from reality and "banal" thoughtlessness.[29]

In Arendt's treatment of both Eichmann and totalitarianism, the contextualized meaning of each serves as a springboard for considering the larger message that each potentially conveys. Her analysis, in other words, moves beyond mere *explanation* and aspires to genuine *understanding*. In making this conceptual shift, she foregrounds the appeal element suggested in each case, and each becomes meaningful to us through our understanding of that appeal. The import of Arendt's analytical approach calls to mind Havel's plays. We do not act merely as external observers, but rather we become implicated, in one way or another, in what we are observing. Arendt's analyses represent encounters with the phenomena through which we are able to read the phenomena in a way that simultaneously makes it possible to read ourselves.

Tom Stoppard and "uncageable" love

While Arendt's studies preceded Havel and may well have influenced his own thinking, Stoppard's contribution to the *explaining/understanding* opposition emerges from a careful reading of Havel's texts written in the period from 1965 to 1990. His 2006 play *Rock 'n' Roll* dramatizes the role played by the musical underground in Czech(oslovak) dissent from the late 1960s up to the 1989 Velvet Revolution. At the same time, it translates the lessons learned from the Czech case into Western (British) terms. Like Arendt, Stoppard directly confronts the appeal component of his theme, and in doing so he offers a new way of framing Havel's *explaining/understanding* opposition.

Two of the main British characters in the play are Max and Eleanor, both professors at Cambridge. Max is a political economist and theorist as well as a committed Marxist, unreformed even in the face of the brutal Soviet invasion of Czechoslovakia in 1968. Eleanor, his wife, teaches the poetry of Sappho, and we learn early in the play that she is suffering from a tenacious cancer. It is through Eleanor's tutorial in Sappho's poetry that we first encounter the *explaining / understanding* opposition, which is embodied in a key and difficult-to-translate word, *amachanon*, in one of Sappho's poems. Sappho used the word to describe Eros, the Greek god of love, and Eleanor's first pupil, Gillian, attempts to translate it as "naughty," an inadequate rendering to which Eleanor immediately objects:

> ELEANOR: Really, Gillian? It's a nice compound, but the interesting word here is *amachanon*. Naughty doesn't get near it. What's the root?
> GILLIAN: I ... *Machan* ... ?
> ELEANOR: Right. *Machan*. Think "machine"...
> GILLIAN (CONFUSED): (Think-machine?)
> ELEANOR: ... contrivance, device, instrument, in a word, technology. So, *a-machanon* – *un*-machine, *non*-machine. Eros is *amachanon*, he's spirit as opposed to machinery, Sappho is making the distinction. He's not naughty, he's – what? Uncontrollable. Uncageable. (Stoppard 2006: 9)

In *(a)machanon*, Stoppard gives us a word that neatly encapsulates Havel's opposition between *explaining* and *understanding*. Eros cannot be pinned down by or reduced to a mechanical explanation. Love, in Sappho's poem as well as in Stoppard's play, is *amachanon*. It is a spirit that transcends the confines of the rationalistic cage, and it acquires meaning and becomes meaningful only to the extent that it is *understood* as a fact of lived-through human experience.

Later in the play, the word and its meaning serve to frame a philosophical (as well as deeply personal) conflict between Max and Eleanor. Max, the philosophical materialist, would like to reduce Sappho's understanding of love to a set of physical symptoms, to reduce *amachanon* mind to *machanon* brain:

> MAX: Her mind *is* her brain. The brain is a biological machine for thinking. If it wasn't for the merely technical problem of understanding how it works, we could make one out of – beer cans. It would be the size of a stadium but it would sit there, going, "I think, therefore I am." (*to Eleanor*) You're very quiet. (Stoppard 2006: 47)

Max's philosophical position is at odds with his personal experience of the world. Eleanor's body has been ravaged by cancer, and she is unusually quiet while listening to Max's abstract theorizing about mind and brain and love and sex, because Max's position is tenable only at the cost of eroding the meaningfulness of his love for her.

In a dramatic exchange at almost the exact middle of the play, Eleanor retorts to Max: "My body is telling me I'm nothing without it, and you're telling me the same" (Stoppard 2006: 50). Max begins to realize his mistake and tries to deny Eleanor's implication, but she presses her argument in the most eloquent and moving passage of the play:

> ELEANOR: It's as if you're in cahoots, you and my cancer ... They've cut, cauterized and zapped away my breasts, my ovaries, my womb, half my bowel, and a nutmeg out of my brain, and I am undiminished, I'm exactly who I've always been. *I am not my body*. My body is nothing without *me*, that's the truth of it ... I don't want your "mind" which you can make out of beer cans. Don't bring it to my funeral. I want your grieving soul or nothing. I do not want your amazing biological machine – I want what you love me with. (Stoppard 2006: 50–1)

Max relents and implicitly renounces his materialist stance in the face of Eleanor's emotional plea. Humanistic *understanding* triumphs over abstract rationalistic *explaining*, spirit over body. Engaged human-level experience in the world trumps detached philosophical theorizing about the world. The implied lesson learned by Max, and dramatically suggested to the audience, is that genuine human meaning is not grounded in theoretical abstraction or reducible to some kind of *machanon* formula.

It is not incidental that Max, shortly after his conversation with Eleanor about love, quietly leaves the Communist Party and begins to retreat from his previous political positions with regard to Czechoslovakia. If *machanon* philosophizing cannot adequately capture the meaning of human love, then its ability to account for meaning at the sociopolitical or philosophical level of human experience is also rendered suspect. Human meaning and meaningfulness are, like love, uncageable.

The opposition as a conceptual tool

Something about the *explaining/understanding* opposition in its various forms has plainly intrigued thinkers across a range of disciplines over the last century. As Stoppard's play indicates, its resonance in Havel's thought is also particularly inspiring. I would propose that what intrigues and inspires is that the opposition functions, like the mosaic principle, as a powerful conceptual tool for making sense of modern human identity. Like Stoppard, my students have also been inspired by the opposition and have personalized its meaning in a variety of ways, extending its application to other experiential domains.

One of my students captured the essence of the opposition in a way reminiscent of Max and Eleanor's *machanon/amachanon* polemic:

> Imagine the experience of accidentally hitting one's hand on the corner of a hard surface. The subsequent pain can be scientifically *explained*: the stimulation of nerve endings can be measured, an increase in blood-pressure monitored. The experience of pain, however, the dilemma of being a creature in pain, the pain's interruption of identity – none of this can be accounted for by a mere explanation of pain. It is what is *unexplainable* about pain that gives it significance.

Other students have focused on modern American society's obsession with classification (take this quiz and find out where you fit in a personal political typology) and discrete quantification (rank your top 10 favourite songs) that serve to reduce, like a Havelian anticode, aspects of our identity to a chart or graph. Members of one group of students once enigmatically began their final presentation for the Havel class by reading a series of numbers. As they subsequently made clear, they were reading their birthdates and ages, the registration numbers for the Havel course, their student ID numbers, grade-point averages, credit scores, checking account numbers, social security numbers, driver's license numbers, and cellphone numbers. Their point was to suggest dramatically the extent to which modern identity has been thoroughly quantified and bureaucratized, as well as the degree to which we are forced to be complicit in this procedure, given that we must memorize, or at least be familiar with, the various numbers that have, taken collectively, come to represent metonymically who we are.

Other students over the years have seen the *explaining/understanding* opposition at work also in the differences between grading and learning, where the former quantifies the latter as a discrete unit (number or letter); verbal instruction about how to ride a bike (drive a car, play a musical instrument) and performing the act itself; classroom instruction in another language and cultural immersion in that language; a travel map or itinerary and the experience of the actual journey; sex in the context of a one-night stand and sex as part of a long-term, committed relationship; linguistic denotation and connotation; pictures of objects arranged in a merchandise catalogue and the same pictures arranged as strips in a collage. In each of these cases, the *understanding* construal encompasses but transcends, in one way or another that is specific to each conceptual domain, the *explaining* construal. Put another way, the *explaining* construal represents a reduction or distillation of the meaning of the *understanding* construal; the meaningfulness of the latter, however, goes well beyond that of the former. In the *understanding* construal, the parts gain value by their participation in the larger whole, and with this observation we see that the *explaining/understanding* opposition is perfectly coherent with, if not a special kind of variation on, the mosaic principle.

Summarizing the opposition

Our experience of meaning transcends attempts to *explain* it. Meaning emerges as a result of our experience in and of the world, and it is richer than any scheme or model that can be devised to capture it. A child's first trip in a plane cannot be meaningfully understood through a report on the plane's technical capabilities. Human meaningfulness is grounded in human *understanding*. Whenever the opposition between *explaining* and *understanding* is invoked by Havel, he demonstrates that *understanding* is not a deficient or degenerate form of meaningfulness, but rather it is a shape or form that models – more accurately than *explaining* – what meaning actually is.

To sum up our examination of the *explaining/understanding* opposition in and beyond Havel and at the same time to anticipate a return to the topic of Havel's plays, it is useful to recall and reconsider the use of the terms "objective" and "subjective" to describe the differences between Havel's essays and plays. These terms were suggested by one of my students, but they badly miss their targets. They are at best misleading and at worst wholly inadequate as characterizations of the differences, and it would make considerably more sense to view the essay/play contrast as emerging from the ways in which *explaining* differs from *understanding*. Unlike the *explaining/understanding* opposition, the *objective/subjective* opposition is dichotomous. The terms are, moreover, marked in relation to truth-value: the "objective" is assumed to be true precisely because it is independent from the vagaries of human conceptualizing, while the "subjective" is somehow suspect in regard to truth – perhaps too emotional, idiosyncratic, elusive, and resistant to generalization; the judgment implicit in the dichotomous opposition between the so-called objective and subjective is that fact and formula (and not human experience, story, or myth) comprise our only meaningful source of truth.

However, as the examples of the *explaining/understanding* opposition from Havel and others have shown, we do not have to (nor should we) reduce truth to a kind of flattened-out and objective explanation. As divergent ways of thinking about or relating to the world, both *explaining* and *understanding* are meaningful and true, but they are so in distinct ways. *Explaining* (or rather *explanation*) is more concerned with the *what* of meaning, and *understanding* with the *how*. The former is at core a *machanon* truth, while the latter enacts truth through a kind of poetically engaged witnessing that places us inside of the flow of meaning.

Understanding Havel's plays

It should be clear by now that an essay differs from a similarly themed play in much the same way that *explaining* differs from *understanding*, which means that the essay/play contrast in Havel's oeuvre represents a token of a larger conceptual type. Reading an essay is more like having a joke *explained* to us: we expect an information-oriented analysis of a question or problem raised by the essay, if not also a rational proposal for its resolution. Watching an appeal-oriented play, in contrast, is more like "encountering" the humour of a joke in its dynamic immediacy. Through our spontaneous laughter, we participate in the joke as a meaningful event and thereby become engaged or embedded in its meaning. Theatrical performance is generative of an *understanding*-orientation towards meaningfulness. It enacts an "embodied meaning" that emerges from the flow of human experience. A play generates forms of meaning that elude the *explaining*-mode characteristic of an essay.

Essays and plays contrast in their respective realizations of the form/meaning nexus, and it is this contrast, which is realized most broadly in the opposition between *explaining* and *understanding*, that proves crucial for a conceptual unpacking of the critical cliché that Havel was "primarily a playwright." By filtering the essay/play contrast through the *explaining/understanding* opposition, we are able to make better sense of Havel's views on theatre as well as of the provocative "weirdness" of his dramatic style. Havel's emphasis on the communal nature of theatre, the centrality of appeal to his style, the predominance of the existential level alongside the interpretive openness of his plays – all of these are meaningful elements of a form of discourse, not to mention an intellectual project, that seeks to promote *understanding* over *explaining*. We can also better understand why Havel took pains to escape – through metaphor, images, and stories – the propositional cage of the essay form. The conceptual effect of these strategies is to shift the emphasis from an *explaining* mode of discourse to one that profiles *understanding*, and recognizing the value of that cognitive shift adds depth to Rocamora's statement that Havel's essays serve as *explications du texte* for his plays.

At the same time that Havel's particular dramatic style can be considered an effective formal vehicle for transcending *explanation* in an effort to convey *understanding*, it is worth noting that absurdist theatre prior to Havel was also viewed as a form that embodied just this kind of conceptual shift. In his monograph on French absurdist theatre, Esslin highlights its relationship to religion and science in a passage that calls to mind not only Havel's views on *explaining* and *understanding*, but also Armstrong's on *logos* and *mythos*:

> In trying to deal with the ultimates of the human condition not in terms of intellectual understanding [Esslin's term for abstract theorizing] but in terms of communicating a metaphysical truth through a living experience, the Theatre of the Absurd touches the religious sphere. There is a vast difference between *knowing* something to be the case in the conceptual sphere and *experiencing* it as a living reality. It is the mark of all great religions that they not only possess a body of knowledge that can be taught in the form of cosmological information or ethical rules but that they also communicate the essence of this body of doctrine in the living, recurring poetic imagery of ritual. It is the loss of the latter sphere, which responds to a deep inner need in all human beings, that the decline of religion has left as a deeply felt deficiency in our civilization. We possess at least an approximation to a coherent philosophy in the scientific method, but we lack the means to make it a living reality, an experienced focus of men's lives. That is why the theatre, a place where men congregate to experience poetic or artistic insights, has in many ways assumed the function of a substitute church. Hence the immense importance placed upon the theatre by totalitarian creeds, which are fully aware of the need to make their doctrines a living, experienced reality to their followers. The Theatre of the Absurd, paradoxical though this may appear at first sight,

> can be seen as an attempt to communicate the metaphysical experience behind the scientific attitude and, at the same time, to supplement it by rounding off the partial view of the world it presents, and integrating it in a wider vision of the world and its mystery. For if the Theatre of the Absurd presents the world as senseless and lacking a unifying principle, it does so merely in the terms of those philosophies that start from the idea that human thought can reduce the totality of the universe to a complete, unified, coherent system. (Esslin 2001: 424–5)

In other words, absurdist theatre was geared, by its very rationale, towards exposing the limitations of the scientific attitude, the constraints on meaning implied by Havel's *explaining* and Armstrong's *logos*. If a central thrust of Havel's project was to promote a shift away from the "metaphysical experience behind the scientific attitude" towards a kind of meaningfulness that is grounded in the spirit of human *understanding*, then he certainly constructed his dramatic style on fertile ground.

We have considered how the fertile ground of absurdist theatre, combined with Czech theatre of the appeal, creates a provocatively weird (*zvláštní*) encounter with meaning, and we have illustrated this in a way that has necessarily shifted our focus from Havel's plays to the larger conceptual type that their form/meaning nexus instantiates. We may take this approach to Havel as a playwright further by using it, on one hand, to analyse the structure of a given play in more depth and, on the other, to propose a more general account of how his plays enact a special kind of truth, a truth that is oriented towards the flow of meaning. In addressing the first, I present a case study of conceptual framing in Havel's thought in general, with a particular focus on his play *The Beggar's Opera*, after which I suggest that Havel's plays serve as enactments of truth by virtue of their status as compressed simulations of selected aspects of our existential reality.

A case study in conceptual framing: "The Beggar's Opera"

As we have seen, Havel was intent on reframing our understanding of theatre itself, arguing in his post-presidential memoir that drama attempts to "uncover something like the structure of Being, to display in vivid terms its internal weave, its hidden structure, and its real articulation" (Havel 2007a: 277 and 2006: 193). There are multiple realizations of this intent in his plays, and the particular structure of each play could be analysed with this existential-level reframing of theatre in mind. To illustrate this point, I will present a reading of one of Havel's most-staged (and arguably most well-crafted) plays, *The Beggar's Opera* (1975). My reading will turn on the role of conceptual framing in the play, and in order best to appreciate *The Beggar's Opera* as a drama that is concerned with the structure of Being (at least with regard to framing), we will first need to consider certain sociological and psychological details related to frame analysis.

The seminal treatise *Frame Analysis* was written by the American sociologist Erving Goffman (1974), and Goffman gave it what is, for the purpose of analysing Havel, a significant subtitle: *An Essay on the Organization of Experience*. Goffman was primarily concerned with the structuring of face-to-face interactions between people (known as "microframing") and with "the unstated rules or principles more or less implicitly set by the character of some larger, though perhaps invisible, entity within which the interaction occurs" (Goffman 1974: xiii) – that is, with sociocultural frames at a level beyond personal interaction. While Goffman examines the framing of social interactions exhaustively and in technical terms, I will apply the notion of conceptual framing to Havel in a mostly non-technical sense, and a broad definition of framing should suffice.[30]

According to Goffman, frame analysis is "the examination via frames of the organization of experience" (1974: 11), and frames are structures which "set the terms for experience" (1974: 182). Frames are pervasive: "we tend to perceive events in terms of primary frameworks" (1974: 24), and "it seems that we can hardly glance at anything without applying a primary framework" (1974: 38). Goffman divides primary frameworks into two classes, "natural" ones (the weather, science) and "social" ones, or frameworks that "provide background understanding for events that incorporate the will, aim, and controlling effort of an intelligence, a live agency" (1974: 22); he illustrates this point with murder (1974: 25), a phenomenon that can be investigated within a natural framework (the coroner searches for the *physical* cause of death) and also within a social one (the police try to determine the *manner* of the crime and the *motive*). Even, however, as "acts of daily living are understandable because of some primary framework (or frameworks) that inform them" (1974: 26), we apply these frames mostly unconsciously. We are not aware of framing experience in a certain way because our primary frameworks are natural to the culture we inhabit. Moreover, because framing is key to making sense of experience, misframing a situation can lead to "systematically sustained, generative error, the breeding of wrongly oriented behavior" (1974: 308), and in a seriously misframed situation, the actors can find themselves "using not the wrong word, but the wrong language" (1974: 309).[31]

It is hardly surprising that Havel, a phenomenologically oriented thinker, would be obsessed with how we organize our experience of the world. Havel's obsession with conceptual framing could be illustrated by a close analysis of almost any of his writings, including (and perhaps especially) his speeches as president. I will, however, limit myself to considering some suggestive details that argue in favour of a frame-analysis reading of Havel, and then detail how framing shapes the directional track, and ultimately also contaminates the larger message, of *The Beggar's Opera*.

Havel (1983b: letter 99) wrote that the "meaning of any phenomenon lies in its being anchored in something outside itself," and thus in its belonging to some higher or wider context – hung, like a picture, against a larger background that constitutes its frame or horizon.[32] Illustrations of this principle are easy to come by: an example that jumps immediately to mind is Havel's notion of the circles of home (Czech *domov*). Our circles of home form a nested hierarchy ranging from the innermost, personal homes (of family and friends) to the outer, interpersonal or even international ones (our educational or class affiliations, our political party, our sense of regional or national identification, etc.). The circles of home figure centrally in many of Havel's presidential speeches.[33] In Havel's understanding, these circles frame key aspects of our identity in the modern world.

The circles of home are just one example of Havel's realization, echoing Goffman, that meaning depends on framing. Much of Havel reads, in fact, like a textbook application of Goffman's conceptual framing without the metatheoretical commentary, and readers of Havel often sense this without being able to capture its systematicity neatly. Like Goffman, Havel could be classified as a "metaphysician of the banal"; he himself suggested that mundane life experiences contain within themselves a wealth of potential poetic meanings, only much of his meticulous dissection of his own life experiences takes the form of frame analysis. That he claims in his post-presidential memoir (Havel 2007a: 207 and 2006: 144) to have written his individual speeches as coherent parts of a larger thematic whole should come as no surprise to readers who understand that questions of framing are fundamental to Havel's thought process.

Havel also noted in his memoir that he is "drawn to everything mysterious, magic, irrational, inexplicable, grotesque, and absurd, everything that escapes order and problematizes it"[34] (Havel 2007a: 335 and 2006: 239), which again points to his sensitivity to framing, but in the sense of someone who is taken with the need to go beyond or transcend conventionally ordered systems (conventional *řády*). In a 1999 address, Havel illustrates this idea, using the figure of Saint Adalbert as a starting point to consider the conventional ways in which human history becomes framed.[35] He argues that official histories often fail to tell complete stories, and that alongside the official historical flow of events "there exist also underground historical currents" that influence the former indirectly but may well be, in the long run, themselves the more decisive historical forms. Official or conventional frames, be they historical or of another kind, seem to serve as guideposts for Havel that direct his attention beyond their boundaries, just as prison impelled him to philosophize about human identity and responsibility in the world outside of it. Concrete, immediate horizons point beyond themselves to broader horizons, to larger circles of home, sometimes even to the absolute horizon, and the more concretely immediate and deeply felt these horizons are (e.g., prison or the post-totalitarian order), the more energetically they seem to point.

In the same address, Havel refers to Saint Adalbert as a *velký zneklidňovač* (in English, a "big trouble-maker")[36] whose historical meaning lies partly in the fact that he embodied "a living, open-ended, unrealized and never fully realizable kind of human transcendence," and the mention of transcendence, especially in conjunction with his characterization of the saint, raises another suggestive motif in Havel's writing that recalls frame analysis. When one begins to read Havel in frame terms, details from his texts take on new life, and a particular detail from "Dear Dr. Husák" that we highlighted in chapter 1 is the phrase "restlessness of transcendence" (*neklid transcendence*): "Life rebels against all uniformity and leveling; its aim is not sameness, but variety, the restlessness of transcendence, the adventure of novelty and rebellion against the status quo" (Havel 1991a: 71 and1999, 4: 93). This phrase occurs towards the end of the letter to Gustáv Husák at a point at which Havel imagines the dissolution of Husák's normalized regime by means of life itself; the language of the letter becomes more and more metaphorical as the essay progresses and as life begins to win out over the regime's attempts regulate it.

What then does Havel exactly mean by the phrase *neklid transcendence*? What are we (or what is life) supposed to (or inevitably going to) transcend? And how can *neklid* (restlessness or disquiet) be a state that leads to transcendence? It is certainly true that *klid* (English "rest," "quiet," "serenity"), like *domov*, is a word that suggests something much more fundamental in Czech than any of its various English translations.[37] It is equally true that there is a *klid*-motif that runs throughout the letter, no doubt as a response to the regime's calls for a post-1968 "return" to *klid*. Thus, in Havel's description of the Husák era, the generally positive term *klid* serves to designate a hypnotic state of non-action and apathy – a sense of *klid* pervades the "normalized" nation, but it is the *klid* of the morgue or the *klid* of the grave (Havel 1991a: 72 and 1999, 4: 95). Havel, however, equates life itself with the restlessness of transcendence. It is not a statement exclusively associated with one particular regime or sociohistorical context, but a suggestive reframing with broader implications.

Both *klid* and *neklid* along with their derivative words are high-frequency terms in Havel's writings, as are references to transcendence: witness his above-cited description of Saint Adalbert that also links *neklid* with a kind of positive and necessary transcendence. The "restlessness of transcendence" that Havel suggests in "Letter to Dr. Husák" is akin to "escaping order and problematizing it." Life itself cannot be ordered or rigidly contained in a ("normalized") frame, nor can the richness of human experience be captured in simple formulations or even in the most poetic of words. Our minds organize experience through conceptual framing, but life itself (as well as our natural, human experience of life) "escapes" that ordering.

Another suggestive detail related to framing is Havel's statement, in "Power of the Powerless," that manifestations of ideology in a post-totalitarian society make up something like a "panorama of everyday life [*panoráma každodennosti*]" (Havel 1991a: 141 and 1999, 4: 242). Havel often suggested that we de-intellectualize abstract concepts like ideology and that we interpret them by analogy to more readily understandable, and more concrete, life experiences. When I ask my students what the concrete, physical panorama – the experiential frame – of their everyday lives in contemporary America consists of, they have tended to answer: highways and roads, parking lots, telephone and electrical poles, sprawling malls and gigantic cineplexes, ubiquitous advertising. It was only, however, while reading Goffman that I fully understood what Havel is suggesting here by "panorama." He is asking us to pay careful attention to those phenomena that comprise the "directional track" of everyday life and that we, under normal conditions,[38] have been trained to *disattend*. These disattended phenomena, like the underground historical currents in Havel's meditation on Saint Adalbert, are more meaningful than they might appear to be. In other words, Havel asks us to see actively the greengrocer and his sign (all the greengrocers of the world with all of their various signs), the smokestacks, the highways and parking lots and malls and electrical poles and advertisements. These are the things left out of our primary cultural frameworks because they have, often perversely, become "natural" background to our everyday lives. In Goffman's words, they form part of our normal *disattend track*, which is a special channel or track in the organization of experience in which locally occurring events are not considered relevant to the main frame (Goffman 1974: 222).

Goffman was aware of the importance of framing for theatre, and he wrote that dramatic scriptings "allow for the manipulation of framing conventions and ... since these conventions cut very deeply into the organization of experience, almost anything can be managed in a way that is compatible with sustaining the involvement of the audience" (1974: 241). Theatre, in this respect, is a special "keying"[39] of reality in which on-stage details are meant to take on semiotic import. We are supposed to pay close attention to (and not "disattend") them (Goffman 1974: 138). At the same time, plays themselves also resist rigid framing, since each performance of a play is unique. Havel's theatre of the appeal is open-ended by its very nature, and we cannot make sense of it without transcending the theatrical frame or going beyond the dramatic frame's "evidential boundary" (Goffman 1974: 216). In this regard, theatrical performances, especially those in Havel's dramatic style, may be understood as concentrated lessons at several different levels in the conceptual strategies that train us to become aware of the frames within which we ourselves are "contained," and they appeal to us to transcend that containment.

Goffman also wrote that (French) theatre of the absurd experiments so much with framing that "one might better call it the theater of frames" (1974: 399), and Havel's plays are a case in point. Many of his plays have titles that frame the play's message ambiguously, and the titles thereby send an explicit appeal to the audience to resolve for itself, or at least puzzle over, their very ambiguity. Depending on how we interpret the title-as-frame, the overall message of the play shifts, and the audience is ideally able to understand the play against the background of the multiple frames simultaneously suggested by the ambiguous title. It is useful to recall here Grossman's thoughts on theatre of the appeal and the theatre of small forms, in which a performance intentionally creates an "empty space" – something left unsaid or undecided – that must be filled up by the audience. In our terms here, the staged play is a frame, or what Goffman refers to as a "keying" of a primary frame (1974: 40ff.), that is intentionally left open, and elements of the performance-frame therefore leak out into the audience's reality.

Of all Havel's plays, perhaps the most explicitly frame-oriented is *The Beggar's Opera*. Havel's play is itself a rewrite (an intentional reframing) of both John Gay's original 1718 play of the same name and Bertold Brecht's 1928 rewrite of it, which he titled *The Threepenny Opera*. Pontuso (2004: 105ff.) traces the differences between Havel's version and the other two, arguing that Havel is, in the meta-literary frame, polemicizing with Brecht's ideological notions of morality. At another interpretive level, in the Czechoslovak post-totalitarian frame, Pontuso notes that the play is a satire of "normalization," and specifically a depiction of those who accommodated themselves to the regime or those who chose to inform on others with the excuse that they could thereby protect those on whom they were informing. Pontuso considers yet a third potential way of framing Havel's intention in rewriting the play, namely to depict an "upside-down world" (111) that is hyperbolically amoral. In this philosophical framing, the play becomes a Heideggerean thought experiment "intended to show the unreality of an amoral world" (114).

Steiner 2001 suggests still another way to frame the play, that is, as a game of "meta-pretending" that Czechoslovaks at the time understood only too well: "By communicating a communicative disorder Havel reframes the double bind of those locked in the primary frame [Czechoslovak 'normalized' society] and offers this reframing for their inspection" (2001: xxxi). In reframing and dramatizing the essential communicative disorder of the time, a kind of collective personal and sociopolitical schizophrenia, the play also enters the frame of politics and becomes, indirectly but emphatically, a political gesture.

The play itself portrays a dance of intrigues or, as Steiner characterizes it, a "self-perpetuating spiral of mutual deception" (2001: xxxi). In other words, the play is about framing, or rather the keying of frames and the fabrication of frames. According to Goffman (1974: 83ff.), keying occurs when all participants in a given frame have the same view of what is taking place (no one is being actively deceived); in a fabrication, however, only the fabricators know that the frame is deceptive, while others are contained or ensnared within the fabrication, which they accept as real. Instances of both keying and fabrication are present in the play, and it is often difficult to differentiate between the two. We could, for example, view Macheath's situation with regard to his two wives in just these terms. Lucy and Polly both initially fabricated a romantic interest in Macheath – or was Macheath aware of this and only too happy to take advantage of it for his own selfish purposes, in which case these would be cases of keying? – and Macheath's polygamy is most certainly a fabrication until his exculpatory prison monologue succeeds in shifting it into the keying category.

Other elements of the play also involve a focus on the framing (or rather the reframing) of conventional expectations. Most of the characters, for example, belong to the criminal underworld, but they speak almost exclusively in high-style, literary Czech. This tension, as Havel himself insisted, is a key element of the play (Steiner 2001: xiii). In Goffman's terms, the linguistic directional track is decidedly at odds with the frame in which it is being used. In addition, the characters refer to the operations of the criminal underworld using language appropriate for conventional business or entrepreneurial undertakings, thus blurring the distinction between the frames of illegal and legal activity. Finally, it might be added that although the world of the play is completely topsy-turvy (underground criminals speak perfect Czech and behave like bourgeois couples, wives are eager to provide their husbands with lovers, the only thoroughly honest character is a petty thief who is executed for his integrity), the actors nonetheless perform as if everything were perfectly normal – that is, as if there were no theatrical framing, keying, or fabrication involved.[40]

The last scene of the play reveals an unexpected plot twist that produces yet another frame within a frame. It suddenly turns out that Lockit, the chief of police, and his wife are secretly at the head of a crime syndicate that has presumably taken control, through underhanded manipulation and intrigue, of both Peachum's and Macheath's rival criminal organizations. The very last line of the play aphoristically conveys its wisdom: "They serve best who know not that they serve. Bon appétit!" (Havel 2001: 84). Steiner writes: "The text's terminus, I would like to emphasize, does not settle the strategic game that animates" the play, but it "merely demarcates one of the loops comprising the self-perpetuating spiral of mutual deception" (2001: xxxi). Within the play, then, the end of the framing spiral has likely not been reached, and we would not be surprised to encounter another keying or fabrication of some sort that would reframe what it is that we think we know. The last line of the play ("Bon appétit!") also represents an indirect appeal in that Havel shifts out of the theatrical frame and serves up the play's message for the audience's consumption. The play warns us of our own loss of authentic identity – our own containment within frames of all kinds – given the roles that we are obliged to play in the various "homes" that we inhabit.[41]

The central question of *The Beggar's Opera* is the role that framing plays in organizing and shaping our experience of the world. The play is about keyed frames and fabricated frames and becoming aware of the difference between the two. Framing is, in Goffman's analysis, an essential part of the "directional track" of human cognition; it is a conceptual mechanism that underlies human meaning-making, but it is not often that we raise it to the level of conscious awareness. *The Beggar's Opera*, like the majority of Havel's plays, is a play that "uncovers something of the structure of Being" by training us to pay attention to that directional track. In this respect, the play represents a kind of semi-interactive instructional manual for reading ourselves through the conceptual anatomy of framing.

The Beggar's Opera does not, like Goffman, *explain* framing to us, but it provides a formal vehicle through which we come to *understand* the conceptual power that framing has over us. Applauding Macheath's self-serving monologue that makes a noble virtue of his polygamy, we become embedded and implicated in the framing game, delighting in Havel's brilliance as a playwright at the same time that we find ourselves vaguely disturbed by the experience of doing so. Like all of Havel's plays, *The Beggar's Opera* is written to disturb – to engender in the audience an experience of *neklid* – because it is only through struggling with this "restlessness" that we may hope to transcend the limitations that it imposes on us.

Havel's plays as compressed simulations

While it is certainly possible to analyse the structure of a given Havel play through the lens of the *explaining/understanding* opposition, it is also possible to distill from this approach a more general account of how Havel's dramatic style might be said to enact a special kind of truth, one that is oriented towards the flow of meaning. Havel's plays serve as enactments of truth by virtue of their status as compressed simulations of selected aspects of our existential reality. To the extent that they "uncover something of the structure of Being," they do so by compressing the daunting complexity of real life (at various levels of our circles of home) into an accessible and human-scale simulation. In this respect, the plays represent simulations of truth not as information or "objective" fact, but rather truth as *understanding*, truth as an experiential form or way of being in the world, and truth as a process by which we establish a relationship to the world. The plays simulate truth as *how* in its inseparability from *what* and *who*.

Pontuso has made a similar argument: "Havel's plays compress reality to bring forth meaning. They 'amplify' reality to 'display' Being" (2004: 75). His argument focuses on the plays as philosophical rejoinders to the German phenomenologist Martin Heidegger. According to Pontuso, Havel paid tribute to Heidegger by using his ideas "as the starting point for, and as a challenge to, his own views" (2004: 49), but ultimately Havel disagreed with Heidegger's stance that Being is mysterious and impenetrable:

> One could almost say that everything Havel has written is a response to Heidegger's philosophy. Havel accepts Heidegger's criticism of modern philosophy, its attempts to fully answer all of life's mysteries by mastering the beings, conquering nature, and fully controlling human destiny. Yet this arrogant effort to place the human will at the center of existence disguises the complexity, spontaneity, and heterogeneity of life. Havel rejects the most important element in Heidegger's principles – the proposition that Being is no-thing. Instead, Havel maintains that there is an absolute ground to human experience, a natural world that is the basis for responsible moral behavior. Havel argues that the validity of his position can be established through a phenomenological meditation on our everyday experience.[42] (Pontuso 2004: 49)

Havel's "complex acceptance and final rejection of Heidegger's philosophy" become most apparent in his plays (Pontuso 2004: 49). In Pontuso's reading, the plays represent Heideggerean thought experiments to the extent that they demonstrate that we can and do understand moral questions, and that we can thereby penetrate the mystery of Being. One reason for this derives from the appeal-orientation of Havel's style: "When the audience must work to provide meaning, in whatever form, the interpretation is truly theirs and has been understood because they formulated it. Havel identifies a ground for human meaning, which negates Heidegger's claims" (Pontuso 2004: 75). Another reason is the way in which certain plays, including and perhaps especially *The Beggar's Opera*, demonstrate "the unreality of an amoral world" (Pontuso 2004: 114). The plays, that is, offer a compressed simulation of the deficiencies in Heidegger's philosophical nihilism. They simulate the ways in which we comprehend morality, and are able to develop a sense of Being even if we are not able to reify these intuitions in the form of a scientifically objective proof. In other words, we come to our knowledge not through objective *explanation*, but through human-level *understanding*.

These considerations are not, of course, applicable only to Havel's dramatic style, but reflect more broadly an approach to theatre as an art form that has a direct connection to human ethics: "Half the art of theater is paying attention to other people, and that is the entire basis of ethics" (Woodruff 2008: x). Theatre is the "art of watching and being watched" (Woodruff 2008), and human-scale compression both facilitates the watching-as-witnessing and renders the ethical angle meaningful in personal terms. We could analyse any number of Havel's dramatic techniques in these terms, and I offer two examples here.

Many of my students have been struck, if not also perplexed, by a defamiliarizing technique that ranks among Havel's favourite rhetorical strategies. In the first chapter, we encountered this technique under the rubric of cross-genre mixing of stylistic levels, which occurs regularly. There are frequent moments in his plays where seemingly important plot developments are abruptly interrupted by characters who feel the need to engage in petty preoccupations like smoking, eating, brushing their hair, and going out for groceries in the middle of a workday. These are activities centred on the self-interest and the personal comfort, in an immediate physical sense, of those engaged in them, and for that reason this technique could be termed the motif of personal comfort. Havel purposefully hyperbolizes these moments in his play, and he often cycles them through a play, much like his playful and repeated reference to the need for a longer hose in the gardens of Prague Castle that appears again and again in his political memoir. When we understand his plays as compressions or minimalist models of a larger existential reality, then the motif of personal comfort as a dramatic technique suddenly becomes meaningful. Instantiations of the motif represent caricatures of a focus on immediate self-interest (on one's own personal comfort) in the midst of much grander goings-on. Havel thereby compresses the broader question of sociopolitical indifference – of retreating, like

Michal and Vera in the Vaněk play *Unveiling*, into one's private space in order to life a quiet (*klidný*) life – into a human-scale dramatic gesture. The gesture prompts us to consider the consequences, both personal and social, of a self-interested obsession with one's own comfort. Havel deploys the motif in such a way that key questions of human existence – What is a meaningful activity? What is the nature of human hunger and desire? What satisfies us? – are implicitly raised; in Pontuso's words, the dramatic gesture compresses and amplifies reality to bring forth meaning and display Being. Moreover, because Havel hyperbolizes the motif and introduces it at moments that frustrate expected plot development, we cannot disattend it. We are forced to confront a world in which these existential forms take, quite literally, centre stage.

There are other aspects of Havel's dramatic style that become focal points in the theatrical compression only by being performed, and my second example, choreographed movement in the plays, is one of these. Havel's plays are tightly choreographed, and precisely timed movements (entrances and exits, mirrored or opposing gesticulations, the "dance" of interlocutors around a stage) become performative gestures that convey a wealth of meaning without resorting to words. The audience is often confronted by what might be called energetic stasis: considerable movement and energy that ultimately goes nowhere because it is self-contained and circular, patterned activity that traps the characters in a frustrating kinetic status quo.[43] At the same time that we find this dynamic inertia frustrating, we may also find it strangely comforting, hypnotic through its very predictability. At a certain point in the play, Havel will disrupt the kinetic pattern and rupture the hypnotic spell. Needless to say, if the actors fail to implement the precise timing of the on-stage choreography, the meaning of the play as an existential-level compression – its *understanding*-oriented appeal – is undermined.[44]

Both of these examples make clear the extent to which Havel's dramatic style becomes meaningful through its realization in performance. Understood as an experiential form or way of being, Havel's truth is performatively enacted. It is modelled or simulated on stage not as a *what* but as a *how*, and the audience becomes embedded in this performative simulation. We watch the characters perform these dramatic gestures and become better "trained" in the art of watching, but watching implies an impassive detachment that is inadequate to capturing our experience of the play as a performative simulation. We come to *understand* the performance as a multidimensional cognitive experience. We do not merely watch it, but are engaged with it in a disturbing existential encounter that has moral implications. In this sense, then, it would be more appropriate to say that we *witness* a performance like we might witness a crime or an accident in all of its (sometimes shocking) immediacy. We experience the event with a degree of empathic projection, as if we could imagine it happening to ourselves.

A relatively recent discovery in cognitive science is the existence of mirror neurons that fire in our brains not only while performing a specific motor action (grasping a cup) but also while watching that action being performed by someone else. Research on mirror neurons suggests that watching even in an everyday sense has something of a witnessing component, or that everyday cognition itself is a kind of "embodied performance" (Cook 2010: 123ff.). Mirror neurons have potentially tremendous implications for a theory of human meaning:

> Mirror-neuron phenomena suggest that *understanding is a form of simulation*. To see another person perform an action activates some of the same sensorimotor areas, *as if* the observer herself were performing the action. This deep and pre-reflective level of engagement with others reveals our most profound bodily understanding of other people, and it shows our intercorporeal social connectedness. (Johnson 2007: 161–2, emphasis in original)

Another scholar has noted that mirror neurons are sometimes referred to in the popular-science press as "empathy neurons" because they potentially allow us to grasp the mind of others not through abstract and disembodied conceptual reasoning, but through empathic simulation, or "[b]y feeling, not by thinking" (Rifkin 2009: 83). Brian Boyd has phrased the idea this way:

> Mirror neurons ... allow an effortless, automatic understanding of the intentions of others through an almost reflex inner imitation. As one mirror-neuron specialist remarks, in a phrase that could not be more relevant to storytelling, "when we (and apes) look at others, we find both them *and ourselves*." (Boyd 2009: 142)

Given this, it should not come as a surprise that theatre scholars have taken note of the research on mirror neurons and have started exploring its implications for the meaning of dramatic performance.[45]

An obvious conclusion to be drawn is that by witnessing an appeal-oriented theatrical performance (by becoming embedded in various ways in its dramatic gestures) we are activating the neural structure of our brains,[46] which gives both a contemporary twist to Grossman's idea of "activation" of the audience as well as new meaning to the old idea that the audience consists not merely of spectators to, but also of spect-actors in, the performance. This becomes potentially even more compelling if we believe, as do certain prominent cognitive scientists, that neural structures are activated in complex chains that relate actions to the consequences that follow from them (Iacobini 2009: 58–9). Mirror neurons may therefore also encode intentions (Iacobini 2009: 76ff.). A dramatic style that maximizes neural activation with regard to action/consequence chains and intention could very well reveal, quite literally in the spect-actors' minds, "something like the structure of Being."

In hinting that Havel's dramatic style is designed to activate our minds in just this way, I am suggesting another way of understanding his plays as compressed simulations. His theatrical simulations are, in this respect, clear-cut examples of what other cognitive scientists, whose research is perfectly compatible with the mirror-neuron model of neural activation, have called conceptual blends. Neural simulation and blending go hand-in-hand in elucidating the status of Havel's plays as conceptual compressions.

Conceptual blending, also known as conceptual integration, was developed by Gilles Fauconnier and Mark Turner (1998 and 2003) as a general theory of human cognition:

> Conceptual blending is a basic mental operation that leads to new meaning, global insight, and conceptual compressions useful for memory and manipulation of otherwise diffuse ranges of meaning. It plays a fundamental role in the construction of meaning in everyday life, in the arts and sciences, and especially in the social and behavioral sciences. The essence of the operation is to construct a partial match between two inputs, to project selectively from those inputs into a novel "blended" mental space, which then dynamically develops emergent structure. (Fauconnier 2001)

Blending operates at the lowest levels of cognition, largely behind the scenes, as a process of mapping and integration that pervades all levels of conceptual organization.[47]

A simple example of a conceptual blend is the familiar computer "desktop" interface. Computer screens depict movable icons on a simulated desktop. The simulation relies on users' experiential knowledge of aspects of the office setting for one of its conceptual "input spaces" –

for example, the office desktop as a space for organizing documents into folders that we can retrieve as needed; documents or folders that have become unnecessary are thrown away in the office trashcan. Experiential knowledge from other input spaces gives meaning to on-screen pointing and dragging, as well as to the way in which we select actionable items from lists or menus. All of these inputs contribute to the imaginative invention or "blended space" that is the computer desktop:

> Once learned, the entire activity of using the desktop interface is coherent and integrated. It is not hampered by its obvious literal falsities: There is no actual desk, no set of folders, no putting of objects into folders, no shuffling of objects from one folder to another, no putting of objects into the trash. The desktop interface is an excellent example of conceptual integration because the activity of manipulating it can be done only in the blend, and would make no sense if the blend were not hooked up to the inputs. (Fauconnier and Turner 2003: 23)

The conceptual blend is not the computer screen itself. Rather it is the mental construction that allows us to use the computer "desktop" effectively: "The user manipulates this computer interface not by means of an elaborate conscious analogy but, rather, as an integrated form with its own coherent structure and properties" (Fauconnier and Turner 2003: 24).

The computer desktop is not only a conceptual blend, but also a conceptual compression. Not all aspects of the office setting are mapped onto the computer screen (there is no water cooler or lunch room), but only selected aspects that prove relevant to the computerized interface. The compression, as a blended space, also has its own logical structure that does not match perfectly with the structure of its input spaces. The computer trashcan, for example, sits on the desktop, not on the office floor. One final point is that the compressed blend of the computer desktop gives rise to forms of meaning not present in the original input spaces. When you copy documents or store them in remote folders on a computer desktop, you do not have to get up and go to the office copy machine or to the file room down the hall.

Fauconnier and Turner have noted that dramatic performances are classic cases of complex blending (Fauconnier and Turner 2003: 266–7). At a simple level, they are deliberate blends (and conceptual compressions) of living people (the actors) with identities that they perform on stage (the characters). The characters may sound and move like real people, and they engage in actions that have counterparts in the real world. The spectators recognize, to one degree or another and in simple or more complicated ways, the links between the represented world in the performative blend and the real world that serves as its main input space (just like we implicitly acknowledge the role of the real office desktop in the computer interface). Spectators can "decompress" the blend to make these links explicit, but the real conceptual power of the performance comes from integration in the blend: "The spectator is able to live in the blend, looking directly on its reality" (Fauconnier and Turner 2003: 266). In rare cases, spectators might become so embedded in the "reality" of the blend that they lose the framing of themselves as spectators to a performance. Fauconnier and Turner cite Goffman here in reporting incidents of theatre-goers who have rushed onto the stage to stop a "murder" from occurring. Most spectators, however, "live" in the blend by selective projection, but even so the "importance and power of living in the blend would be hard to overestimate" (Fauconnier and Turner 2003: 267). In drama, the very ability to live in the blend serves as the motivation for the entire activity.

The theatrical blend of a Havel play – the imaginative world that it depicts and in which the actors and audience "live" – acts as a conceptual compression of selected aspects of the non-stage world. The play can be associated with the non-stage world only indirectly, and this association is mediated via conceptual expansion of the dramatic compression, that is, by "unpacking" the blend (sometimes referred to as "running" the blend). Havel's plays are, in this respect, like existential maps, and maps represent another classic case of conceptual blending. Maps are not the same as what they depict, but we cannot find our way without imagining the map first. A map is a compression of complex topography to a human scale that allows us to orient ourselves in the real world, and we do so by unpacking the compression and running the decompressed topographic simulation in our minds. Maps are blends that compress reality in order to "amplify" it; in other words, "we experience what the maps make it possible to perceive" (Cook 2010: 26).

That the plays certainly are compressions, in the sense of existential maps, becomes clear when we recall our discussion of the Vaněk plays from the first chapter. Compression is "one of the governing principles of conceptual blending theory" in which the complicated is miniaturized into the simple to facilitate understanding (Cook 2010: 31). Considered as a coherent trilogy, the Vaněk plays compress a set of complex political and social questions, questions that are directly relevant to post-totalitarian Czechoslovakia but applicable to all modern consumer-industrial societies, into a human scale, and the plays thereby facilitate a human-level response to this complex of problems that we, as individuals, find overwhelming. The plays blend the personal and sociopolitical layers of human identity, and Havel suggests that the former can serve as a ground for our understanding of the latter.[48] In the blend, the larger problems become, to a significant extent, subject to an individual's control. Their human dimensions are revealed, and they are rendered accessible by being framed with this "human content." By unpacking the compression or running the blend, we are meant to discover, perhaps to our surprise, ways in which the seemingly powerless become potentially powerful.[49]

Vaněk is less a character than he is a dramatic principle personified, and he plays a special role in the blended compression as both the spectators' on-stage proxy and off-stage goad. He binds together the various spaces that comprise the blend, and he forces the audience to reflect on questions that prove to be both personal and sociopolitical at the same time. These levels themselves are conceptually blended not only in the on-stage compression but also on life's larger stage. Who are we, and what is our relationship to other people in the society in which we live? Do we have the same identity in our personal and interpersonal existential "homes," and how does one influence the other? Who should we be or who might we become? In the Vaněk blend, Havel does not give us fixed answers to these questions. He purposefully refrains from filling in the details of the conceptual mapping. Is the brewmaster in *Audience* an agent of the regime? Is Vaněk a hero or model for us to follow? Havel metadramatically problematizes the conceptual mapping and guides our attention to the very *how* of the blend, a directional track that we would otherwise be liable to disattend.

The motif of personal/sociopolitical compression is characteristic of Havel as a playwright beyond the Vaněk trilogy, and is realized in different forms in other plays. In *The Garden Party*, for example, there are obvious parallels between Hugo's (bourgeois) home life and the (socialist) professional world that Hugo enters to make a career. One way to read this play, through blending and compression, is as a conceptual reframing and parody of the relationship between petty-bourgeois and socialist ways of being:

> Life guided by the socialist ideal turns out to be as soulless and degenerate as that of the petite bourgeoisie. It is governed even to a larger degree

> by conformity and opportunism, with people acting and speaking without sense. The only real difference is in their replacing one type of verbal gesture by another. The "conservative" maxims of Pludek Senior [Hugo's bourgeois father] are superseded by the mechanical repetition of official statements, slogans, and ideological clichés. (Trensky 1978: 110)

Similarly, Macheath's "knife's-edge" speeches in *The Beggar's Opera* could be read as indications of the character's own personal deficiencies, but also as parodies of the official speech of the regime at the time (Štěrbová 2002: 46), if not also as a parody of a type of widespread modern-day discourse that falls squarely into the category of "bullshitting" (Frankfurt 2005). In the dramatic compression, the variant interpretations simultaneously coexist. In the spectators' existential encounter with the play, the variant interpretations are "blended" together. At the very least, the audience is "activated" to think along these lines as they unpack the compression by running the blend.

Combined with an understanding of Havel's plays as conceptual compressions, blending theory provides a cognitive dimension to many other aspects of Havel's dramatic style that we have also discussed. It should, for example, be clear that the overall thrust of the appeal is aimed at encouraging the audience to treat the play as a compressed blend that must be unpacked or "run." Absurdist techniques entertain, but they also reinforce the appeal component by preparing the ground for it. By defamiliarizing, they disrupt our conventional ways of seeing and knowing, and they challenge us to make sense of the play, and its relation to our lives, in new terms. Some of Havel's dramatic strategies are directed at embedding us in the blend so that we "live" it. We are confronted with odd manifestations of the motif of personal comfort, familiar to us from our own lives, at inappropriate times. We become entranced by the choreography, and we give, almost despite ourselves, Macheath's duplicitous monologue a standing ovation. Actors are encouraged to treat the plays not as farces, but rather to act as if the absurd world inhabited by the characters were completely normal, and this facilitates audience identification with the blended space as a simulation or model of the off-stage world. Indeed, if the plays are staged primarily for comic effect (as they sometimes are), they lose their status as blends. The prompt or appeal to the spectators to try to understand the on-stage world as a compression of certain existential aspects of their off-stage world is entirely undermined.

Other Havelian strategies profile the simulational aspect of the plays-as-compressions by prompting us to unpack or run the blend. As we have already seen, many of his plays end by seemingly starting over again, and we take this impression with us as we leave the theatre. We thus re-enter the spaces of our everyday lives with the simulation of the blended world of the play foremost in our minds. Staging details often serve to reinforce the link between on-stage and off-stage worlds – between, for example, actors as characters and actors as people. In this regard, I vividly recall the ending of one production of Havel's *Largo Desolato*. The main character in the play, Leopold Nettles – a "dissident" in spite of himself who has spent the entire play having a nervous breakdown, and who is a psychological mess by the play's end, slouched and nearly shaking on a couch at the centre of the stage after a climactic psychotic episode – dramatically stands up and slowly walks, getting gradually taller and more confident as he moves, directly towards the audience. During that short walk to the edge of the stage, "Leopold" transforms himself from a psychologically crushed character to an actor with his human dignity fully restored. His transformative walk concludes the play by bridging the worlds of the blend. The play's final dramatic gesture encapsulates and simulates the "running" of the compression. As the house lights are gradually turned up, the charismatic actor remains standing calmly at the front of the stage, smiling and bowing. The other actors rush on stage to join him, and the audience acknowledges their performances with enthusiastic applause.

Conclusion

Given its diversity of congruent themes, this chapter's structure is reminiscent of the structure of a conceptual blend. It may be helpful, as a first step in this conclusion, to unpack the blend systematically.

I set the stage for the chapter with a vignette about the "weirdness" of Havel's plays. Unlike the two communication undergraduates, we should consider the plays "weird" in the provocative sense of the Czech *zvláštní*. This chapter has illustrated how and why this could be so. In the chapter's opening scene, I portrayed a duel between essays and plays, which represent contrasting ways of realizing the form/meaning nexus, with the former focusing on the *what* and the latter on the *how*.

The first scene also included selected details from some of Havel's plays (Hugo's alliterative feats in *The Garden Party* and Macheath's "knife's-edge" monologue from *The Beggar's Opera*) that capture what is at stake in the essay/play contrast and illustrate the form/meaning nexus of Havel's dramatic style. These details led into an account of Havel's own views on the meaning of theatre, which then initiated a more philosophical discussion about the nature of human meaning. In this regard, Havel's views have affinities with the American pragmatic tradition, as it finds expression in Dewey's *Art as Experience*, with its emphasis on embodied meaning and meaning as flow of experience. In blending together Havel's account of the meaning of theatre and a cognitive account of human meaningfulness, we understand that it is our participation in the plays as aware theatre-goers or spect-actors (as engaged witnesses to the performance) that enacts the meaning or message of the plays.

In scene two, we reimagined the philosophical discussion of human meaning, as well as its relationship to the meaning of theatre, in terms of the conceptual opposition between *explaining* and *understanding*, which I argued must be considered a central thread in the fabric of Havel's thought. I exemplified key moments in Havel's writings at which the opposition appears at the same time that I argued that it has intrigued and inspired thinkers beyond Havel. Like the mosaic principle, the opposition serves as a conceptual tool for reading our own modern-day selves.

That the essay/play contrast can be thought of as a localized realization (or strategic compression) of the opposition between *explaining* and *understanding* became clearer as we explored the contours of the latter, and scene three was devoted, rather paradoxically, to *explaining* Havel's dramatic style as a meaningful and serious form of *understanding*-oriented discourse. To make this case, we saw that Havel's obsession with the "organization of experience" is woven into the structure of *The Beggar's Opera* in such a way that a performance of the play becomes a vehicle for instructing (and implicating) the audience in the cognitive power of framing. *The Beggar's Opera* represents, in this respect, a dramatic compression of the conceptual role played by framing in the off-stage world. Basing the discussion in recent research in cognitive science, I then argued that Havel's plays in general serve as simulations of selected aspects of our existential reality that have been compressed to a human scale. Cognitively speaking, the plays are concentrated conceptual blends that the audience must decompress or unpack, and much that is associated with Havel's dramatic style serves to activate the spectators in the running of the blend.

Put another way, Havel's plays are existential maps that compress aspects of our reality in order better to "display Being." They are compressed simulations that activate neurons in logically related chains, and one of their primary functions, then, is to foster recognition of the decompressed situation that they model. The crux of our existential encounter with a Havel play involves running the blend as a simulation. His plays are ultimately a kind of metadrama, the message of which lies not in a dogmatic *explanation* of the world, but rather in teaching us to *understand* the world and its associated conceptual "directional track."[50]

Havel's dramatic style – a style that he chose as a formal vehicle best-suited to convey his message – may well have served as a more appropriate form than the essay to promote an intellectual project aimed at a reorientation from *explaining* to *understanding*. Dramatic performance allows for possibilities of transcendence that the essay form does not, because the "presence" of transcendence is represented in a less-mediated form in the former than in the latter. Havel's dramatic style borders on a kind of spiritual therapy. Existential forms are enacted on stage that have, through decompression of the blend, disturbing implications for our off-stage identities, but the theatrical setting and the absurd humour of the staging give the audience a measure of critical detachment from the situation. As spectators to the performance, we laugh at existential realities that may prove disturbing to us in our off-stage lives, and humour gives us a measure of control over those realities. As the psychologist Victor Frankl once observed, laughing at a situation represents, from a psychoanalytic viewpoint, restoration of trust in Being via existential reorientation (1986: 240). If psychological therapy is understood as a form of "reading" human identity, then Havel's plays are instruction manuals for "reading" ourselves in the modern world.

One essential instruction in Havel's manual for reading ourselves encourages us to rethink our conventional definition of truth. Truth in Havel's plays is not an objective thing. It is not a piece of information that the play transmits to us ready-made and packaged to bring home. Havelian truth is not an *explanation* as much as it is a process of reflection and self-reflection that is embodied in the personal struggle that we undergo in unpacking the compression. Truth is a form of *understanding* that is oriented towards meaning as flow of experience. It is a *how*, not a *what*, and the plays are designed to enact truth-as-flow and embed the audience, as engaged witnesses, in that enactment.

It is in this way that an encounter with one of Havel's plays may lead members of the audience to a kind of personal existential catharsis, one that takes place, as Havel describes in *Disturbing the Peace*, in a collective setting:

> Even the toughest truth expressed publicly, in front of everyone else, suddenly becomes liberating. In the beautiful ambivalence that is proper only to theatre, the horror of that truth (and why hide it – it looks worse onstage than it does when we read it) is wedded to something new and unfamiliar, at least from our reading: to delight (which can only be experienced collectively), because it was finally said, it's out of the bag, the truth has finally been articulated out loud and in public. In the ambivalence of this experience there is something that has been a part of theatre from the beginning: catharsis. (Havel 1991b: 200–1 and 1990: 174)

Given that catharsis is a matter of "human content" and that *explanation* lacks that spirit, it is the *understanding* orientation of theatre of the appeal that makes catharsis possible.

Taken together, these considerations shed light on Havel's claim, in the epigraph to this chapter, that his plays depict, whether he wants them to or not, an almost obsessive concern with the theme of human identity. Human identity, Havel noted elsewhere, "has always been intrinsically related to the phenomenon of theater."[51] We are beings who are aware of our own Being, and theatre enacts this awareness. The very logic of the world of a play "forces a confrontation between the way people legitimate themselves and the way they really are." Every play raises, in its own complex fashion, "the question of identity as the most fundamental question of existence." That the theatre always deals with this theme, then, is not a conspiracy of playwrights, but rather in the nature of the art form itself; the playwright is merely a "medium" for channeling this dramatic potential.

3 Understanding East and West: The World in Existential Crisis

But I know that people in the West in general tend not to admit that humanity is in a state of crisis and that therefore their own humanity is in a state of crisis too. Whenever I have a chance to talk to Westerners, I try to raise this matter.

– Václav Havel,
Disturbing the Peace[1]

In their encounter with Havel's 1984 essay "Politics and Conscience," the more attentive readers among my students are usually quite taken aback when they come upon passages like this one:

> Let me repeat: totalitarian power is a great reminder to contemporary civilization. Perhaps somewhere there may be some generals who think it would be best to dispatch such systems from the face of the earth and then all would be well. But that is no different from an ugly woman trying to get rid of her ugliness by smashing the mirror that reminds her of it. (Havel 1991a: 260–1 and 1999, 4: 432)

This passage (and indeed, the entire essay) argues for a radical reconsideration of the conventional wisdom surrounding the Cold War relationship between East and West. In Havel's understanding, the (post-)totalitarian East is not the opposite of the democratic West, but rather the former serves as a warning for the latter. Sociopolitical systems in the East

> ... warn of something far more serious than Western rationalism is willing to admit. They are, most of all, a convex mirror of the inevitable

> consequences of rationalism, a grotesquely magnified image of its own deep tendencies, an extreme offshoot of its own development and an ominous product of its own expansion. They are a deeply informative reflection of its own crisis. (Havel 1991a: 260 and 1999, 4: 431)

Havel's ambition in "Politics and Conscience" is to "consider, in a most general and schematic outline, the spiritual framework of modern civilization and the source of its present crisis" (Havel 1991a: 254 and 1999, 4: 422), and realizing that ambition first requires a fundamental rethinking of the East/West relationship.

The conventional framing	*Havel's reframing*	
	HUMANITY IN EXISTENTIAL CRISIS	
EAST ≠ WEST COMMUNISM ≠ CAPITALISM	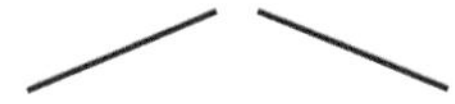	
	POST-TOTALITARIAN SYSTEM	DEMOCRATIC SYSTEM

Students have found it useful to visualize Havel's conscious reframing of the East/West relationship as in the figure above. In the conventional view, the opposition between East and West is dichotomous: "communism" and "capitalism" share nothing in common, and Havel's critique of the East is therefore not in any way applicable to the West. In Havel's reframing, however, East and West are understood as two sides of the same modern coin. They represent different but related realizations of an existential or spiritual crisis that encompasses the modern world. It is in this sense that post-totalitarian systems in the East can be understood "for what they ultimately are – a convex mirror of all modern civilization and a harsh, perhaps final call for a global recasting of that civilization's self-understanding" (Havel 1991a: 259 and 1999, 4: 431). While we cannot compare East and West directly, Havel's strategy is to invite an indirect comparison through the mediating structure of a world civilization in existential crisis.

Given that Havel's reframing of East and West is not confined to "Politics and Conscience," we should consider its status in Havel's thinking. Questioning the place of Havel's reframing within his larger body of work is of particular importance given that Havel has not yet been taken seriously by the great majority of his English-language commentators in this regard. There are those scholars, like John Lewis Gaddis (2006), who read Havel exclusively as an anti-communist crusader and fail to take into account Havel's more nuanced treatment of the Cold War relationship between East and West. Other scholars, like Suk (2013), are aware of Havel's reframing, but limit themselves to a historical account in which there is no clear place for critical discussion of it.[2] Some commentators on Havel acknowledge the reframing, but readily dismiss its seriousness: Kaiser, for example, suggests that Havel is on "thin ice" (2009: 157) in advancing this kind of argument, and Judt, although an obvious admirer of Havel as an intellectual "dissident," writes somewhat glibly about Havel's East/West analysis (1988: 233ff.), and seems to imply that it can be reduced to a "distaste for material goods and the benefits of modernity" (1988: 234).[3] Only a handful of scholars have both taken Havel seriously on this point and explored the implications of the reframing for the post-1989 world.[4]

My ambition in this chapter, then, is to outline in detail Havel's East/West argument. This is a necessary first step towards appreciating the argument's status in Havel's overall project, and to my knowledge it is a step that has yet to be taken. In order to disagree with Havel's reframing of East and West, we first need to understand what we are disagreeing with and appreciate its value in Havel's thought. We might think of Havel's reframing as an attempt to provide a coherent background narrative for understanding the crisis of modernity, and as such it acts as a conceptual framework within which we may best position ourselves to confront that crisis adequately.[5] Havel's reframing represents, then, his most general intellectual appeal.

First and foremost, it must be recognized that Havel's East/West reframing is a localized variant of a grander hypothesis that also represents an overarching thread in Havel's thought, one that has received little attention in the critical literature. Havel's restructuring of the conventional Cold War dichotomy emerges from his belief that the twentieth century represents the dawn of a transitional era in human history, a shift from one great age of humanity – the Modern Age (Czech *novověk*), with its implicit faith in rationality and science – to another age that is beginning to take shape but that has yet to define itself fully. Humanity is in the throes of redefining itself, searching for a new self-understanding. The mediating structure of a world in existential crisis is given hypothetical substance, and the East/West relationship is understood to be one particular manifestation of a larger phenomenon.

I first consider in some detail Havel's East/West reframing. This then leads into a discussion of the grander hypothesis of humanity in an age of transition. To explicate the latter, I analyse one of Havel's major presidential texts, his 1995 address at Harvard University, and I also summarize studies by two intellectual historians whose views dovetail with Havel's own. Those analyses shed light on the status of this hypothesis in Havel's thinking and beyond. I conclude the chapter by reflecting on the value of these interrelated hypotheses for reading Havel as well as for making sense of the phenomenon of post-totalitarianism – that is, for rendering it "meaningful" in Arendt's sense of the word.

East and West reframed

Havel always explicitly rejected, from his earliest writings through his presidential and post-presidential texts, a conventional reading of the Cold War in which post-totalitarian East represents the antithesis of democratic West.[6] Havel reworks the conventional reading of the East/West relationship in two major essays: "Power of the Powerless" (1978) and "Politics and Conscience" (1984). In both of these essays, the reframing is overtly "explicated": Havel's views are rationalized and realized in a logical argument. Moreover, the argument is unambiguous, and it is hard to imagine how it could be glossed over by an attentive reader.[7]

In the first essay, "Power of the Powerless," for example, Havel argues that both East and West share fundamentally the same value system, a value system that underlies any modern consumer-industrial society. East and West, however, exemplify different specific forms of realizing the system of shared values (Havel 1991a: 131 and 1999, 4: 229). In this view, post-totalitarianism is a face of the global crisis of human civilization that represents a "special and extreme version" of consumer-industrial society (1991a: 207 and 1999, 4: 321). The East should therefore serve as a warning to the West:

> [I]n the end, is not the grayness and emptiness of life in the post-totalitarian system only an inflated caricature of modern life in general? And do we not in fact stand (although in the external measures of civilization, we are far behind) as a kind of warning to the West, revealing to it its own latent tendencies? (1991a: 145 and 1999, 4: 246)

The "automatism" that the post-totalitarian system represents is, in Havel's reframing, "merely an extreme version of the global automatism of technological civilization," and the "human failure that it mirrors is only one variant of the general failure of modern humanity" (1991a, 207 and 1999, 4: 321). Moreover, despite the clear political differences between the systems, Western democracy in its current form does not provide a solution to humanity's existential crisis. On the contrary, because ideological manipulation in the West is "infinitely more gentle and refined" than its counterpart in the East, the crisis is more hidden, more elusive, and therefore more difficult to confront (1991a: 208 and 1999, 4: 322).[8]

As we see from the above citation, Havel coined the term "post-totalitarian" to describe a system that is "totalitarian in a way fundamentally different from classical dictatorships, different from totalitarianism as we usually understand it" (Havel 1991a: 131 and 1999, 4: 230). He suggested thereby that the West misread totalitarianism in the East. Havel's post-totalitarianism is different from Arendt's focus on the brutal regimes of Hitler and Stalin, and the difference lies in method, not essence. The post-totalitarian system that Havel describes is a refined version of Arendt's model, a version that brings it closer to the West in terms of its existential contours.[9]

In Havel's reframing, the East is understood as an extreme version of the West in the sense that it represents the West's "vain ratiocentrism" pushed to its logical (and ultimately absurd) end.[10] This situation is reminiscent of the structure of Havel's plays, in which the kernel of a realistic situation – a conversation between boss and employee (*Audience*), a dinner party with a married couple (*Unveiling*), a visit to an old friend (*Protest*) – rapidly takes on absurd dimensions, and in this respect the structure of Havel's plays may also serve as a model for the East/West reframing. Post-totalitarian regimes are, in other words, grotesquely exaggerated forms of the late twentieth-century consumer-industrial society that has been perfected in the West.

This same theme is considerably developed in the later essay "Politics and Conscience," in which Havel invokes Czech philosopher Václav Bělohradský's term "eschatology of the impersonal" to describe key points of existential contact between the Eastern and Western versions of consumer-industrial society. Both represent, to different degrees and in different local forms, the "rule of a bloated, anonymously bureaucratic power, not yet irresponsible but already operating outside all conscience, a power grounded in an omnipresent ideological fiction which can rationalize anything without ever having to come in contact with the truth" (Havel 1991a: 260 and 1999, 4: 431). This type of impersonal power "has achieved what is its most complete expression so far in the totalitarian systems" (Havel 1991a: 258 and 1999, 4: 429), but the phenomenon is by no means limited to these systems.

As Havel makes clear in "Politics and Conscience," post-totalitarianism is less a political phenomenon than it is a matter of human identity, and to get to the root causes of its evil and not merely treat the symptomatic sociopolitical manifestations of the problem, we need to confront it at the level of the human spirit. Havel writes that the "best resistance to totalitarianism is simply to drive it out of our own souls, our own circumstances, our own land, to drive it out of contemporary humankind" (1991a: 268 and 1999, 4: 441). East and West face

> ... one fundamental task from which all else should follow. That task is one of resisting vigilantly, thoughtfully, and attentively, but at the same time with total dedication, at every step and everywhere, the irrational momentum of anonymous, impersonal, and inhuman power – the power of ideologies, systems, apparat, bureaucracy, artificial languages, and political slogans. We must resist its complex and wholly alienating pressure, whether it takes the form of consumption, advertising, repression, technology or cliché – all of which are the blood brothers of fanaticism and the well-spring of totalitarian thought. (1991a: 267 and 1999, 4: 439-40)

In both the Marxist and the capitalist frameworks, identity becomes materialized, commodified, ritualized, and automatized. In both types of society, economic or material aspects of being are taken to be primary, although in different (if not opposing) ways. Both Marxism and capitalism represent, in other words, deeply materialist philosophies or consumer-industrial ways of being. Human meaning in both becomes a matter of one kind of "scientific materialism" or another, and the differences between them become mere surface-level symptoms of a shared systemic structure.[11]

Havel's reframing of the East/West dynamic is rationally explicated in the essays, but it is modelled or simulated in the plays. In Havel's reworking, the mediating structure for the East/West relationship is the spiritual crisis of modern humanity, which derives from the materialization and commodification of being. The existential layer of interpretation so prominent in the plays – a layer that allows for the interpretive "openness" of the plays as well as of other works like the anticodes – is representative of this mediating level. In the plays, Havel does not so much explicate the East/West reframing as assume its existence and its influence: the existential level includes and encompasses the "domestic" interpretive level. If, in other words, East is a grotesque caricature of West, then the existential and domestic interpretive levels are conflated, with the former subsuming the latter.

Given the centrality of Havel's reframing to the arguments that he makes in the essays as well as to an interpretive reading of the plays, it is puzzling how often scholarship on Havel has ignored this line of argumentation or minimized its significance. In most scholarship on Havel, the East/West hypothesis is simply not discussed, and this is likely because it falls outside the scope of a reading that focuses on contextualizing (biographizing and historicizing). These forms of scholarship do not seem to know what to do with Havel's hypothesis. Scholars like Aviezer Tucker (2001) and Paulina Bren (2010) directly address Havel's reframing, but do so dismissively. Bren, for example, notes that to a certain extent,

> Havel staked his claim in political philosophy based on the recognition that what he had to say about the human condition in late communism was just as relevant in any postmodern, consumer-oriented society – that, on some level, Western societies were just as troublingly post-totalitarian as was Czechoslovakia's normalization. (2010: 110)

Raising this point without citing the relevant passages from Havel's own writing or presenting Havel's line of thinking, she dismisses it some pages later by citing the writer Paul Berman whose "blunt assessment" of Havel is that he "'became merely one more slightly befuddled left-wing reader of Martin Heidegger'," and a poorer cousin of the sociologist and philosopher Herbert Marcuse, who is called the "Cassandra of consumer society" (2010: 198). Abruptly ending discussion, Bren remarks: "There is something to be said for Berman's demystification" (2010: 198).

It is telling that scholars who ignore or dismiss Havel's East/West framing tend to be those who focus on his essays.[12] Those scholars who are primarily interested in his plays have found it difficult to avoid confronting the existential level of interpretation that is built into Havel's dramatic style. As an example, we might consider Phyllis Carey's 1999 analysis of the play *The Memorandum*, in which she argues that Havel's plays in general (and this play in particular) focus on the "institutionalization of language in closed systems," and that *The Memorandum* "was and is relevant not only to those in politically totalitarian regimes but also to those in an increasingly technocratic global society" (1999: 174). In Carey's reading of the play, Havel's project is to awaken readers

> ... to the subtle, pervasive, and dehumanizing conditioning that accompanies our increasingly technological existence. Such conditioning includes an impersonal objectifying of reality; the reduction of humans to consumers; the measuring of the real exclusively in quantifiable terms; a focus on means as ends in themselves; efficiency and productivity as unquestioned but absolute values; the exploitation of nature and other humans in the name of progress; a standardizing and normalizing of consumers under the guise of a variety of choices; intrusive informational gathering for the sake of data and/or manipulation; and the reliance on technological solutions for the problems caused by the wholesale reliance on the technological. (Carey 1999: 174)

She notes that while we are much more conscious of technology's advantages and tend not to dwell on its consequences, *The Memorandum* forces us to think again and examine

> ... the depersonalizing and dehumanizing elements that tend to accompany business as usual as the technological holds sway over more and more aspects of human existence. In presenting the effects on the human of a totalized system, the play evokes a hunger for a genuine human response to the other, a responsibility that would begin to transform the system or at least mitigate its effects. (1999: 182)

She concludes by stating that while Havel's play does reflect the domestic political situation in communist Czechoslovakia, "it also reflects, especially for Western audiences, the succumbing of the individual and society to a world view that increasingly disregards human responsibility" (1999: 182).

The existential level, in other words, subsumes the domestic level, and in this way the plays enact Havel's reframing of the East/West dynamic, which he then rationally explicates in the essays. By not taking Havel's essayistic explication of the reframing seriously, critics have a rather difficult time reconciling the essays with the plays. This is one reason for the strong tendency to engage in a fragmentary reading of Havel's genres. If we do not appreciate the value of the East/West reframing for Havel's thought as a whole, it is even more difficult to see the coherence between his pre- and post-1989 incarnations. If the conventional view of the Cold War is explicitly or implicitly accepted, then the 1989 Velvet Revolution and the fall of Central/Eastern European post-totalitarianism render Havel's pre-1989 literary and political engagement obsolete in the post-1989 world. If East is the opposite of West, then how could Havel's keen pre-1989 analyses of Central European post-totalitarianism be relevant in a post-1989 world? Havel the "dissident" is put safely under glass in the museum display case.

Not surprisingly, Havel did not see things in these terms, and many of his speeches as president, particularly in the early 1990s, insist on the East/West reframing. Some of the better-known examples of this insistence include his description of communism as a "perverse extreme of the modern age" in a 1992 speech to the World Economic Forum and his argument that the post-communist challenge represents a general human challenge or the search for a "new type of self-comprehension for man," which is one of the central themes of a 1993 speech given at George Washington University. While most of the references to the East/West reframing are made in international speeches, he revisits the theme in a late speech aimed specifically at a Czech audience (Státní svátek 2001). He specifically argues that the structure of thought under capitalism is fundamentally the same as it was under communism in that both systems attempt to explain all of life by "banal schemas" that give primacy to "economic being" and that those in power want to create the impressions that they are "the only owners of the truth."[13] Havel, at least, saw strong continuity and coherence between his pre- and post-1989 faces, and the glue that binds these faces and time periods together – that makes them tiles in the same intellectual mosaic – is his reframing of the East/West relationship.

Another recurrent (and related) theme of Havel's presidential texts is the proposition that the East has something important to offer the West and that therefore the aid provided to the East by the West following 1989 is not unreciprocated. He mentions this theme in one of his first speeches as president in a January 1990 address to the Polish Sejm and Senate. Havel dramatically claims that Central Europe has awakened and that Central Europeans now have a collective responsibility to rouse those in the West who have slept through the true meaning of this event. He defines the awakening, and the East's potential contribution to the world as whole, primarily in spiritual and moral terms: "What we have to offer are spiritual and moral impulses, courageous peace initiatives, under-exploited creative potential, and the special ethos created by our freshly won freedom." Havel sees an opportunity to "transform Central Europe from what has been a mainly historical and spiritual phenomenon into a political phenomenon," that is, to import the spiritual awakening into the realm of politics. This would allow Central and Eastern Europe to "approach the richer nations of Western Europe, not as poor failures or helpless, recently amnestied prisoners, but as countries that can make a genuine contribution."[14]

The essence of that contribution lies in the moral lesson bound up with the experience of post-totalitarianism. In a 1991 address for a conference on European ecology, Havel suggests that one aspect of this moral lesson is that a successful society cannot be built on ideological hubris. This kind of hubris, Havel claims, was the "basic mental stance" of post-totalitarian ideology, but Havel's detailed description of this arrogant mental stance – as an ideology that turned people into lords of all creation, owners of all truth, and rulers over the whole world – is not limited in its scope to the pre-1989 East. Bridging East and West and the 1989 divide, he calls for a spiritual reorientation all across the modern world, one that would understand people not as lords, but as creatures of nature and the cosmos. Havel advocates here, as elsewhere, for an existential or spiritual revolution that will return mankind to its proper place in the world and thereby cultivate a renewed sense of responsibility towards the world.

Havel is uncharacteristically hesitant and uncertain in his development of the theme of the East's potential contribution to the West, and he revisits it only late in the 1990s. In a 1999 address celebrating the anniversary of the Polish newspaper *Gazeta Wyborcza,* Havel casts doubt on whether the East has in fact given anything to the West in return for the latter's post-1989 material aid. He again suggests that the unique experience of life under a post-totalitarian regime carries with it a moral lesson that would be instructive for the post-1989 world – and not just because it might prevent the return of such sociopolitical systems, but also for deeper reasons that touch on the spiritual health of modern civilization. The post-totalitarian experience offers a moral perspective on freedom, independence, human rights, prosperity, and sacrifice that would, according to Havel, benefit even the wealthy, democratic West. People in the East learned the value of moral self-reflection, and this is what the modern world needs in order to avert civilizational collapse. Havel ends his address pessimistically, doubting whether the East has fulfilled its historical task to act as a warning to the West in this regard.

A similar speech is Havel's 1999 address to a conference titled "Europe: A Culture of Shared Causes," in which he laments that he and others have not articulated well enough what the East has to offer the West.[15] At the same time, he again insists that the experience of post-totalitarianism is generally important for everyone and has far-reaching consequences even for those who did not live under such a system. Havel mentions, in particular, that life under post-totalitarianism taught the need to live an ethical life and to develop an ability to transcend the framework and habits of modern civilization, and in these he includes consumerism as well as an orientation to the "dictatorship" of the media and advertising. He warns that Western Europeans (or post-1989 Europeans in general) have yet to overcome these destructive civilizational automatisms.

While the West gave the East material aid in the aftermath of 1989, Havel is proposing that the East ought to have repaid the West with spiritual aid. He makes this explicit in a 2001 conference address titled "Political Culture in a United Europe."[16] Havel's point is that the East ought to have offered the democratic West a "spiritual contribution toward a better mutual future," which would arise from the moral lessons learned by life under post-totalitarian circumstances. He states that he tried to write about this topic in his pre-1989 essays (and we have indeed seen that this is true), and that the essence of the lesson lies in the experience of living in a system in which the roles of victim and perpetrator of a violent crime were mixed together. The post-totalitarian system was, in its own particular way, able to "unfold over the whole of a society a peculiar kind of complicity." To different degrees, everyone was implicated in the system, and everyone was at the same time a victim of it. All were, through particular threads, entangled in the system. In this address, Havel sees in the post-totalitarian experience a lesson – and once again a warning – for humanity. He speculates that it may prove impossible to communicate the experience and the lesson that derives from it, but that all who lived under a post-totalitarian regime should not give up trying to do so and that the post-1989 democratic West should welcome this instructive discussion.

Without recognizing Havel's reformulation of the East/West relationship, we cannot make proper sense of his insistence on the East's spiritual contribution to the West. It is a theme that develops from

Havel's reframing of the conventional view of the East/West dynamic and depends upon understanding the post-totalitarian regimes in the East as inflated caricatures of modern society in general. The facile, politically tendentious, and culturally convenient story of the triumph of Western capitalism over Eastern communism is thereby defamiliarized and undermined.

Humanity in an age of transition

Havel's East/West reframing is encompassed by a grander hypothesis that provides broader background for it.[17] The focal point of this grander hypothesis is a whole world in existential crisis, the conceptual bridge that mediates between East and West. What is, in Havel's view, the essence of the modern civilizational crisis? In *Disturbing the Peace*, he summarizes the crisis in the following terms:

> In the first place, I think that the reasons for the crisis in which the world now finds itself are lodged in something deeper than a particular way of organizing the economy or a particular political system. The West and the East, though different in so many ways, are going through a single, common crisis. Reflecting on that crisis should be the starting point for every attempt to think through a better alternative. Where does the cause of the crisis lie? Václav Bělohradský puts it very nicely when he writes about this late period as one of conflict between an impersonal, anonymous, irresponsible, and uncontrollable juggernaut of power (the power of "megamachinery"), and the elemental and original interests of man as a concrete individual ... I'm persuaded that this conflict – and the increasingly hypertropic impersonal power itself – is directly related to the spiritual condition of modern civilization. The condition is characterized by loss: the loss of metaphysical certainties, of an experience of the transcendental, of any superpersonal moral authority, and of any kind of higher horizon. (Havel 1991b: 10–11 and 1990: 13–14)

The loss of an experience of the transcendental is tied to Havel's belief that humanity at the end of the twentieth century is in transition from one great age in its history – an era that we could call the Age of Science and Rationality or, more succinctly, the Modern Age – to another great age whose exact form and content have yet to be determined.

Havel maintains that we are searching for a new self-comprehension, a new way of framing who we are. His own search for form could be said to parallel what he believes humanity as a whole is facing: a need to find a new way of being in the world that recovers or (re)discovers a sense of the transcendental. This is, according to Havel, a rare historical opportunity for humanity, one that must be seized to make the world a better place. Business as usual will not suffice, and that is precisely his point as well as the crux of his radical thinking. If the modern world seems topsy-turvy, then we ought not to continue to pretend that everything is fine with it; that is, we ought not to act like the characters in his plays, who behave as if the absurd situation they find themselves in is completely normal and acceptable.[18]

Put another way, Havel suggests that humanity's current cultural-historical, hyper-rational home (our modern existential *domov*) is unstable, and this modern-age frame for our collective identity needs to be transcended. We cannot afford to remain "contained" within it; by closing ourselves up in its conceptual infrastructure, we endanger ourselves and the world in which we live. This grand hypothesis of humanity in an age of transition can be read as the mother-frame of the strategic and localized reframings that Havel undertakes. Havel himself did not subject this hypothesis to exhaustive analysis or commit to one particular way of understanding its implications, preferring instead to assume its general validity and to take for granted that other intellectuals would agree with him on this point.[19] At the same time, however, there are several interrelated ways to make sense of the hypothesis, all of which Havel considers at various points in his pre- and post-1989 writings.

First and foremost, the hypothesis of humanity in an age of transition posits the end of the Modern Age, a loss of belief in the transcendent power of science. We have reached the limits of a mindset (or, more generally, a way of being) oriented primarily towards Havel's *explaining* or Armstrong's *logos*. In this version of the hypothesis and as we have already seen, post-totalitarianism represents a grotesque caricature of modern society in general, an *explaining*-oriented system pushed to one logical and absurd extreme. Humanity cannot rely on science and rationality to provide a technical "fix" to the problems that plague us because the root cause of these problems is existential or spiritual; its roots lie, that is, in *understanding* and *mythos*. Havel had in fact already explored this thesis in his typographic poems from the 1960s. Many of the anticodes playfully challenge the idea that human meaning can be captured in a graph or chart or some kind of rational exposition, and they suggest that this is the essential contradiction of the era in which we live.

When Havel suggests that the Age of Science and Rationality is coming to an end, he is not saying that we are going to rid ourselves of technology. His point is rather more philosophical in that he suggests that an age dominated by science and rationality no longer provides us with a deep sense of meaning. We are spiritually restless, disquieted, troubled, and disconnected. We are in search of a new kind of human identity, a new spiritual or existential home. There is an empty space inside modern man, a longing for a kind of meaningfulness that society does not provide, a deep-seated yearning for comfort coupled with a sense of connectedness and belonging.[20] Although it provides us with many advantages, science does not fill that emptiness, just as Armstrong argues that *logos* does not and cannot satisfy the human need for *mythos*.

We have seen this argument in Havel's writings before in the line of thinking that connects the essay "Power of the Powerless" (1978) and his letters from prison (1979–1983) with the essays "Politics and Conscience" (1984) and most especially "Thriller" (1984).[21] In the last essay, Havel refers to the end of the Modern Age as an awkward (but nonetheless necessary) phase that humanity must go through to reach a higher level of maturity, like a child who must survive the anguishes of puberty to emerge into young adulthood:

> I am unwilling to believe that this whole [modern] civilization is no more than a blind alley of history and a fatal error of the human spirit. More probably it represents a necessary phase that man and humanity must go through, one that man – if he survives – will ultimately, and on some higher level (unthinkable, of course, without the present phase), transcend. (Havel 1991a: 286 and 1999, 4: 507)

This is perhaps yet another reason why "Thriller" has not received its due in the critical literature on Havel; it is not only a condensed and powerful presentation of Havel's reframing of the Cold War, but it contextualizes that reframing within the grander hypothesis of humanity in an age of transition. Both of these represent themes that readers of Havel from the "West" seem to be either too uncomfortable with, or perhaps find too radical, to confront.

For Havel, the end of the Modern Age is also associated, on a sociopolitical level, with the collapse of the post-totalitarian systems in Central and Eastern Europe and the subsequent dismantling of the bipolar geopolitical structure that dominated the world in the era of the Cold War. Havel sees the disintegration of the bipolar geopolitical system as a step in humanity's transition to a new age in which genuine multipolarity becomes the norm. This theme becomes central to Havel's description of humanity in an age of transition in the post-1989 presidential texts. This is hardly surprising given that the events of 1989 brought the Cold War to an end, rendering Havel's East/West reframing obsolete. Havel is obliged to shift the emphasis in his thinking to a more explicit focus on the mediating level of the reframing, that is, to a world in existential crisis. In other words, his concern with the East/West reframing gives way to, or rather transitions into, the theme of a multipolar, multicultural, and globalized world.

The argument that Havel develops in a succession of presidential addresses and texts from the early 1990s through his 2006 political memoir, *To the Castle and Back*, are complex. Instead of presenting them in step-by-step detail, I will focus on one major text, Havel's 1995 address upon receiving an honorary doctorate at Harvard University, in which the segue from the East/West dynamic to a global civilization in moral crisis is fully (if subtly) realized. I will cite the Harvard address at length, and its wording will make greater sense to us given our previous discussions of both the *explaining/understanding* thread and the East/West reframing hypothesis.

Havel opens the address by describing an evening he had recently spent in a restaurant:

> One evening not long ago I was sitting in an outdoor restaurant by the water. My chair was almost identical to the chairs they have in restaurants by the Vltava River in Prague. They were playing the same rock music they play in most Czech restaurants. I saw advertisements I'm familiar with back home. Above all, I was surrounded by young people who were similarly dressed, who drank familiar-looking drinks, and who behaved as casually as their contemporaries in Prague.

He then reveals, undoubtedly after a dramatic pause, that he was not in Prague and not in Europe or the United States, but rather in Singapore.

Havel uses this engaging opening gambit to lead into the main thesis of the address, which concerns the emergence of a globalized society:

> I sat there thinking about this and again for the umpteenth time I realized an almost banal truth: that we now live in a single global civilization. The identity of this civilization does not lie merely in similar forms of dress, or

> similar drinks, or in the constant buzz of the same commercial music all around the world, or even in international advertising. It lies in something deeper: thanks to the modern idea of constant progress, with its inherent expansionism, and to the rapid evolution of science that comes directly from it, our planet has, for the first time in the long history of the human race, been covered in the space of a very few decades by a single civilization, one that is essentially technological.

Havel symbolizes and instantiates the technological ground of this civilization by reference to the telecommunications network that criss-crosses the globe like capillaries in a human body, carrying not only informational content but also integrated models of social, political, economic, and legal behaviour. The modern life of humanity is fully interconnected not only "in the informational sense, but in the causal sense as well," a claim that he illustrates by again evoking Singapore: "[A]ll it takes is a single shady transaction initiated by a single devious bank clerk in Singapore to bring down a bank on the other side of the world." The shape of this technological civilization, Havel asserts, derives from the Western tradition. It is a Euro-American export to the world as a whole, and Europeans and Americans must therefore bear a heightened sense of responsibility for it.

Havel argues, however, that there is "something not quite right" with this global society. There are "dangers that threaten humanity in spite of this global civilization, and often directly because of it." Many of the problems faced by the world today emerge from the fact that the global civilization evident everywhere "is no more than a thin veneer over the sum total of human awareness." It is a superficial, young, fragile civilizational structure that has come into being so quickly that humanity has not had a chance to get used to it or the time to develop it into a workable form. This new way of being – Havel metaphorically describes it as a "single epidermis of world civilization" – conceals deep contrasts in cultural, spiritual, and historical traditions that lie hidden beneath its surface. As this "epidermis" of world civilization expands, "this 'underside' of humanity, this hidden dimension of it, demands more and more clearly to be heard and to be granted a right to life."

Havel also adds that the new globalized order is deeply paradoxical:

> [W]hile the world as a whole increasingly accepts the new habits of a global civilization, another contradictory process is taking place: ancient traditions are reviving, different religions and cultures are awakening to

> new ways of being, seeking new room to exist, and struggling with growing fervour to realize what is unique to them and what makes them different from others. Ultimately they seek to give their individuality a political expression.

A further aspect to this paradox is that the reviving cultural traditions that are struggling for political expression use "weapons provided by the very civilization that they oppose" in order to "defend their ancient heritage against the erosions of modern civilization." Europe and America have thus

> ... equipped other parts of the globe with instruments that not only could effectively destroy the enlightened values which, among other things, made possible the invention of precisely these instruments, but which could well cripple the capacity of people to live together on earth.

These circumstances represent, in Havel's view, "a clear challenge [*výzva*] not only to the Euro-American world but to our present-day civilization as a whole." The challenge is for the world to begin to understand itself as a genuinely multicultural and mulitpolar civilization "whose meaning lies not in undermining the individuality of different spheres of culture and civilization but in allowing them to be more completely themselves."

Havel remarks on the "dual nature" of the global civilization that encompasses the consciousness of modern humanity. The marvellous achievements of this technological civilization that often serve to enrich individuals and society "can equally impoverish, diminish, and destroy our lives." The trappings of this civilization can enslave people instead of serving them:

> Almost every invention or discovery from the splitting of the atom and the discovery of DNA to television and the computer can be turned against us and used to our detriment. How much easier it is today than it was during the First World War to destroy an entire metropolis in a single air-raid. And how much easier would it be today, in the era of television, for a madman like Hitler or Stalin to pervert the spirit of a whole nation. When have people ever had the power we now possess to alter the climate of the planet or deplete its mineral resources or the wealth of its fauna and flora in a space of a few short decades? And how much more destructive potential do terrorists have at their disposal today than at the beginning of this century?

At this point in the address, Havel invokes the Modern Age focus on *explaining* – and the accompanying loss of emphasis on *understanding* – by saying that the rational part of the human brain that "has made all these morally neutral discoveries" has become exceptionally developed, while the development of the brain's other part, the one that "should be alert to ensure that these discoveries really serve humanity and will not destroy it," has catastrophically lagged behind. While we may not be able to rein in the technological progress of civilization, we must hope that human conscience "can catch up to our reason, otherwise we are lost."

While we have become "masters at describing the crises and the misery of the world" (at *explaining* it), we are "much less adept at putting things right" (at *understanding* the world and rendering its problems "meaningful" to us). In this address, as we have seen elsewhere, Havel suggests that there is only one way to put things right and thereby save humanity: we must radically renew our sense of human responsibility by divesting ourselves "of our egoistical anthropocentrism, our habit of seeing ourselves as masters of the universe who can do whatever occurs to us." To do so requires (re)discovering and then cultivating a respect for the transcendent:

> We must discover a new respect for what transcends us: for the universe, for the earth, for nature, for life, and for reality. Our respect for other people, for other nations, and for other cultures can only grow from a humble respect for the cosmic order and from an awareness that we are a part of it, that we share in it and that nothing of what we do is lost, but rather becomes part of the eternal memory of Being, where it is judged.

This is equivalent to imbuing our newly globalized civilization with a spiritual dimension. The main responsibility for achieving this lies with the "cultural sphere" that originally exported this form of civilization to the world at large and that therefore "taught humanity its destructive pride." Europe and America must "now return to [their] own spiritual roots and become an example to the rest of the world in the search for a new humility."[22]

In this address and in the presidential texts taken as a whole, Havel has obviously and necessarily moved beyond a narrow focus on the East/West dynamic by incorporating it into his larger hypothesis of humanity in an age of transition. It is only by taking into account this larger hypothesis that we can make sense of Havel's insistence on the destructive "hubris" of post-totalitarian ideology as a warning to all of modern civilization. In the post-1989 texts, then, Havel suggests the contours of the new age of humanity that may be dawning, and he develops a compelling narrative for this new age in the hope that it may stick. He appeals to his readers and listeners to think about the problems confronting the world in a new way, and he seeks to persuade them that his own version of the narrative, which frames a call for action, deserves attention.

It has seemed, however, difficult for scholars to understand or appreciate Havel's points in this regard, almost as difficult as it is for the naive readers of Havel in my monograph course who are asked to rethink their entrenched understandings of the Cold War and its value for contemporary history and human identity. Without being consciously aware of it, we are invested in a conventional understanding of the East/West dynamic, perhaps because the conventional story underpins a cultural and sociopolitical "framework of intelligibility" that we take for granted, and Havel's reframing – along with the associated, and even more provocative, hypothesis of a transitional age of humanity – therefore confronts us with a significant intellectual, if not also existential, challenge.[23]

It may help us to confront that challenge if we note that Havel is by no means unique in positing that humanity is in an age of transition, and consider the views of other thinkers who have professed the same belief. I will limit myself here to discussing the views of two such thinkers, the first a Western scholar who was almost certainly unknown to Havel and the second a Czech scholar who was Havel's friend and whose ideas strongly influenced him.

Stephen Toulmin and the dismantling of the Newtonian cosmopolis

In his 1990 book *Cosmopolis: The Hidden Agenda of Modernity*, the British philosopher and intellectual historian Stephen Toulmin argues that the approach of the new millennium represents the end not only of a numerical age but also the end of an age of humanity "in a deeper, historical sense" (Toulmin 1990: 3).[24] Toulmin traces the history of the Modern Age and suggests that humanity is now in the process of transitioning from one kind of modernity to another:

> Approaching the third millennium, we are at the point of transition from the second or the third phase of Modernity – or, if you prefer, from

> Modernity to Post-Modernity. Placed at this transition by changes beyond our control, we have a choice between two attitudes toward the future, each with its own "horizons of expectations." (1990: 203)

Much like Havel, he sees this transitional period as an opportunity for humanity to welcome the prospect of change to shape a better future, but at the same time worries that we may turn our backs on this opportunity and retreat "back into the future" in a fit of fearful nostalgia.

Toulmin recognizes the difficulty of dating the exact beginning (and ending) of the Modern Age (1990: 5), and his strategy is to consider several different but related measures by which to judge the inception of Modernity as well as to compare and contrast modernity with the humanistic revival of the Renaissance, the age that immediately preceded Modernity and that, in Toulmin's analysis, laid a substantial part of the groundwork for it. One measure of the "modern" for Toulmin is the rise of the nation-state system, which succeeded the medieval Church as the central sociopolitical structure in Western Europe (1990: chapter 3). The nation-state emerges as a sovereign and dominant political entity from 1600 to 1650, and is securely in place by the late seventeenth century. The Modern Age is thus at its height from 1700 until 1914, and this is the high tide of nationhood when "few people seriously questioned that the nation-state was the central political unit, in either theory or practice" (1990: 139).

This dating coincides with another possible measure of the modern, namely the rise of Newtonian mechanistic science. If the scientific (in Havel's terms, the *explaining*) mentality is associated with the work of the British mathematician and physicist Isaac Newton, then this would put the start of the Modern Age in the late seventeenth century. Toulmin, however, suggests that it was the French philosopher René Descartes who set the stage for Newton's intellectual paradigm-shift, which pushes the date back to about 1630. Descartes and Newton laid the intellectual foundation for a scientific system that changed the world. Modern scholarship initiated a shift to rationality in philosophical and scientific inquiry that then spread into other more "practical" spheres like law, politics, and diplomacy (1990: 9).

In Toulmin's argument, the coincidence of these two measures of the modern are not incidental. Newton's scientific ideas, grounded in Descartes' emphasis on rational cognition, contained a "hidden agenda" that was not evident in their surface meanings (the physics and mathematics, which most people were unable to understand) but was "implicit, below the surface, in the way his ideas were commonly understood" (1990: 118). The Newtonian spirit, in other words, exerted a deep cultural influence. At stake was not so much science as a new "cosmopolis" implied by Newton's work (1990: 128ff.). Toulmin argues that this Newtonian cosmopolis gave "a comprehensive account of the world, so as to bind things together in 'politico-theological,' as much as in scientific or explanatory, terms" (1990: 128). Toulmin writes:

> The comprehensive system of ideas about nature and humanity that formed the scaffolding of Modernity was thus a social and political, as well as a scientific device: it was seen as conferring Divine legitimacy on the political order of the sovereign nation-state. In this respect, the world view of modern science – *as it actually came into existence* – won public support around 1700 for the legitimacy it apparently gave to the political system of nation-states as much as for its power to explain the motions of planets, or the rise and fall of the tides. (1990: 128)

The welcome of Newtonian thought represents, then, a kind of Quest for Certainty that fits into the social and political framework of its time (1990: 132).[25] Put another way, the assumptions of Newtonian science became so widespread that they came to represent a "framework of intelligibility" for European society at the time.

Interestingly for a discussion of Havel's views, Toulmin compares and contrasts the Newtonian modern cosmopolis with the Renaissance humanism of the sixteenth and seventeenth centuries. In the received or standard account (1990: 13ff.), the Modern Age began in the seventeenth century and represented a transition from medieval to modern modes of thought and practice that rested on the adoption of rational methods in all serious fields of intellectual inquiry. In Toulmin's "revised narrative" for Modernity (1990: 21), however, the cultural break with the Middle Ages did not occur in the seventeenth century, but had already taken place a hundred or more years before, during the late Renaissance. Toulmin reads seventeenth-century ideas less as revolutionary advances and more as a "defensive counter-revolution" to the humanistic revival in the period immediately prior. In this view, Modernity represented

> ... an intellectual and practical agenda that set aside the tolerant, skeptical attitude of the 16th-century humanists, and focused on the 17th-century pursuit of mathematical exactitude and logical rigor, intellectual certainty and moral purity. Europe set itself on a cultural and political road that has

> led both to its most striking technical successes and to its deepest human failures. (1990: x)

Modernity was a "new way of thinking about the world" (1990: 9) whose goals partly overlapped and partly contrasted with late-Renaissance humanism.

In Toulmin's revised narrative, seventeenth-century scientific thinkers did not expand the scope for rational or reasonable debate, but rather narrowed it: reason came to mean only formal, abstract reason (1990: 20). The Modern Age thus has two distinct origins. The first is the literary and humanistic phase of the late Renaissance, and the second is a seventeenth-century scientific focus on the rational method. The latter "turn[ed its] back on the former," and modern science can therefore be understood as a kind of counter-Renaissance or a reversal of late-Renaissance values (1990: 23). In this regard, Renaissance humanists were religious, but not dogmatically so (1990: 30): they appreciated diversity of opinion and complexity of thought. In the late Renaissance, intellectual and spiritual tolerance was promoted, but these insights and this approach were lost in the seventeenth-century Quest for Certainty (1990: 36).

While Renaissance humanism represented a "commitment to intellectual modesty, uncertainty, and toleration" as well as a kind of "humane wisdom" (1990: 174), seventeenth-century philosophy reacted against this and was concerned with theoretical ambitions and intellectual (as well as spiritual) constraints (1990: 42). In comparing the late Renaissance and the Modern Age and tracing the lasting influence of the former on the latter, Toulmin cites C.P. Snow's famous 1959 "Two Cultures" lecture, in which the latter decried the gulf between "literary intellectuals" (modern humanism) and scientists (modern rationalism):

> If the Two Cultures are still estranged, then, this is no local peculiarity of 20th-century Britain: it is a reminder that Modernity had two distinct starting points, a humanistic one grounded in classical literature, and a scientific one rooted in 17th-century natural philosophy. (Toulmin 1990: 43)

The dramatic tension between the sources of the modern cosmopolis, which we can imperfectly analogize to Havel's opposition between *explaining* and *understanding*, continues to be felt.

By the middle of the twentieth century, Modernity as a program has ceased to carry with it "anything like the same conviction" that it used to; the tide of the age no longer flowed as strongly as it once did (1990: 3):

> What looked in the 19th century like an irresistible river has disappeared in the sand, and we seem to have run aground. Far from extrapolating confidently into the social and cultural future, we are now stranded and uncertain of our location. The very project of Modernity thus seems to have lost momentum, and we need to fashion a successor program. (1990: 3)

The assumptions of Newtonian science have come "under damaging fire," and a critique of Modernity broadened "into a critique of Rationality itself" (1990: 12). Demolition of the intellectual "scaffolding" of Modernity occurred bit by bit (1990: 144). In Toulmin's account, the dismantling of the "less critical timbers" had already begun by 1750, but the entire task took well into the late twentieth century (1990: 145). Toulmin asserts that by this time not one timber of the scaffolding related to Modernity's views of Nature was fully accepted by scientists or non-scientists:

> Today, we need no longer assume either that nature is generally stable, or that matter is purely inert, or that mental activities must be entirely conscious and rational. Nor do we any longer equate the "objectivity" of scientific work with "non-involvement" in the processes being studied. Least of all, do we see the distinction between "reasons" and "causes" as necessitating the separation of Humanity from Nature. (Toulmin 1990: 143)

The science of ecology here has been key because ecology cannot ignore "the engagement of humans in the causal processes of nature," and "once we undo that knot, the rest of the fabric quickly unravels" (1990: 143).

The gradual undermining of the foundational tenets of Newtonian science have their parallel in the sociopolitical sphere in the waning influence of the nation-state model, which is no longer "the self-sustaining political unit that it was in the 17th and 18th centuries" (1990: 7). Toulmin agrees with Havel that we live increasingly in a globalized world, and this calls out for new institutional arrangements – new forms of being – that "overlap national boundaries and serve transnational social and economic needs" (1990: 7). Globalization is also resulting in the decline of Euro-American political supremacy (1990: 3). The emergence of a multicultural and multipolar world is gradually transforming our geopolitical landscape, and this phenomenon represents, in both Toulmin's and Havel's accounts, a key event in human history, the meaning of which we may be in danger of misreading.

At the risk of oversimplifying matters, we observe much that is common in Toulmin's account of the Modern Age and Havel's hypothesis of humanity in a transitional epoch. First and foremost, both believe that how we view the past is important for how we understand the present and future. The narratives of the past that we construct and believe in (like the conventional story of the Cold War) tell us a great deal about ourselves and strongly influence the decisions we make regarding our future. Related to this point is the fact that both Toulmin and Havel see the Modern Age not just as a mindset or mentality that we can accept or reject as the circumstances require (in other words, not as a way of thinking that is ultimately under our rational control), but as a form of identity or mode of being in the world. Cartesian and Newtonian rationality is understood as a zeitgeist that permeates social and, to a great extent, individual consciousness. Even if you do not understand Newtonian science, you are shaped by the implications of its principles. We are, in other words, citizens of the cosmopolis, sometimes even in spite of our propensities to the contrary.

Both Toulmin and Havel also believe that the story of the Modern Age offers us a moral lesson. In Toulmin's case, there is a civilizational lesson to be learned at the end of the Modern Age, which he describes in terms of an urgent need

> ... to reappropriate the wisdom of the 16th-century humanists, and develop a point of view that combines the abstract rigor and exactitude of the 17th-century "new philosophy" with a practical concern for human life in its concrete detail. Only so can we counter the current widespread disillusion with the agenda of Modernity, and salvage what is still humanly important in its projects. (1990: xi)

This is similar, or in certain respects supplemental, to Havel's discussion of the opposition between *understanding* and *explaining*, in that the former captures the essence of Toulmin's late-Renaissance humanism with the latter characterizing the Cartesian and Newtonian age that followed. In Toulmin's terms, then, we could say that Havel longs for a return of ideas and modes of thought and discourse that pre-dated the Modern Age, which is not the same thing as a nostalgic return to a pre-industrial or pre-rational past, but is rather a revival of humanistic ideals that have been lost.

It is, in other words, not the death of rationality as such, but a reframing, in the Havelian spirit, of rationality's meaning. Toulmin makes this point particularly clear, arguing that the end of the Modern Age does not inevitably lead to the conclusion that the intellectual program of Modernity, grounded as it was in Newtowian rationality, was a failure (1990: 172) as much as it was a case of intellectual overreach (1990: 175). We are perhaps starting to learn (or relearn) not to ground all of our knowledge in universal, timeless systems, because we have realized that the formal, abstract rationalist "dream" – Havel's "vain ratiocentrism" – is an illusion (1990: 172). The end of the Modern Age may then mark "our awakening from a transient, ambiguous daydream" through a realization that rationality is just not systemic: "If, instead, we reanalyze 'rationality' in non-systemic terms, there need be nothing 'absurd' in that" (Toulmin 1990: 172).[26]

For both Toulmin and Havel, the way forward as we enter the "second or third phase" of Modernity (in the former's estimation) or another age of humanity (in the latter's) is clear. We must drop the artificial opposition between objective and subjective, science and humanism, *explaining* and *understanding* – that is, between Snow's "two cultures." In order to do so, we must reappropriate the reasonable and tolerant (but neglected) legacy of humanism (Toulmin 1990: 180). Our task is "to find ways of moving on from the received view of Modernity… to a reformed version, which redeems philosophy and science, by reconnecting them to the humanist half of Modernity" (Toulmin 1990: 180).

Toulmin is an example of an intellectual who believes that humanity is in the throes of a transitional age. Although the details of Toulmin's views and Havel's less-studied beliefs may not fully coincide, we nonetheless see in the former a confirmation of the latter's assumption that intellectuals generally acknowledge the truth of his grand hypothesis. A belief that may seem in Havel's post-1989 texts to be radically provocative, if not also enigmatic, instead turns out to be in the mainstream of thought among intellectual historians.

Radim Palouš and the rise of the World Age

Radim Palouš is another such intellectual, but one whose particular views on the Modern Age (*novověk* in Czech) directly influenced Havel's own. Palouš is a Czech philosopher, educator, and former dissident who served as a spokesperson for Charter 77 in the early 1980s. In January 1990, he became chancellor of Prague's Charles University and served in this capacity for four critical years following the Velvet Revolution of 1989. Palouš was also one of the unnamed addressees of Havel's letters from prison and a key figure for the development of Havel's philosophical reflections. We ought therefore to pay particular attention to Palouš's views on humanity in an age of transition in order better to understand Havel's, and this is especially true given that Havel himself does not theorize the hypothesis, while Palouš does so at length.

In a 1991 presidential speech, Havel refers to Palouš's book on the subject of humanity in a transitional age, noting that planetary civilization is entering a global era and experiencing an accompanying existential crisis. These are indications, Havel says, that one of his friends takes as signs of a shift from the Modern Age to another age that his friend has called the World Age (*světověk* in Czech).[27] Havel describes the World Age in the following terms: "[E]verything today is interconnected, and all of today's crises have both a global context and global consequences, and it is only possible to deal with these crises also globally." If we do not admit this simple fact and begin to coordinate with each other in earnest, then Havel warns that the world is "doomed to catastrophe."

In Palouš's view, we are in fact already living in the World Age, or at least we have been actively engaged in transitioning to it since the mid-twentieth century. Palouš notes the traditional division of the ages of humanity into three distinct periods, the Czech names for which are derivationally systematic: *starověk* (the Ancient World), *středověk* (the Middle Ages), and *novověk* (the Modern Age).[28] This periodization, according to Palouš, came about during the beginning of the Modern Age (in Toulmin's humanistic late Renaissance), and was fully in use by the end of the seventeenth century. Unlike Toulmin, Palouš provides a detailed philosophical and historical justification of the methodology of historical periodization as such, and the justification proves to be inseparable from Palouš's understanding of the historical ages themselves.[29]

In the first place, Palouš asks whether historical periodization has any conceptual validity or any reality beyond historiography. Is it merely an analytical convenience of the historian (not to mention a handy aid in the history classroom), or is there something more to it? He answers unequivocally that periodization is not a random or hollow procedure on the part of historiographers, but rather an attempt to get at the "meaning of an age" (*smysl doby*) by extrapolating from individual events and figures – the various facts, symptoms, or acts of a given period of time – to the "common meaning" (*společný smysl*) towards which these point (1985: 15). Individual historical events become truly meaningful only as emblems of the broader cultural-historical spirit of the time in which they occur, Palouš argues, in much the same way that what happens in the individual acts of a well-conceived theatrical play serves to suggest the meaning of the play as a whole (1985: 15). The meaning of the historical era is alive in different ways in the various events that comprise it, but all of these ways point to a unity of meaning that is real and discoverable, and it is only by searching for and recovering this unity of meaning that we can hope to understand history (1985: 15).

Periodization, then, is not an obvious matter and cannot by carried out on the basis of a logical calculus or through rational formulas (1985: 17). Since periodization as a methodology is about discovering meaning, it has a spiritual ground and represents a "search for the spiritual unity of events" (1985: 19).[30] Periodizing requires transcendence, through both a certain distancing from local events and an active awareness of how various phenomena share a "meaningful sense of togetherness" (*smysluplná sounáležitost*), and this cannot be deduced mechanically from a pile of data (1985: 3).[31] To make this key point clearer, Palouš notes the different approaches to (historical) time implied by the Greek words *chronos* and *kairos*, the former of which treats time in a quantitative, impersonal, and mechanistic sense, while the latter treats the passage of time in its human and spiritual dimensions.[32] Periodization is then a form of kairology in which the historian is open to the meaning of the age in its spiritual contours, and not merely as a stretch of time devoid of meaningful substance (1985: 19).

A central focus of Palouš's book characterizes the meaning of the Modern Age in relation to the spirit of the emerging World Age. In terms of the former, Palouš's account largely parallels Toulmin's, with different points of emphasis. First and foremost, the Modern Age is characterized by modern science (*novověká věda*), which also serves as the conceptual foundation for modern spirituality and modern identity (Palouš 1985: 47). The spirit of the age is defined by the division of people and the world into subjects and object: humans have seemingly escaped the natural order by standing to the side of it, and have reduced nature (and here Palouš cites the twentieth-century scientist and Nobel Prize laureate Ilya Prirogine) "'to a blind game of forces and the indifferent movement of atoms'" (1985: 47). Human beings have become experimenting subjects who are ostensibly in control of nature, which we adapt to our own goals; if human artefacts in past ages have, for the most part, supplemented the natural world, modern "scientific technology" (*vědotechnika*) has gradually transformed the natural world and has ended up destroying it for its own purposes (1985: 48). Even God, notes Palouš, has not been immune from the spirit of the age. Cartesian dualism created a god who exists *for* humans. In this view, God came to serve man instead of the other way around (1985: 56).

Like Toulmin, Palouš see faith in the spirit of the Modern Age as already on the wane by the mid-twentieth century. Palouš cites thinkers who see the shaken faith as a loss of belief in the modern idea of progress. The motto of "always forward [*vpřed*] and always better" begins to lose its luster with increasing awareness of the hazards of modern technological civilization (1985: 28).[33] In short, humanity in the twentieth century began to find itself increasingly in crisis, and the sources of this existential crisis – two world wars, the development of weapons of mass destruction with world-wide consequences, the rise of global ecological threats – largely represented an indictment of blind faith in the spirit of modernity (1985: 37). Like Toulmin and Havel, however, Palouš sees the crisis as an opportunity, and he notes that the word "crisis" derives from Greek *krinein*, which had a number of contextualized meanings that were joined together by an implicit awareness of a crossroads or boundary (1985: 27). In its original sense, then, "crisis" meant not only a potentially threatening situation to find oneself in, but also an opportunity to discover corrective courses of action that would lead the way out of the crisis towards salvation and redemption (1985: 27). Without crises, Palouš notes (1985: 28), there can be no maturation, neither in the life of an individual nor in the history of a nation or of the world.

For Palouš, humanity's mid-twentieth-century existential crisis initiated a shift in understanding our relationship to the world, and he suggests that the invention (and use) of the atomic bomb symbolizes this shift well (1985: 30ff.). The atomic bomb is a weapon that can cause massive destruction beyond certain limited geographical zones, or even result in the destruction of the world as a whole. As soon as it became clear that humanity had in its hands power over the whole world at once, our relationship to the world's fate was in question – for the first time in human history. In other words, our ability to engage in massive destruction on a world-wide scale led naturally to reflection on our responsibility and our obligations towards the planet as a whole.

While the advent of the atomic bomb symbolizes a shift in humanity's relationship to the fate of the world, the single event that Palouš chooses as decisive in the turn from the Modern Age to the World Age is the 1969 moon landing. This was an event that symbolized "the end of the Modern Age and the European Age and the beginning of the World Age: for the first time man left the Earth, stood on the Moon, and then came back" (1985: 87).[34] We left the planet, and, for the first time in human history, saw the whole world at once with our own eyes (1985: 32). For Palouš, the return of the astronauts back to Earth is key, and their return symbolizes the deeper meaning of the moon landing, which is not about the trip itself but rather about the shift in human understanding that emerges from it (1985: 88). The Earth is no longer perceived merely as an indifferent planetary body rotating senselessly around its axis and orbiting the Sun through the frigid cosmos. It becomes instead humanity's *domov* or home (1985: 88).[35] Thus, 1969 is a symbolic boundary that divides the spirit of the Modern Age from the spirit of the World Age, because it represents both a recognition that humanity belongs to the Earth and, more philosophically speaking, a turn away from a focus on the particular (e.g., man as an individual) to a focus on the holistic (our relationship to the rest of humanity and to the planet as a whole) (1985: 89). All previous European ages, Palouš argues, were *ne-světověky* ("non-World Ages") to the extent that they emphasized, each in its own way, particularity, whereas 1969 made us both "earthlings" and "cosmopolitans" (in the sense of creatures of the cosmos) (1985: 92).

Palouš spends considerably more effort outlining the spirit of the newly emerging age than Toulmin does in his analysis. Palouš's World Age is characterized first and foremost by the assumption of a unitary civilization, and this is playing out across various levels or layers of contemporary human identity. Scientific thinking, led by the ecological sciences, is undergoing a shift in emphasis: the world is being perceived more and more as one interconnected, holistic system (1985: 59). The same is becoming true at sociopolitical, cultural, and historical levels, and for the first time, in the emerging World Age, we stand before the question of the meaning of our history not as a mere conglomeration of individual cultures and beliefs, but rather as a unified and truly human society (1985: 71).[36] Palouš notes that this is also true at a personal level to the extent that by the second half of the twentieth century people began to experience events happening in other parts of the world as pertaining, in some deeply felt way, also to themselves. Previously, such events were viewed from a distance and tended to seem more like curiosities, and only now are we beginning to feel that the age in which we live does indeed have a "unitary meaning" (*jednotný smysl*) (1985: 64).

We might borrow a term from Toulmin and suggest that, in Palouš's view, the underlying foundation of the human cosmopolis has dramatically changed at the dawn of the World Age. Philosophically, this is manifested in a new kind of *světověk* spirituality in which man is once again part of a larger rational but humanly meaningful world (1985: 56). Man, then, is no longer an external observer of (*divák*), but rather a participant in (*účastník*), the world (1985: 59). The divide between human subject and object characteristic of the Modern Age is being brought to an end, and we are beginning to see a refocusing from an objective account of "what is" to reflections on "what should be." This is, in Palouš's view, a return to understanding ourselves in the context of what transcends us, and it is a conceptual shift that is supported by science itself (1985: 61). The World Age is, in short, an age in which the Newtonian Quest for Certainty has given way to a quest for common meaning and human meaningfulness, and if this remains true in the foreseeable future, then it is an age that opens up new opportunities for human transcendence (1985: 71).

As is clear from this sketch of Palouš's study, Palouš is focused not on *explaining* history but rather on attempting to *understand* it in human terms. The spiritual dimension of each historical age is key both to justifying periodization as a methodology and to rendering the history of that age meaningful to us. History is not merely about the facts of an age – not only about historical events and their dates, the rulers and the rebels and the dramatic tension between them. These serve instead as contextual markers for making sense of history in a way that profiles the spiritual or moral contours of the larger age in which they occurred. Attempting to understand history in this way gives Palouš access to each age's transcendent meaning or message.

Palouš's account both complements and amplifies Toulmin's. While these intellectual historians may not agree on all of the details and use different terminologies that imply different intellectual emphases, they agree that humanity is currently in an age of transition. They also largely agree on not only the reasons underlying the transition, but also the broad contours of the ages that we are transitioning from and to. Palouš and Toulmin supply historical and theoretical grounding for this age of transition that Havel in his own discussions merely assumes. The views of both scholars lend intellectual credence to Havel's grand hypothesis, and give us a better understanding of its value in intellectual discourse as well as its status as a conceptual thread in Havel's thought. It is a hypothesis that has clear intellectual resonance beyond

Havel, and deserves to be taken more seriously in the context of Havel's writings than it has been.

From existential crisis to existential revolution

The modern crisis of humanity that Havel describes in his pre- and post-1989 writings, a description with which Toulmin and Palouš largely concur, exists in dimensions once shared by both East and West, even as they were manifested in each territory in distinct ways. To summarize, these dimensions include: the modern primacy of "vain ratiocentrism" and "egoistical anthropocentrism," or rather an *explaining* way of being pushed to its logical (and absurd) extreme; the commodification, materialization, and bureaucratization of Being in modern consumer-industrial society, which is also a type of society in which people are made complicit in a system that exploits them; extreme ideological hubris of one kind or another that precludes a healthy sense of humility inasmuch that we set ourselves up as "owners of truth" and attempt to explain everything through "banal schemas"; the ever-increasing rule of anonymous, impersonal, and inhuman power, and the accompanying erosion of a sense of individual, human responsibility; the loss of the experience of transcendence and a deepening sense of spiritual restlessness; and an ever-strengthening feeling that our modern "home" has become, in a number of different respects, unstable. Many of these dimensions were manifested in more acute forms in the pre-1989 post-totalitarian East than in the democratic West, and this then is the reason for Havel's view that the East should serve as a warning – or teach a moral lesson – to the West. The post-totalitarian East should, that is, be understood as a "convex mirror" or "inflated caricature" of modern civilization in general. At the same time, these dimensions are interrelated realizations of Toulmin's and Palouš's shared thesis concerning the gradual but increasing collapse of faith in the Modern Age cosmopolis, and the resulting shift from a Quest for Certainty towards a presumed and hoped-for quest for common meaning.

These considerations facilitate a return to Havel's 1995 address at Harvard University. As is now clear, the address captures many of the dimensions of the existential crisis that appear elsewhere in Havel, and also in Toulmin's and Palouš's accounts. One of its main focal points is a description of the civilizational structure of Palouš's emerging World Age. Like Palouš, Havel attempts to *understand* the transitional process in its various manifestations and with its intriguing paradoxes. In doing so, he also attempts to render its implications meaningful to us. Like both Toulmin and Palouš, he sees the crisis brought on by the collapse of the modern cosmopolis as an opportunity for renewal. The age of transition is a "challenge" (*výzva*) that humanity must successfully confront in order to survive.

If, as Havel asserts in the Harvard address, human conscience has lagged behind human technological capabilities, then the key to confronting this challenge lies in ridding ourselves of hubristic and egoistical anthropocentrism or, in Palouš's and Toulmin's terms, in erasing the subject/object division characteristic of the Newtownian cosmopolis. That this must necessarily involve an existential revolution should not be too surprising. A point that emerges from Havel's description of the modern crisis as well as from both Toulmin's and Palouš's accounts is that the transitional age is first and foremost a matter of a shift in understanding ourselves and our relationship to the world. It is a question of human identity, which is at heart an existential-level phenomenon. If the root problem is existential in nature, then it must be confronted at that level and in those terms. In other words, the existential and spiritual crisis of modern humanity needs to be addressed existentially and spiritually. The mediating structure of the existential level in Havel's East/West reframing is indicative of this need.[37]

Havel presents the idea of an existential revolution in the Harvard address, and indeed throughout his writings, in the form of an appeal. The addressees (or readers) are invited to think about the modern world in a fundamentally different way, much like we have seen in Toulmin's and Palouš's accounts, and also in Havel's own description of the various dimensions of the crisis. Havel's appeal results in a radical reframing of how we conventionally understand modern history, both the immediate past and its influence on the present. The appeal is intended to lead towards existential catharsis. Only by reframing the conventional narrative – by taking the first step towards existential revolution – can the crisis become an opportunity for renewal. In this sense, then, the idea of an existential or spiritual revolution is not abstractly idealistic or hopelessly mystical, but pragmatically grounded in the reality of the challenge that confronts us.

Indeed, in the Harvard address, Havel presents a pragmatic program for an existential revolution by advocating a quest for what he calls a spiritual "common minimum we can all share, one that will enable us to go on living side by side." Despite the diversity of cultures and spiritual traditions in the newly and rapidly globalizing world, there exist "genuine spiritual roots hidden beneath the skin" of that society that are shared across it. There are, in other words, essential similarities across cultures that can serve as a "unifying starting point for [a] new code of human coexistence that would be firmly anchored in the great diversity of human traditions," and these are common elements at the core of most world religions and cultures that take many different forms. These include a respect for the transcendent or for imperatives "that come to us from heaven, or from nature, or from our own hearts"; a belief that our deeds will live after us; a respect for our families and neighbours, and for certain kinds of authority; a respect for human dignity and for nature; and a sense of solidarity and benevolence towards guests who come with good intentions. These elements of a common spiritual minimum represent "basic commandments of [an] archetypal spirituality in harmony with what even an unreligious person, without knowing exactly why, may consider proper and meaningful." In sketching the ground for a possible common spiritual minimum, Havel is giving shape to Toulmin's and Palouš's visions of the "opportunity" that emerges from the crisis of Modernity.

Havel characterizes the goal of the program that he outlines as a return to human responsibility to and for the world around us, and this is also consistent with both Toulmin's and Palouš's visions for a future age in which the subject/object division has been erased. The spiritual dimension of the program is an ideal that we must keep in mind if we are to develop the practical logistics of a new world order from which a renewed sense of responsibility can naturally emerge. An existential revolution is necessary to develop an agreed-upon spiritual or moral vision functioning as a conceptual whole (like the big picture of a mosaic) that calls out, and gives meaning to, its various parts.

Havel is clear that his hypothesized existential revolution cannot be an ideologically imposed, top-down, or forced transformation. It is, rather, a practical, everyday task for "teachers, educators, intellectuals, the clergy, artists, entrepreneurs, journalists, people active in all forms of public life," and, above all, it is a task for politicians, who must learn to put the long-term interest of humanity before the short-term interests of their political parties and their careers. Havel's hypothesized revolution is, unfortunately, also not a change that will be realized without further trials. Havel asks, "Who knows how many horrific cataclysms humanity may have to go through before such a sense of responsibility is generally accepted?," and he surmises that it is the very survival of the human race that is at stake.

In the Harvard address, Havel frames the appeal component of this pragmatic quest for an existential revolution through one of his famous rhetorical questions:

> Is humanity capable of such an undertaking? Is it not a hopelessly utopian idea? Haven't we so lost control of our destiny that we are condemned to gradual extinction in ever-harsher high-tech clashes between cultures, because of our fatal inability to cooperate in the face of impending catastrophes, be they ecological, social, or demographic, or of dangers generated by the state of our civilization as such?

He answers the question himself on a non-committal but optimistic note: "I don't know. But I have not lost hope." As with his plays, Havel's rhetorical appeal in the Harvard speech ultimately shifts the burden of responsibility for reflecting on his proposed reframing of modern humanity's existential crisis – as well as for realizing the kind of spiritual revolution that he envisions will transform the crisis into a historic opportunity – onto his audience.

Conclusion

The idea of an existential or spiritual revolution was not, of course, a newly conceived theme for Havel at the time of the Harvard address. It had a strong presence in his pre-1989 writings, essayistic and otherwise, and he summarized its meaning in the following passage in *Disturbing the Peace*:

> It seems to me that if the world is to change for the better it must start with a change in human consciousness, in the very humanness of modern man. Man must in some way come to his senses. He must extricate himself from this terrible involvement in both the obvious and the hidden mechanisms of totality, from consumption to repression, from advertising to manipulation through television. He must rebel against his role as a helpless cog in the gigantic and enormous machinery hurtling God knows where. He must discover again, within himself, a deeper sense of responsibility toward the world, which means responsibility toward something higher than himself. (1991b: 11 and 1990: 14–15)

The idea is closely bound up with Havel's East/West reframing, as the problems of the world are not confined to one particular sociopolitical system or economic -ism. The world as a whole is undergoing "a single, common crisis" (1991b: 10 and 1990: 13–14), and we must reflect on this crisis as a necessary "starting point for every attempt to think through a better alternative" (1991b: 10 and 1990: 14).

In this chapter, I have traced the trajectory of two interwoven ideas, Havel's reframing of the East/West relationship and the hypothesis of humanity in a transitional age, across the 1989 divide. I have argued that Havel's pre-1989 texts present (or assume) a counter-narrative to the conventional story of the Cold War. The conventional story of the East/West dynamic is both formal skeleton and cage. It is a conceptual blend that compresses the many nuances and human complexities of the Cold War into a simple form, and we have come to inhabit the blend's conceptual space and "live" in the world that emerges from it. East and West reduced to a dichotomous opposition is still, almost twenty-five years after the revolutions of 1989, a deeply entrenched cultural frame that suggests to us a certain way of understanding history, both past and present, and it therefore also suggests a certain way of understanding ourselves and our future. Havel's conscious reframing of the conventional story is an attempt to transcend this conceptual cage.

It is not, however, merely that Havel reframes the traditional East/West dichotomy into an East and a West both actively undergoing more or less the same modern existential crisis. This reframing itself takes place within an even broader frame; it is hung, like a picture, against the background of the passing of one great age of humanity, the Modern Age (represented in its grotesque extreme by post-totalitarianism), into another age that has yet to be defined, but whose general contours, as intellectual historians agree, have been coming into shape since at least the mid-twentieth century. The trajectory in Havel's writing is to shift naturally away from specific discussion of the East/West dynamic and towards discussion of the broader hypothesis that subsumes it, and this becomes especially true post-1989 with the end of the Cold War and the emergence of a multipolar and ever more-globalized world.

While tracing the development of Havel's thinking with regard to East and West, I have also addressed the status of this line of thought in his oeuvre as a whole. Havel's reframing of the Cold War and the hypothesis of humanity in a transitional age are not incidental threads in the overall weave of his thought. They cannot be easily isolated from Havel's larger project and dismissed as ideas unto themselves without doing violence to the remarkable coherence and consistency of his thinking. If we radically downplay the value of these hypotheses, we are unable to appreciate fully the relationship between Havel-the-playwright and Havel-the-essayist, and we cannot adequately reconcile the pre- and post-1989 faces of Havel with each other. These hypotheses, then, are central threads running throughout Havel's intellectual project; remove them, and the fabric of his thought as a whole begins to ravel.

Taken together, these interrelated hypotheses also represent Havel's narrative attempt to *understand*, and not merely *explain*, the Cold War. Through the mediating structure of a world in crisis, Havel renders the experience of the East meaningful, in Arendt's sense, to the West.[38] It is, moreover, with this in mind that we should read and understand Havel's views on the West and Westerners as they are captured in this chapter's epigraph.

In light of the centrality of this complex thesis for Havel's project, it is shocking that commentators on Havel's writings and life have generally ignored or dismissed it, and I have taken pains to detail both parts of the thesis precisely because of this. Part of the reason for this attitude is perhaps obvious. As the crux of Havel's provocative appeal to his "audience," the meta-frame of humanity in an age of transition presents difficulties for scholars intent on historicizing Havel in one way or another. The meaning of an appeal transcends contextualization, and contextualizing forms of scholarship do not know how to address this central aspect of Havel's thinking effectively. The path of least resistance has been simply to avoid engaging it. Ideally, of course, a Havelian appeal is meant to "activate" its "audience." We can agree or disagree with it and argue our respective stances accordingly, but it is not intended to fall, as it largely has, on deaf ears.

We cannot, in other words, comfortably confront Havel's thesis regarding the meaning of the Cold War and the end of the Modern Age through contextualization alone, because we ourselves – our sense of self and our way of being – are directly implicated in it. Historicizing or biographizing Havel cannot adequately address the questions that the appeal raises. Like the East's proposed spiritual repayment to the West, it is a moral lesson that needs to be taken to heart and mind.

Havel's depiction of a world in existential crisis also provides a conceptual framework in which and through which we might read ourselves. It is a conceptual tool that suggests ways of reshaping our personal sense of self through a reframing of modern history. It is, moreover, a conceptual tool that is consistent with both the first chapter's discussion of the mosaic principle and the second chapter's discussion of the *explaining/understanding* opposition. And as we will see in the next chapter, it is also compatible with a focus on the semantic and cultural resonance of keywords in Havel's thought.

4 "Metaphysical reconstruction": Translating Havel's Keywords

There can be no doubt that distrust of words is less harmful than unwarranted trust in them. Besides, to be wary of words and of the horrors that might slumber inconspicuously within them – isn't this, after all, the true vocation of the intellectual?

– Václav Havel,
A Word about Words[1]

Reflecting on the difficulties involved in translating Havel's master essay "Power of the Powerless," Paul Wilson, Havel's English translator, notes that "many of the words carried a different burden of meaning than their dictionary equivalents in English" (2006: 12). The main example that Wilson cites is Havel's coinage of the term *samopohyb* (from *samo-* meaning "self" and *pohyb* meaning "motion") to describe the juggernaut nature of the post-totalitarian system. The term *samopohyb* certainly poses a challenge for the translator: while English "self-propelled" or "self-generating" capture the particular semantic combination of the roots, neither is, like the Czech original, a noun. Wilson's solution was to use another favourite Havelian word with a not unrelated meaning, "automatism," as his principal recourse. *Samopohyb* is a clear-cut example because it represents an extreme case, but other words present similar challenges for reasons that are less immediately apparent. Their "burdens of meaning" relate to their grounding in Czech culture and the unique semantic resonance that results from this grounding.

Taking seriously the different "burdens of meaning" conveyed by Havel's words in the original Czech and in English translation is crucial for two reasons. In the first place, Havel is a Czech writer who achieved world renown primarily through the translations of his texts into English. Two questions logically follow from this: how do the English translations of the original Czech texts differ, and how might these differences influence our reading and interpretation of them?[2] This is especially the case with regard to key concepts or keywords in the texts. While Wierzbicka (1997) uses the term "key word" in application to a language or culture, it would also seem productive to apply the same strategy to literature, that is, to search for and analyse words that occupy a key position in a work (or even the entire oeuvre) of a given author because they exhibit a special organizational and semantic potential for that work or for that particular author's whole system of thought.[3] A focus on Havelian keywords raises the question of the extent to which the meanings of their English translations are indeed equivalent to the meanings of the Czech originals. What aspects or nuances of meaning might be, quite literally, lost in translation?[4]

In the second place, Havel himself understood only too well that words and their meanings matter.[5] Words have "anatomy" and are agentive in that their meanings actively frame our understanding of the world in particular ways. We need only consider the epigraph to this chapter to get a sense of Havel's healthy "distrust" of words and their conventional meanings, as well as to understand his belief in an intellectual's commitment to being "wary" of words.

In another context, Havel expands on his interest in words and language in the following way:

> Another thing I should mention here is an interest in language. I'm interested in its ambivalence, its abuse; I'm interested in language as something that fashions life, destinies, and worlds; language as the most important skill; language as ritual and magic charm; the word as a carrier of dramatic movement, as something that legitimizes, as a way of self-affirmation and self-projection. (Havel 1991b: 193 and 1990: 167)

Throughout much of his career as a writer, and especially in the 1960s and 1970s, Havel was particularly interested in the phraseological cliché (Czech *fráze*), and the way in which such clichés organize modern life by expropriating human identity: the cliché has a tendency to be taken as more "real" than reality itself (Havel 1991b: 193 and 1990: 167). In this view, then, words and phrases are forms of embodied and experiential cognition. They are conceptual compressions that reduce the complexities of our experience in the world to a simpler story, and different cultures often have different versions of the story.

To provide an example of how language actively frames meaning, consider the phrase "global warming," which is certainly a "key phrase" in modern society and modern politics. As a term used to describe our current ecological crisis, it is misleading for a number of reasons. In the first place, and as many have pointed out, it suggests that "warming" is the focal symptom of the crisis, which has allowed so-called sceptics to ridicule the idea in the face of harsh winter weather or other meteorological conditions that do not support a "warming" trend. In the second place, however, it is a merely descriptive term that does not speak to cause. It is the "globe" that is "warming," and if this is a problem, then it is the "globe" that apparently deserves the blame. The alternative phrase "climate change" manages to get around the singular focus on "warming," and has therefore become more standard as a description of the crisis, but "climate change" is also just descriptive, and implies that the cause of the change lies with the "climate" itself. Perhaps a more proper term – and this is a term that Havel would undoubtedly have embraced, given how he treats the threat of "climate change" in his presidential texts – would be "civilizational crisis." As Palouš and Havel remind us, it is modern humanity's very civilizational structure that has led to the current ecological crisis. We are the cause of dramatic changes in the climate simply because of how we live, and it would be useful to reflect this fact in how we talk about it.

Language, in other words, maps a certain reality, and differences in linguistic phrasing frequently reflect differences in conceptual construal. As one linguist has written: "Language is a kind of informal plebiscite: when we adopt a new word or alter the usage of an old one, we're casting a voice vote for a particular point of view" (Nunberg 2007: 3). More often than not, the way in which language maps reality takes place below the level of conscious awareness. It is with this in mind that we can better appreciate Havel's coinage of the term "post-totalitarianism" in "Power of the Powerless" as well as his reconceptualization of the meaning of a series of other keywords in the same essay.[6] These systematic, strategic forays into semantic analysis are characteristic of Havel as a writer. They are also entirely consistent with an understanding of Havel as a frame-oriented thinker, or rather as an intellectual concerned with transcending the limitations of conventional frames.

It was the influential British economic thinker E.F. Schumacher who once wrote that the task of his generation was "metaphysical reconstruction," and Schumacher had specifically in mind the "need to reconstruct the meaning of ideas like wealth, knowledge, work, economics, development, and progress" (Robertson 1999: xi). Havel would have undoubtedly (and enthusiastically) agreed with Schumacher's delineation of the generational task, and would have expanded the list of terms in need of such reconstruction well beyond Schumacher's. Indeed, is not "metaphysical reconstruction" largely what Havel's existential revolution is about? And what better place to start than by reconceptualizing the "anatomy" of culturally loaded (and key) words and phrases?

My contention in this chapter is that Havel's keywords present different maps of reality for a reader of the original Czech and a reader of Havel in English translation, and that an explicit discussion of these differences – that is, a semantic reconstruction and juxtaposition of these cognitive-cultural maps – proves illuminating for reading Havel. Keywords in Havel's oeuvre are not difficult to identity. They act as conceptual threads woven into the fabric of thinking. They are running motifs in his writing that cut across genres and time periods (the pre- and post-1989 faces of Havel), and they serve as intellectual touchstones around which many of his larger ideas coalesce and take shape. Havel extends and subtly reconceptualizes the basic Czech meanings of his keywords, and the reframed meanings act as compressed images that encapsulate in micro-form Havel's larger project of "metaphysical reconstruction." We have already partially analysed the meaning and import of one of Havel's keywords, *neklid* ("restlessness"). After returning briefly to *neklid*, I will add three other terms that we have also encountered in earlier chapters, but have yet to examine in depth: *domov* ("home"), *svědomí* ("conscience"), and *duchovnost* ("spirituality").[7]

It is fortunate that methodologies exist for engaging in semantic analysis across languages, a line of research that is often referred to as (comparative) ethnolinguistics.[8] According to Jerzy Bartmiński, ethnolinguistics:

> ... deals with manifestations of culture in language ... It attempts to discover the traces of culture in the very fabric of language, in word meanings, phraseology, word formation, syntax and text structure. It strives to reconstruct the worldview entrenched in language as it is projected by the experiencing and speaking subject. (2010: 10)

That culture is cognitively (and linguistically) entrenched is increasingly confirmed by research in cognitive neuroscience. For example, in an appendix to his 2007 book (287ff.), Doidge discusses the cognitive perspective on the "culturally modified brain" and he asserts, among other things, that to *"a larger degree than we suspected, culture determines what we can and cannot perceive"* (2007: 300).[9] Ethnolinguistic analysis provides tools for investigating the entrenchment of culture in language, as well as for comparing the meaning of words across different languages. It is not concerned with *explaining* linguistic meaning in some abstract and formal sense, but with *understanding* language and rendering it meaningful to us on a human level. My analyses of Havel's keywords in this chapter will be grounded in and inspired by the ethnolinguistic approach.[10]

This chapter presents, then, case studies in Czech-English ethnolinguistic analysis that are simultaneously studies in translating and reading Havel. We will see that the conventional meanings of Havel's keywords in Czech provide fertile ground – a ground that does not exist in quite the same way in English – for his extensions of their meaning that transform them into crucial components in his larger project to understand modern human identity and the role of the transcendent within it. Ethnolinguistic analysis of the conventional meaning of Havel's keywords provides a necessary starting point for considering his elaboration or reshaping of their meanings. To understand the conceptual value of a transformative redefinition, we need to start by considering the word's already familiar (entrenched) meaning, and semantic familiarity is the very thing that ethnolinguistics attempts to uncover and describe. Put another way, if defamiliarization is one of the main functions of literature, then it is helpful to know the starting point of that process, that is, the "familiar" meaning that the writer seeks to reshape and reframe. Such an awareness helps us arrive at an appreciation of the literariness of the writer's project at the same time as it also allows us better to visualize our personal relationship to that project.

In that regard, ethnolinguistic analysis of Havel's keywords will prove illuminating not only for reading Havel, but also for reading ourselves. As we have seen in earlier chapters, the very strategies that Havel uses to analyse the existential crisis of the modern world are equally useful as conceptual tools for analysing ourselves. Comparative semantic analyses of *neklid* ("restlessness"), *domov* ("home"), *svědomí* ("conscience"), and *duchovnost* ("spirituality") will serve as vehicles to "activate" our sense of what these words personally mean to us, and it will become clear that these words are "key" not only for understanding Havel, but also for understanding modern identity in general.

The remarkable semantic range of Czech *(ne)klid*

Czech *klid* and its derived opposite *neklid*[11] do not have stable English translation equivalents. Depending on the context, *klid* can be rendered as "rest," "quiet," "calm(ness)," "peace," "standstill," "silence," "composure," "tranquility," "serenity," and even "leisure." For this reason, it is a keyword in Havel's thinking that does not come across as such for those reading Havel in translation. In English, its range of possible translations both obscures its use as a motif in the letter to Husák and effaces its overall status as a Havelian keyword. Indeed, in its separate appearances in the Husák letter, *klid* is rendered variously as "quiet life," "rest," "calm," and "peace and quiet," while *neklid* is systematically translated as "restlessness." The situation in the Husák letter becomes even more complicated when we consider other derived terms based on the *klid* root; for instance, the verb *uklidňovat* (i.e., to give *klid* to someone) is translated as "to reassure" while its nominalized form *uklidnění* becomes "assuaging." We have seen an echo of Havel's use of *uklidňovat* in the Husák letter in his later assertion in *Disturbing the Peace* that theatre of the appeal should not "reassure" the audience in their preconceived views but rather "disquiet" or disturb them to provoke thought (Havel 1991b: 194 and 1990: 168).[12]

This instabilty in translation reflects the fact that Czech *klid* has an astoundingly broad range in terms of the domains that it can reference. A partial listing of the domains in which *klid* is conventionally used, with brief illustrations of each, would include: human emotions (*vnitřní klid,* "inner peace"), interpersonal relations (*do rodiny se vrátil klid,* "a sense of tranquility returned to the family"), work (*mít k práci potřebný klid,* "to have the necessary peace and quiet for work"), health and sickness (*hemorroidy jsou v klidu,* "my hemorrhoids are quiet"), death and sleep (*klid zesnulých,* "the peace of the dead"), diplomacy (*klid zbraní,* "silencing of weapons" or "cease-fire"), history (*neklidná doba,* "a troubled time"), ethics (*klidné svědomí,* "an untroubled conscience"), and natural phenomena (*moře bylo klidné / sopka se uklidnila,* "the sea was calm" / "the volcano quieted down"). An example that illustrates *klid*'s semantic as well as stylistic range is an advertising slogan for a Czech country music station: *Klidné rádio do neklidné doby* (one possible translation would be "Soothing radio for a troubled time").[13]

It is certainly true that *klid,* like the keyword *domov,* is a term that suggests something more fundamental in Czech than can be captured by one word (or root) in English. This is not to say that English cannot convey the meanings that *klid* and words derived from it do, but just that English does not do so in the same lexically systematic way, and that Czech *klid* therefore represents a ready-made conceptual slot that English lacks. In its application to a range of domains, *klid* spans both human experience and non-human phenomena. Internal and external states of being are all collectively implicated in the *klid* spectrum. The same root covers (and implicitly associates) internal and potentially moral calmness, external peace and quiet that still falls within the realm of human activity, and the tranquility of natural phenomena. If we were to push these reflections on *klid's* remarkable semantic range, we might say that Czech *klid* implies a folk model of the relationship among human states of mind, the human social order, and the non-human natural order. It suggests a harmony between the internal (*klid* of the soul) and the external in a way that is linguistically systematic. The word *klid* conceptually spans our circles (which are really, as we shall see, our layers) of home.

It is precisely this unique range and resonance of Czech *klid* that Havel takes advantage of in his argument against Husák's normalized regime. On one level, the *klid* motif is Havel's response to the Husák regime's call for a post-1968 return to *klid* in the sense of a "quiet (*klidný*) life" (Bolton 2012: 73ff.), and the regime itself was playing on the special "burden of meaning" associated with the word. As Havel moves from describing the true nature of a "normalized" society to prophesizing its inevitable dissolution, metaphoricity in the essay increases. Whereas *klid* was used in the earlier part of the letter to stand for a "quiet life" that could be secured by cooperation with the regime (1991a: 58 and 1999, 4: 76–7) or the "tranquility" that people find by turning away from the public sphere through a focus on their own private lives (1991a: 58 and 1999, 4: 77), in the later sections *klid* is metaphorized both directly and indirectly.

The turning point is Havel's characterization of the consequence of living a life directed towards consumer gratification and limited to one's innermost circle of home: the regime promotes this because it wants "not [to] excite people with the truth, but to reassure [*uklidňovat*] them with lies" (1991a: 66 and 1999, 4: 87). Shortly after this assertion is the key passage that figured prominently in our analysis of Havel's genres in the first chapter:

> Just as the constant increase of entropy is the basic law of the universe, so it is the basic law of life to be ever more highly structured and to struggle against entropy. Life rebels against all uniformity and leveling; its aim is

not sameness, but variety, the restlessness of transcendence [*neklid transcendence*], the adventure of novelty and rebellion against the status quo. (1991a: 71 and 1999, 4: 93–4)

It is life itself with its *neklid transcendence* that will ultimately undermine and erode the post-totalitarian system, because the system is representative of a false *klid*, the *klid* of the morgue or the grave (1991a: 72 and 1999, 4: 95). Havel then indirectly invokes the concept of *(ne) klid* in metaphorical images that model the disintegration of the regime: the images he uses are grounded in the domains of human health and sickness or sexual physiology, natural phenomena (a tornado, an earthquake, an erupting volcano), and sleep and death (a death-like slumber from which society will eventually awake).[14] Through these metaphors and the "restlessness of transcendence" embodied in them, Havel then predicts the collapse of the regime. The regime's collapse is inevitable because it is *naturally* unavoidable. The regime forces people to maintain *vnější* (external) *klid* (1991a: 103 and 1999, 4: 103) but life as internal *neklid transcendence* will ultimately burst forth and prevail.

It could be argued that *klid* is a keyword not only in Havel's thinking, but in Czech culture in general.[15] Even more generally, the import of how Havel plays with the "burden of meaning" inherent in *(ne) klid* is obviously not limited to the post-totalitarian East: its meaning ought to figure prominently in an attempt to understand the complexities of modern human identity even (or perhaps especially) in a post-Cold War world. The range of domains that *(ne)klid* spans implies a kind of transcendence that characterizes Havel's larger project of exisential revolution via metaphysical reconstruction. Understanding the Czech meaning of *(ne)klid* allows us to appreciate more fully that Havel's restlessness of transcendence is a provocative appeal to move beyond conventional ways of thinking, acting, and being in the world. It is a metaphysical restlessness that is necessary to avoid spiritual and intellectual petrification in rigid, ideological forms. It is a transcendent disquiet that offers a way out of the automatisms of modern cliché-oriented thought, and the fatalistic *samopohyb* that inevitably comes with it.[16]

The layers of Czech *domov*

Unlike *(ne)klid*, Czech *domov* has a more or less stable English translation equivalent in the word "home." Wilson has written, however, that *domov* "suggests something more fundamental than home in English"

(1999: 29), and we might ask ourselves in what way the burdens of meaning differ and how these differences bear on reading Havel in translation.

Havel's clearest treatment of the word occurs in *Summer Meditations* in a discussion of the "circles of home" (*kruhy domova*) that comprise the basic existential background of modern experience and identity (1993b: 30ff. and 1999, 6: 409ff.). The circles of home are understood as a set of concentric circles (*soustředné kruhy*) with the individual at the centre. Our *domov* is, in concrete terms, the room and house we live in, and it is also the village or town in which we are born and where we spend most of our lives. In less concrete terms, it is our family and friends, our workplace, and the country we live in, along with its culture. It is the native language that we speak, our gender, and our political affiliation (if we have one). It is also our education, upbringing, and social milieu – and the list of our circles could be extended as needed. Havel argues that these circles of home shape our identity and that in a healthy society, every circle should be given its due: "All the circles of our home [*všechny vrstvy našeho domova*], indeed our whole natural world, are an inalienable part of us, and an inseparable element of our human identity. Deprived of all the aspects of his home, man would be deprived of himself, of his humanity" (1993b: 31 and 1999, 6: 411).[17]

Havel borrows the notion of "circles of home" from the Czech philosopher Jan Patočka, wrestling philosophically with it in his letters from prison before applying it to his exposition of civil society in *Summer Meditations*.[18] Recognizing this influence does not, however, address the issued raised in Wilson's observation that there is something more fundamental (and more intensely felt) by Czechs when they use the word *domov* than by English speakers using the word "home." We may trace an answer to this by considering the range of usage of the word *domov* in its basic meaning, the grounding of the Czech word in its larger cultural context, and also the connotative aspects of meaning associated with each term. Across all three of these ethnolinguistic dimensions we see a stark contrast with the meaning of English "home."

A standard Czech-English dictionary (Fronek 2000) lists five primary translation equivalents for *domov*: "home," "home town," "native country," an institutional "home" for children or the retired (as in a "retirement home"), and an animal "habitat." This list already suggests that the Czech term has, like *klid*, a broad semantic and pragmatic range, certainly much broader than English "home." In conventional usage, the word's meaning extends outward from narrow realms ("home" or "home town") to encompass larger experiential circles (a whole nation as *domov*), and it also crosses from human to animal domains.[19]

The multilayered and hierarchical meaning of Czech *domov* finds an instructive parallel in the origin and historical development of the meaning of the English word "abroad." This latter descends from the Old English phrase *on brede*, which meant something like "at wide," and its original meaning was "outside of one's normal home" in, one must imagine, an often rather localized sense. Over the centuries, however, the meaning shifted to refer to wider circles of home, and the original sense of "out of doors, away from home" led to the main modern sense of "out of one's country, overseas," which is attested from the mid-fifteenth century. Whereas English "abroad" definitively shifted its meaning through association with wider and wider circles of home, Czech *domov* synchronically incorporates that variety of geographical layers under one umbrella term.

We might be tempted to say, then, that the very notion promoted by Patočka and Havel of circles of home that form a nested hierarchy from our innermost and personal homes (self, family, and friends) to our outermost ones (city, state, country, the world) is already contained, in seminal form, in the basic hierarchical meaning of *domov* itself.[20] In fact, Czechs have yet another way of expressing the same range of contextualized meanings in a common phrase, *u nás*, that is close in its meaning to *domov*. As with *domov*, the phrase *u nás* in its full range of usage is not translatable into English by one word or phrase. Sayer (1998: 193) notes that *u nás* (not to mention *domov*) has strong associations with the National Revival and therefore with Czech nationhood, and that it is a "phrase full of homely potency: it can mean 'at our home,' 'in our country,' 'among us,' or simply 'here.'" He adds: "Not all languages provide so economical a means of expressing the identities whose assertions are so fundamental to modern national statehood" (1998: 193). We might respond to Sayer's claim by suggesting that neither *domov* or *u nás* is primarily a means to express national or state identity. Nationhood merely represents one possible layer in a semantically complex and multilayered term, and the real semantic "potency" of these expressions – one that Havel seizes on as the essence of *domov* – lies in the nested hierarchy of meanings implicit in each.

In everyday usage, Czech *domov* occurs in a range of contexts that parallel its range of implicit hierarchical meanings. It is used in concrete everyday expressions like *odejít z domova* ("to leave home," which can mean to leave one's house or one's home town or even, depending on the context, country), as well as in newspaper headings to refer to what North Americans would think of as the section for national news (Czech *zprávy z domova*). A lyrical or poetic extension to a meaning of "found homeland" is also conventionally associated with *domov* (but not, of course, English "home") through the title of the Czech national anthem, *Kde domov můj?* ("Where is my home[land]?"). In connection with this last point, Macura noted that the Czech anthem begins with a question and "betrays uncertainty and a feeling that the homeland is inaccessible and not self-evident" (1993: 29). It is, somewhat paradoxically, a national anthem that problematizes the very existence of a concrete, national *domov*.

One of the ways in which Havel subtly extends the conventional meaning of Czech *domov* is by attempting to emphasize the concentricity of the various circles of the "homes" that we inhabit. In fact, the word that Havel uses most often in the key *domov* passage from *Summer Meditations* is not *kruhy* ("circles") but rather *vrstvy* ("layers") of home.[21] Havel's use of "layers" places greater emphasis on the concentric nature of the circles. The word *vrstvy* is also used in Czech to refer to social classes (*společenské vrstvy*) as well as styles or registers (e.g., *neutrální vrstva spisovného jazyka* or "the neutral register of the literary language"), and these semantic associations in Czech must have influenced Havel's word choice. Havel's emphasis on "layers" of home additionally lends itself to temporal transposition, which would then result in a focus on history as a key component of human identity (like the civilizational layers of an archaeological site).[22]

One implication of Havel's focus on "layers" is that a spiritually healthy individual ought to inhabit "homes" that are arranged harmoniously, and in which one's sense of self is not disjointed or fragmented – not, that is, dispersed across circles of identity that do not substantially overlap. The notion that modern identity is disjointed and fragmented represents, as we have already seen, a recurrent motif in Havel's anticodes, plays, and other writings from the 1960s and 1970s. In a 1975 interview, he prefigures the image of identity dispersed across divergent circles of home in a simple yet powerful trope involving sports teams. With the loss of a connection to the transcendent, Havel asserts, modern man

> ... has lost a kind of absolute and universal system of coordinates, to which he could always relate anything, chiefly himself. His world and his personality gradually began to break up into separate, incoherent fragments

> corresponding to different, relative coordinates. And when this happened, man began to lose his inner identity ... It's as if we were playing for a number of different teams at once, each with different uniforms, and as though – and this is the main thing – we didn't know which one we ultimately belonged to, which of those teams was really ours. (Havel 1991a: 94–5)[23]

Both the team analogy and the circles of home are also variant forms of Havel's mosaic image, in which fragmentation of human identity can be understood as the shattering of the mosaic.

Another way that Havel reshapes the meaning of *domov* for his own purposes is to expand it outward to encompass layers or circles beyond the outermost level of "country" that is part of *domov*'s conventional meaning. In a 1997 speech given in Bonn, Havel analyzes the etymology and meaning of German *Heimat* and its Icelandic equivalent, arguing that these two words, like Czech *domov*, refer to both a concrete "home(land)" and a philosophical one at the same time.[24] Havel asserts that the meaning of *Heimat* mediates between an individual person and the larger universe in that one's experience of a concrete *Heimat* (or *domov*) serves as a bridge to a more philosophical or expanded understanding. The concept of *domov* is, then, not a closed structure, and Havel's extension of its meaning follows the trajectory implied by the word's conventional semantics.

Not unrelated to the multilayered semantic scope of *domov* and its cultural grounding in the Czech context are connotative aspects of meaning associated with the use of the word. In his analysis of a similar Polish concept, Bartmiński notes that the Polish word suggests a system of values, and therefore must be described, like a kinship term, in its relation to people and their experience of the world (2010: 163). One way to understand this is that Czech *domov* means something to Czechs beyond its concrete manifestation as a "house" (*dům*). In other words, a Czech understanding of *domov* transcends the concrete and the material, and includes the range of emotional and experiential connotations associated with the various layers of its meaning: the home in which a Czech was born, the home town that she or he grew up in, the geographical region in which that home town is located, and the Czech Republic as the country in which that region is situated.[25] Not surprisingly, Havel assumes the existence of these connotative aspects of meaning in his use of *domov,* and insists in a number of different contexts on the distinction between a mere "dwelling place" (*bydliště*) and a proper *domov*.[26] We might also recall here Palouš's focus on the 1969 moon landing as the key event in the emergence of the World Age. The trip to the moon represented a symbolic return to earth in the sense that the planet as a whole was perceived, for the first time in history, as not just a *bydliště* but rather as our collective human *domov*.

As may already be clear, the meaning of English "home" contrasts strongly with the meaning of its Czech counterpart *domov*. In the first place, the concentric and hierarchical circles of home that are profiled in the meaning of *domov* are largely absent in the English concept. This is not to say that we cannot imagine the Czech perspective by extending our understanding of "home" outward to encompass larger and larger experiential circles, but merely that the basic meaning of "home" does not already communicate, as a matter of course, these hierarchical relationships. English also does not problematize or philosophize the meaning of "home" to the same extent that Czech culture, largely from historical necessity, has done with the meaning of *domov*.

In fact, the decisive trend in English seems to be towards concretizing the meaning of "home" or, in other words, to head in exactly the opposite direction of *domov* and Havel's extension of it. In its most recent definition of "home," the Oxford English Dictionary contains a special comment that illustrates the extent of this trend towards concretization: "In N. America and Australasia (and increasingly elsewhere), [home] is frequently used to designate a private house or residence merely as a building." While in the Czech mind the "house" (*dům*) is the material prototype for the "home" (*domov*), and therefore lies at the centre of the concentric circles that comprise the latter concept (Vaňková 2012), in the English mind the difference between the concepts "house" and "home" is increasingly minimized. Put another way, the everyday meaning of "home" is shrinking towards the concrete prototype of "house." To borrow phrasings from chapter 3, its meaning is becoming increasingly materialized, if not also commodified. English "home," then, is not a fundamentally relational concept (in Bartmiński's sense of the term), and the connotative aspects associated with it are effectively minimized.[27]

Like perhaps *klid*, *domov* is a keyword not only in Havel's oeuvre but in Czech culture as a whole. Given this, it is hardly surprising that the word resonates quite differently in Czech than its translation via "home" does in English, and Wilson's intuition about the different burdens of meaning carried by *domov* and "home" follows directly from this. With its wide semantic range, the special role that it has played in Czech cultural history, and the connotations deriving from both of these factors, *domov* does suggest something more fundamental than "home."

This special burden of meaning also makes *domov* a decidedly appropriate cornerstone concept for Havel's program of metaphysical reconstruction. The crux of Havel's larger project is, after all, a focus on transcendent elements in human experience. Without a sense of transcendence in our lives, we lose meaning; without a relationship to the transcendent, we lack a true "home" and settle for a mere "dwelling place" (Neubauer 2010: 88). Havel's use of *domov* as a keyword takes, in this respect, the form of an appeal. Like *klid*, *domov* proves to be a concept worth thinking about beyond the borders of Central and Eastern Europe. Following the lead of *domov*'s semantic trajectory, Havel invites us to rethink the scope of responsibility that we have to the world around us. He seeks to move us out of the narrow confines of those conventional "homes" or "dwelling places" that are prioritized by the modern world and into the conceptual space of a more philosophical, transcendent, and ultimately truly human "home."

Czech *svědomí* and the voice of Being

Our third case study in reading Havel in translation concerns the Czech word *svědomí*, which has, in almost every instance except one, a necessary translation into English via "conscience." While the first two case studies largely focused on differences in semantic range between the Czech and English words, the contrast between *svědomí* and "conscience" suggests a more nuanced story that involves two conceptual dimensions. In the first place, we will see crucial differences in the semantic associations that each word has in its respective language, and in the second place, we will uncover subtle but meaningful differences in how Czech *svědomí* and English "conscience" are conceptualized. The conclusions that we will reach after the story of the semantic contrast has been told will, however, be the same as for *(ne)klid* and *domov*: that Havel grounds himself in the Czech conceptualization, which provides a more fertile ground for his program of metaphysical reconstruction, and that it is the Czech meaning that we must take as our familiar starting point if we want to make sense of Havel's arguments.

Svědomí, especially in its relationship to a kind of responsibility (*odpovědnost*) that lies at the core of human identity, is a key concept in Havel's thought that cuts across both time periods and genres. It is a keyword in his pre-1989 essays and comprises, as we have already seen, a central motif in the 1984 essay "Politics and Conscience" as well as in its companion essay "Thriller." Although not represented verbally, *svědomí* is, as we will see, a major focus of his plays, and in particular the Vaněk trilogy.[28] It is also one of a handful of words that make up the core vocabulary of his philosophical letters from prison. Finally, *svědomí* is a touchstone concept in Havel's post-1989 presidential speeches and other texts. In analysing Havel's reshaping of the meaning of *svědomí* and its relationship to the conventional Czech understanding of the word and to English "conscience," I will first trace the development of Havel's thought and then provide a comparative ethnolinguistic account to ground it.[29]

In "Politics and Conscience," Havel problematizes the contemporary meaning of the word by arguing that modern man has privatized conscience. He metaphorically dramatizes the privatization of conscience by suggesting that we have locked our consciences up in our bathrooms and thereby cut them off from engagement with the world. Conscience (along with a sense of responsibility that ought to come naturally with it) is reduced to a personal matter, or what Havel more philosophically terms a "phantom [*přelud*] of subjectivity" (1991a: 255 and 1999, 4: 425). An echo of the conscience-in-the-bathroom image appears in "Thriller" where Havel imagines modern "demons" in business attire who inflict moral ruin on the world as the "gods" sequester themselves in the refuge of individual conscience: "The demons simply do what they want while the gods take diffident refuge in the final asylum to which they have been driven, called 'human conscience'" (1991a: 288 and 1999, 4: 510).

Indeed, Havel is not the only modern intellectual to have raised the question of the privatization or individualization of conscience. The American legal scholar and writer Jedediah Purdy, for example, has noted that in the American cultural tradition, "free conscience" came to be understood as "being true to oneself," which risks failing to look beyond oneself and thereby falling into a solipsism "that is often as banal and derivative as it is self-impressed" (2010: 21). In more hard-hitting terms than Havel, Purdy wonders "whether the spirit of conscience that Burke called 'the dissidence of dissent' has arrived at the end of history as full-blown narcissism" (2010: 22).[30]

In "Politics and Conscience," Havel places the phrase *lidské svědomí* ("human conscience") at the very end of the essay as the culminating term in a rhetorical question that he leaves for the reader to ponder. Does not hope for a better future, Havel asks, lie in making "a real political force out of a phenomenon so ridiculed by the technicians of power – the phenomenon of human conscience?" (1991a: 271 and 1999, 4: 445).

The essay as a whole defamiliarizes a conventional understanding of conscience, and specifically its relationship to politics. By liberating conscience from the confines of the individual mind (by freeing it from Purdy's narcissism), Havel presents a possible way out of the existential crisis that engulfs the modern world.

The groundwork for Havel's reframing of conscience in the essays of the mid-1980s was laid in his 1979–83 philosophical letters from prison, in which reflections on *svědomí* comprise a central theme. Foreshadowing the bathroom image, Havel notes that conscience as an active force in the world is but a shadow of what it ought to be; it has become perfunctory, ritualized, a mere formality. The crisis of the modern world is a crisis of human identity and human responsibility, but Havel insists that an "orientation toward Being," which conscience somehow embodies, has not disappeared: after all, "who would dare to deny that they have a conscience?" (1983a and b: letter 142). The "voice of Being" has not died out: "we know it summons us, and as human beings, we cannot pretend not to know what it is calling us to" (1983a and b: letter 142). We have many ways in the modern world of drowning out that voice ("[i]t is just that these days, it is easier to cheat, silence or lie to that voice"), but no matter how badly we behave, there is always a voice in some corner of our spirit saying that we ought not to have done so (1983a and b: letter 142).

Throughout the letters from prison, Havel emphasizes the dialogic nature of conscience and its inherent relationship to what he terms the "voice of Being" (*hlas bytí*). This frees conscience from its cage of narcissism, as conscience is understood to be not so much an inner, personal voice but rather an internalized manifestation of the voice of Being itself. In letter 139, Havel claims that while the *hlas bytí* informs the voice of conscience, it is greater than that personal voice. At the same time, the personal voice of conscience manifests the interconnectedness of two worlds, the world of man (the concrete human here and now) and the world of the transcendent (of gods, of the absolute). These worlds are one and the same, but our access to Being is necessarily grounded in the former: "Being is one, it is everywhere and behind everything; it is the Being of everything and the only way to it is the one that leads through this world of mine and through this 'I' of mine" (1983a and b: letter 139). Conscience is internal to the individual only in the sense that its personalized voice represents a concrete realization of the transcendent voice of Being. Rather than saying that conscience (Being) is in us, it would be more true to say, in Havel's interpretation, that we are in conscience (Being).[31]

Havel hangs his philosophical argument concerning conscience on one concrete and seemingly rather trivial experience: you are in an empty night tram and have to decide whether or not to pay the fare for the ride. Your "voice of conscience" is activated, and Havel insists that the resulting inner dialogue takes the form of an exchange between your ego and a "partner" that is outside of your ego and therefore not identical with or reducible to it (letter 137):

> This "partner," however, is not standing beside me; I can't see it, nor can I quit its sight: its eyes and its voice follow me everywhere; I can neither escape it nor outwit it: it knows everything. Is it my so-called "inner voice," my "superego," my "conscience"? Certainly, if I hear it calling me to responsibility, I hear this call within me, in my mind and my heart; it is my own experience, profoundly so, though different from the experiences mediated to me by my senses. This, however, does nothing to alter the fact that the voice addresses me and enters into conversation with me, in other words, it comes to my "I" – which I trust is not schizoid – from the outside. (1983a and b: letter 137)

One thing seems clear to Havel: that if our "I" has not completely suppressed its orientation towards Being, then it

> ... has a sense of responsibility purely and simply because it relates intrinsically to Being as that in which it feels the only coherence, meaning and the somehow inevitable "clarification" of everything that exists ... because it hears within and around itself the "voice" in which this Being addresses and calls out to it. (1983a and b: letter 137)

In another letter, Havel defines responsibility (*odpovědnost*) in terms of being responsible to or for something else that is usually concrete and immediate, although not only so. The "particular incarnation" of one's responsibility does not exhaust the matter: "there is always something 'more,' something 'outside,' something that transcends [*přesahuje*] it," and sometimes we call this feeling "conscience," and in doing so "we localize it within ourselves" (1983a and b: letter 109).

Havel's reframing suggests a latent dramatic potential in the voice of conscience and its relation to the voice of Being. The "absolute horizon" of meaning (the voice of Being) is "present in us not only as an assumption, but also as a source of humanity and a challenge [*apel*]" (1983a and b: letter 95). Conscience is, then, a uniquely human experience that serves as a challenge or appeal (*apel*), a characterization that explicitly references Havel's style as a writer of plays associated, as we have already discussed, with the "theater of the appeal" (*divadlo apelu*).

By the time Havel becomes president of first Czechoslovakia and then the Czech Republic, his conceptual reframing of *svědomí* has been established. The presidential speeches and other published texts from this time reinforce and extend the reframing, continuing to insist on the importance of conscience (as Havel describes it) for confronting the existential crisis that defines the modern world. In his treatment of *svědomí* in the presidential texts, we see echoes of many of the themes highlighted in earlier chapters of this book. A non-exhaustive list of post-1989 contexts that both reinforce and extend his reframing includes the following:

(1) The argument that conscience ought not to be understood as "localized" in our minds or "psychologized" is reinforced in, among others, a 2002 speech in Malta. Havel polemicizes with the notion that conscience is "a particular segment of our brain, identifiable with a certain area, or some kind of singular feature of the human being." Conscience as a source of moral responsibility is "more complicated than that" because it entails an "awareness that there is someone who watches us," and we are "intrinsically conscious of that silent eye." In Havel's first speech before a joint session of the US Congress (1990), he similarly defines "conscience" as the "interpreter or mediator [*tlumočník*]" between an individual and a "higher authority" that he equates, in a purposefully vague description, with the "Order of Being."[32]

(2) Conscience as a point of access to the transcendent is consistently reinforced: it is subjectively through our individual consciences that we establish a connection with the metaphysical order that both includes and transcends us.[33] In a 1996 speech at Trinity College, Havel explicitly defines conscience and responsibility as "a certain attitude of man toward that which reaches beyond him, that is, toward infinity and eternity, the transcendent, the mystery of the world, the order of Being ..." Modern Europeans hesitate, Havel says, to understand conscience and responsibility in these terms, and continue to consider them a kind of private or personal hobby "that does not belong on the public scene of politics." This is akin to "[s]hrinking from the

transcendental aspect of one's own endeavours" and is, in modern circumstances, a "very dangerous attitude" to have.

(3) A final pre-1989 theme reinforced in the post-1989 texts is that conscience is the hope for the future, a sleeping force whose potential has yet to be tapped: "A conscience slumbers in every human being, something divine. And that is what we have to put our trust in" (Harvard University 1995).

(4) Havel also extends his pre-1989 account by granting conscience a key role in bringing down the socialist regimes in Central Europe (see Davos speech, 1992) with the corollary that an understanding of politics as moral conscience was what the post-1989 East could offer the West. As we saw in chapter 3, this was for Havel the true meaning and lesson of the dissident movement in Czechoslovakia, Poland, and elsewhere: "Our fundamental experience has taught us very clearly that only politics that is preceded by conscience really has any meaning"[34] (*Gazeta Wyborcza* Anniversary 1999).

(5) A further extension derives directly from the argument made in "Politics and Conscience" as well as in (as we have already seen) Havel's plays: that the technological, scientific age of humanity – an age that privileges *explaining* over *understanding* – lacks a conscience in the sense that Havel conceives of it. In a February 1990 speech to commemorate the anniversary of the 1948 communist-party putsch in Czechoslovakia, Havel notes:

> Science [*věda*] does not have a conscience. It is certainly beautiful and important ... but the human spirit is not mere rationality [*rozum*]. It is judgment. Deliberation. Conscience. Decency [*slušnost*]. Tact. Love for those close to us. Responsibility. Courage. Stepping away from the self. Doubt. Even humor.[35] (Prague, 25 February 1990)

In other speeches, as we have already seen, he similarly suggests that human conscience lags behind technological and scientific knowledge, which may very well be the modern world's defining dilemma.[36]

(6) Havel's final post-1989 extension is his suggestion that conscience plays the same key role in shaping modern democratic political communities as it played in the dissident community under socialism. Democracy is defined as an "unending journey" and a "constant appeal [*trvalá výzva*] to the human spirit and human conscience" (Prague, 12 March 1996). The task of Europe – the meaning of which ought not to be reduced to cooperation on

economic and political matters – is once again to find its conscience and sense of responsibility in the world (see Aachen speech, 1996). Cultivating this extended understanding is the chief responsibility of intellectuals, who are the "conscience of society" (see Wellington speech, 1995).

By way of summing up Havel's reshaping of the meaning of conscience over the course of his literary and political career, we might consider a passage from a 1995 presidential text in which Havel plainly pins his hopes for the future of humanity on the awakening of "human conscience":

> We know quite well what threatens our world today, but there is precious little will to deter those threats. Or rather: it is not enough to speak the truth, it is necessary to awaken our human conscience.[37]

What Havel means by this is just what we have explored in this section on conceptualizing conscience as a literary figure in Havel's writings. The awakening of human conscience – and Havel frequently insists on the adjective "human" in reference to conscience as if to emphasize continually the responsibility that having a conscience places on us as human beings[38] – presupposes a reconceptualization of its spiritual and cultural meaning. While a degenerate understanding of conscience that ultimately leads to solipsism localizes conscience in the individual's mind as an exclusively internal dialogue, Havel imagines conscience as a transcendent dialogue with Being and an appeal for engagement in and with the world, one that has the potential to be a game-changing political and moral force.

If lexis, as Bartmiński argues, is a classifier of social experience that "provides access to the conceptual sphere, to the realm of ideas and images important in a given culture" (Bartmiński 2010: 17), then Havel seeks to influence the cultural sphere through a careful and nuanced redefinition of the meaning of human "conscience." The extent to which Havel's reshaping of *svědomí* differs from the conventional meaning of the concept, however, remains to be determined. In other words, if Havel subtly defamiliarizes, then what is the familiar ground of his starting point? And to extend this line of thinking: is that ground the same for Czech *svědomí* as it is for English "conscience"?

In comparing Czech *svědomí* with English *conscience*, we first note that they are, etymologically speaking, parallel: each has a prefix meaning "with" (*s*- and "con-" respectively) attached to a suffixed root with the original meaning "knowledge" (*-vědomí* and "-science"). The origin of both words implies a form of mental deliberation that comes "with knowledge" of the world, and this brings them close to Havel's extended definition: conscience establishes a relationship between ourselves (our inner voice) and events in the world at large (the Order of Being). In other words, conscience responds to questions that are raised by our experience in and knowledge of the world. What we know should therefore be closely related to what we do and how we act (Ralston Saul 1997: 181).

The etymological identity already exposes, however, a crucial difference in how the words resonate in each language: the Czech root for "knowing" (*-věd-*) is more etymologically and semantically transparent in a host of other common words related to knowledge, consciousness, and awareness than the comparable English root (*-sci-*), which, if anything, might tend to associate English "conscience" with a particular (scientific) kind of knowledge. A partial list of Czech words in which *-věd-* is immediately perceivable includes the following: *vědět* ("to know"), *věda* ("scholarship" or "science"), *vědomí* ("consciousness"), *povědomí* ("awareness"), and *uvědomit si* ("to realize, become aware of"). By comparison, the *-sci-* in conscience is conceptually opaque: even the connection between "conscience" and "consciousness" is, at best, only tenuously felt. Whereas Czech has one root that serves as a semantic locus for many experiences of "knowing," the multiplicity of English roots for "knowing" fails to activate the connection between "conscience" and Being that Havel highlights and then extends in his interpretation.

A crucial concept in the Czech *vědomí-svědomí* nexus proves to be the Czech terms for witnessing: *svědek* ("witness") and *svědectví* ("testimony"). English here has yet another root ("wit"), but the Czech words derivationally conflate knowledge, witnessing, and conscience. In Jungmann's entry on *svědomí*, the second meaning is listed as *svědectví*, glossed as Latin *testimonium*, and it is this witnessing connection that is arguably more activated in the meaning of Czech *svědomí* as opposed to English "conscience." The association of *svědomí* with *svědectví* also helps lay the groundwork for Havel's creative extension of the meaning of the former. Indeed, in an analysis of faith and belief in Havel's writings, Milan Balabán sees Havel's concept of the "absolute horizon of Being" as "the most important witness [*svědek*] ... of the deliberations that we have with ourselves on a daily basis" (2009: 43–4). In other words, *svědomí* in Havel's extended philosophical sense is a dialogue with the *svědek* of Being, and this is an active kind of witnessing because we, who also belong to Being, simultaneously observe and participate in it.

Although Balabán does not mention it, it would be productive to read Havel's plays within what might be called a "witnessing framework." Theatre of the appeal activates conscience by transforming theatre-goers in the audience into witnesses. This witnessing element in Havel's dramatic style is embodied in particular by the character (or rather dramatic principle) that is Vaněk, for reasons made clear earlier. It is in this way that *svědomí* (via its association with *svědectví*) is a key concept in Havel's plays, even though the word itself is not used.

If the semantic development of Czech *svědomí* in relation to other words in the same etymological and derivational network reaffirms a connection to witnessing, the meaning of English "conscience" seems to have shifted away from the knowledge-witnessing relationship towards the more personalized or privatized understanding of conscience with which Havel aggressively polemicizes in "Politics and Conscience" and elsewhere. This development also seems to have run parallel to the narrowing of the meaning of English "conscious" as outlined in Humphrey (1999: 117ff.). Humphrey notes the etymological structure of the word and states that the original meaning of the Latin verb *conscire* (from which the adjective *conscius* is derived) was "to share knowledge widely." As time passed, the usage changed, "and it shifted to mean sharing knowledge with some people but not others, sharing it within a small circle – and thus being privy to a secret" (1999: 118). This knowledge circle narrowed even further "until eventually it included just a single person, the subject who was conscious" (1999: 118). Humphrey sums up:

> Thus, as the English language has evolved (and perhaps as the users of the language have become more self-concerned and introspective), the meaning of the word "conscious" has not only become narrower and narrower, it has in effect turned around. Rather like the word "window," which has changed in meaning from "a hole where the wind comes in" to "a hole where the wind does *not* come in," "conscious" has changed from "having shared knowledge" to "having intimate knowledge *not* shared with anyone except oneself." (1999: 119)

The parallel with a privatized conscience (or one that is locked up in the bathroom) is rather striking.

At the very least, the narrowing of the dialogic aspects of English "conscious" – its journey from sharing to not sharing – is similar to the way in which the "voice" of conscience has come to be internalized. Both *svědomí* and "conscience" share a conventional metaphorical association with a voice (Uličný 1999), but the schema suggested by the voice metaphor is open to a variety of elaborations. Is it a voice entirely inside one's head, an inner dialogue with oneself, or, as Havel advocates, an inner voice that instantiates a connection with the very voice of Being?

This distinction evokes Erich Fromm's writing on modern identity and specifically the opposition that he details between, on one hand, *having* or *using* and, on the other, *being*. Fromm writes:

> Man became a collector and a user. More and more, the central experience of his life became *I have* and *I use*, and less and less *I am*. The means – namely, material welfare, production, and the production of goods – thereby became the ends. (2005: 21)

In Fromm's terms, then, a privatized conscience is one that we *have* and that we *use*. Opposed to this is Havel's understanding of conscience, which is an understanding grounded in the knowing-witnessing nexus and which is much less a matter of practical utility and much more a matter of who we fundamentally *are*. Fromm's analysis of the distinction between *having/using* and *being* is reminiscent of Havel's (and Stoppard's) conflation of capitalism and Marxism/socialism in terms of their shared focus on the material aspects of being. "Conscience," is, in this respect, part and parcel of a modern identity that has become strongly materialized and commodified.

Existing scholarship on the conventional meaning of *conscience* confirms a tendency towards conceptual narrowing (personalization) and a *having/using* interpretation. Miroslava Nejedlá (2001) studied the semantics of Czech *vědomí* ("consciousness") and *svědomí* in comparison to English, and concluded in part that English "conscience" seems to be understood as more of a mechanism than Czech *svědomí*: with "conscience," more of an element of individual will makes its function potentially controllable by an exertion of that will (2001: 29). This correlates with a sense of duty or moral obligation in "conscience," a sense not as strongly felt in the meaning of *svědomí* (2001: 29). The qualms or pricklings of Czech *svědomí* "are considered to be phenomena independent of the will of the subject who is undergoing them" (2001: 30).[39] Perhaps another way of making the same point would be to say that English "conscience," in comparison with Czech *svědomí*, is conceptualized more as an ability, one that we *have* and that we *use*.

In this connection and in the North American context, we might mention the American scholar Stanley Fish's discussion (Fish 2009) in the *New York Times* of the so-called conscience clause that allows medical professionals to deny healthcare (e.g., contraception) that they believe runs counter to their own moral or religious beliefs. Fish notes that it is so named "because it affirms the claims of conscience – one's inner sense of what is right – against the competing claims of professional obligations"; he then, however, demonstrates that the meaning of "conscience" has changed radically over time. Fish cites the seventeenth-century English philosopher Thomas Hobbes, who had quite a different sense of the word and who argued that considering conscience to be "the private arbiter of right and wrong" was a "corrupted usage" invented by those who desired "to elevate 'their own ... opinions' to the status of reliable knowledge and try to do so by giving them 'that reverenced name of Conscience.'" The sense, then, that "conscience" represents an inner mechanism for determining right from wrong is entrenched in modern English to such an extent that it has become the substance of legal manoeuvring, but at the same time, this entrenched sense is not beyond dispute.

Fully consistent and compatible with Nejedlá's analysis as well as illuminating for Fish's discussion is Anna Wierzbicka's tracing of the historical development of the English concepts "right" and "wrong" and the extension of these originally conversational words into the ethical realm, a realm that includes "conscience" (Wierzbicka 2006). Wierzbicka argues that the rise of "right" and "wrong" is a language- and culture-specific phenomenon, and it sets English apart from other European languages in which "good" and "bad," which have a more general meaning and are also less subject to an individual's will, still hold sway. She writes: "[T]he ascendancy of 'right' and 'wrong' over 'good' and 'bad' seems to reflect a more rational, more procedural, more reason-based approach to human life and a retreat from a pure distinction between GOOD and BAD unsupported by any appeal to reason, procedures, methods, or intersubjectively available evidence" (2006: 72). In Wierzbicka's analysis, ethical decision-making has evolved into a matter of good thinking (like scientific thinking) and interpersonal validation: "It is a rational ethics, an ethics that doesn't need to be grounded in metaphysics (in particular, in God) but can be grounded in reason" (2006: 72).[40]

The concepts of "right" and "wrong" are, in this view, Anglo cultural constructs (2006: 65). When other concepts are defined in terms of "right" and "wrong," these concepts are then imbued with the Anglo-specific associations related to "right" and "wrong." In this regard, Wierzbicka specifically mentions "conscience," which is defined in the *Oxford Companion to Philosophy* as "the sense of right and wrong in an individual" (2006: 66). She notes that this was not, in fact, how philosophers who were not speakers of modern English understood "conscience," and gives the example of the thirteenth-century philosopher and theologian Thomas Aquinas: "[F]or Aquinas, conscience was *not* 'the sense of right and wrong,' but rather the sense of *bonum* and *malum*, that is, 'good' and bad' ... For speakers of most modern European languages, too, 'conscience' is usually linked with the notions 'good' and 'bad,' rather than 'right' and 'wrong'" (2006: 66).

If Nejedlá and Wierzbicka are correct, then we could conclude that conventional usage of English "conscience" strongly implies the kind of understanding that Havel cautions against: it has been privatized and rationalized, reduced to a mechanism in each of our minds that is more or less subject to our control. The conventional meaning of Czech *svědomí*, however, seems to resist this process, whether it be because the concepts of *bonum* and *malum* still predominate over "right" and "wrong" (Wierzbicka) and individual will is less emphasized (Nejedlá), or (and this might be stating the same idea in different terms) the relationship between an individual and her or his awareness (*vědomí*) of the world, a relationship mediated by *svědomí* and its semantic/derivational network, is more foregrounded. In Fromm's terms, English "conscience" privileges a *having/using* mode, while Czech *svědomí* leaves more semantic space for an interpretation in the *being* mode, a space that Havel uses to full effect in his conceptual reimagining of the import of *svědomí* for the modern world.

In this regard, the basic meaning of *svědomí* provides more fertile ground for Havel's argument than does the meaning of "conscience." While it is not by any means impossible for an English reader of Havel to understand or even endorse Havel's argument, he or she is obliged to make a greater leap of faith in following the line of Havel's thought given the ways that "conscience" is not, from an ethnolingusitic perspective, a semantic equivalent for *svědomí*. As we have seen, the basic Anglo understanding of "conscience," like our understanding of "home," tends in entirely the opposite direction from that in which Havel would like to go in extending and elaborating the Czech understanding of *svědomí.*

As a result, many instances in which Havel discusses *svědomí* prove potentially misleading if we read him in English translation. A few examples may suffice to make this clear, the first of which is a passage that we have already seen from Havel's 1999 address in Warsaw. In this speech, and as we have discussed, Havel expands on the theme of the East's moral debt to the West, and he unequivocally states that the experience of post-totalitarianism has taught humanity "that only politics that is preceded by conscience really has any meaning." Havel's "conscience" here is actually Czech *svědomí*: it is not a privatized, mechanized understanding of the concept, but rather a "conscience" with transcendent social and moral dimensions and a connection to the voice of Being. Immediately after stating this, Havel goes on to argue that human "conscience" will lead to a renewed sense of responsibility for the future of the world as a whole. While this hopeful and hoped-for conclusion emerges directly from the basic meaning of Czech *svědomí,* its correlation with English "conscience" appears, to say the least, more problematic.

The second example represents the only instance that I have found in which Czech *svědomí* is translated into English by a word other than "conscience." The passage is taken from *Summer Meditations,* and Havel's topic, familiar to us from chapter 3, is a hypothesized "existential revolution." The English translation reads:

> I once called this coming to our senses an existential revolution. I meant a kind of general mobilization of human consciousness [*svědomí*], of the human mind and spirit, human responsibility, human reason. Perhaps, in light of this view, it makes sense that I cannot consider upbringing, education, and culture as mere ornaments to decorate and beautify life, and enrich our leisure time. (Havel 1993b: 116 and 1999, 6: 507)

Wilson chooses to render *svědomí* here as "consciousness" perhaps because he senses that English "conscience," which represents a rationalized sense of "right" and "wrong" that an individual has and uses and a "phantom of subjectivity" that is locked away in the privacy of our bathrooms, is hardly amenable to general mobilization. "Consciousness," however, shifts the focus beyond the mind of one individual and away from a fully rationalized understanding. It avoids the potential for interpreting "conscience" in a solipsistic and narcissistic fashion.

Wilson's translation calls to mind British historian and author Timothy Garton Ash's characterization of the 1980–1 Solidarity movement in Poland as a "revolution of consciousness [that] changed, lastingly ... not institutions or property relations or material circumstances, but people's minds and attitudes" (Garton Ash 1990: 106).[41] "Consciousness," in other words, evokes a process-oriented sense of "awareness" that transcends individuals. It is less an ability that we have and use selectively to determine right from wrong than a general sense of being "with knowledge" of the world around us. This is an understanding that comes much closer in meaning to Havel's *svědomí* as a moral and ultimately political force that has the potential, if awakened, to change the world for the better.

Czech *duchovnost* and transcendence

Our final case study in translating Havelian keywords concerns the Czech noun *duchovnost* and its related adjective *duchovní*. *Duchovnost* and *duchovní* have path-of-least-resistance realizations in English as "spirituality" and "spiritual," respectively, and these renderings arise by reference to the root word *duch*, which is typically translated into English as "spirit." By far the most frequent term in Havel's writings is the adjective, which I will concentrate on while also mentioning, where relevant, the two nouns.[42] Although *duchovní* strongly tends to be translated as "spiritual," we will see that this is not the only possible, or even an adequate, translation, and this is largely because *duchovnost* resonates quite differently in Czech than "spirituality" does in English. An ethnolinguistic comparison of the terms will uncover why this is the case, as well as elucidate Havel's fixation on *duchovnost* as a keyword.

Martin C. Putna (2010) has suggested that there are two ways to approach the question of spirituality in Havel. We can focus on the details of the texts themselves and carry out a "philosophical, religious-philosophical, or theological analysis" of them, or we can place Havel's ideas concerning spirituality "into [the] wider context of Havel's intellectual forbearers and contemporaries" (2010: 354). Putna takes the latter approach. My strategy here has affinities with Putna's first proposal in that I will be concerned with textual details, but deviates from it in the suggestion that a comparative ethnolinguistic analysis, which is neither philosophical nor theological in nature, may also contribute to our understanding of Havelian spirituality. Indeed, for readers of Havel in English translation, a comparative analysis of the Czech terms related to spirituality and their English translations is, as I will show, a necessary step in coming to terms with the status of *duchovnost* in Havel's thought.

Duchovní is a keyword that cuts across genres and time periods in Havel's oeuvre. It is a verbal motif in the pre-1989 essays, comprises part of the core vocabulary in *Letters to Olga*, and is a recurring and prominent word in the presidential speeches.[43] In this book, we have seen a number of instances in which Havel highlights *duchovnost* in his writings, notably in our discussion of the opposition between *explaining*, which lacks a "spiritual" component, and *understanding*, in which such a component is strongly profiled. *Duchovnost* also surfaced as an integral part of Havel's hypothesized existential (or "spiritual") revolution. The structure that mediates, in Havel's view, between East and West as variants of a modern consumer-industrial society is also fundamentally "spiritual" in nature. What, then, is the meaning of this "spirituality" that proves so crucial in Havel's thought process, and how does the meaning of the Czech concept, which is Havel's familiar ground, differ from the meaning of its English counterpart?

To answer these questions, as well as to clarify Havel's understanding of the concept, I will first cite and discuss prototypical cases in which the translation into English is via the path-of-least-resistance "spiritual," then I will move on to non-prototypical instances in order to sketch out the differences, from an ethnolinguistic viewpoint, between Czech *duchovní* and English "spiritual." Illustrations will be selected from a range of Havel's texts.[44] At issue will be the semantic range of each concept in its respective language, each word's scope of relevance and connotative associations, and, finally, the status of *duchovnost* as a keyword in Havel's thinking, along with a consideration of the extent to which English "spirituality" provides, or rather fails to provide, an appropriate conceptual starting point.

Prototypical cases in which *duchovní* is rendered as "spiritual" (or *duchovnost* as "spirituality" as well as *duch* as "spirit") represent the majority of examples. Two examples will suffice, the first taken from

Letters to Olga and the second from Havel's 1984 essay "Politics and Conscience":

(1) Jde o zkušenost povýtce **duchovní**, resp. něčeho povýtce **duchovního**. ["It is an extremely **spiritual** experience or an experience of something extremely **spiritual**."] (Havel 1983a and b: letter 95)

(2) Zamýšlím se pouze ... nad tím, co zakládá **duchovní strukturou** moderní civilizace, a v čem je tudíž třeba hledat i nejvlastnější příčiny její krize. ["I wish no more than to consider ... the **spiritual framework** of modern civilization and the source of its present crisis."] (Havel 1991a: 253 and 1999, 4: 422)

In the first instance, Havel is writing about his relationship with God, and he considers it necessary to use the word *duchovní* in two (related) ways. On one hand, the phrase "extremely spiritual experience" seems to suggest a religious understanding of the term. On the other hand, "an experience of something extremely spiritual" does not exclude, but also does not emphasize, a religious association. In the second passage, *duchovní* can obviously not be limited in its meaning to a religious understanding: the word has a broader semantic scope in the context of modern civilization as a whole. For Havel, the second type of contextualization for *duchovní* is characteristic. We could add that the very phrase *duchovní struktura moderní civilizace* appears more than once in his collected works.

In addition to these prototypical instances, there are examples in which the translation of *duchovní* via "spiritual" is qualified by a supplemental phrase. One example of this is from "Power of the Powerless," in which Havel writes about the pre-political roots of political processes:

(3) Ty skutečné životní intence mohou mít přirozeně nejrůznější podobu: jednou to mohou být elementární zájmy materiální, sociální či stavovské, jindy určité **zájmy duchovní**, jindy nejzákladnější požadavky existenciální. ["The real aims can naturally assume a great many forms. Sometimes they appear as the basic material or social interests of a group or an individual, at other times, they may appear as certain **intellectual and spiritual interests**; at still other times, they may be the most fundamental of existential demands."] (Havel 1999, 4: 257; 1991: 156)

In this context, Wilson evidently felt that "spiritual" alone would not capture the entire original sense of Czech *duchovní*, and he added the phrase "intellectual and ..." to the English translation. This is a frequent strategy for translating Czech *duchovní*. In another section of the same essay, Havel writes about the *duchovní klima* surrounding Charter 77, and the translation reads "spiritual and intellectual climate." It is equally possible to cite a number of passages from Havel's speeches that illustrate the same strategy: *duchovní impulzy* ("spiritual and intellectual stimuli"), *duchovní rozměr politiky* ("the intellectual and spiritual dimensions of politics"), *středoevropský duchovní svět* ("Central European spiritual and intellectual world"), *duchovní tradice* ("spiritual and intellectual traditions"), *duchovní vlivy* ("spiritual and intellectual influences"), and *duchovní základ* ("intellectual and spiritual basis"). In these instances, the translators apparently consider English "spiritual" an inadequate semantic equivalent for Czech *duchovní*.

The most intriguing cases are those in which *duchovní, duch,* and *duchovnost* are rendered into English not by the words "spiritual," "spirit," and "spirituality," but rather by wholly different expressions. In these cases, that is, the translator has opted entirely against a path-of-least-resistance translation. These instances are rare, but telling. The first example here is from "Power of the Powerless," the second from "Dear Dr. Husák," and the final one from a 1990 speech before the Polish Sejm and Senate.

(4) ... jde [tu] de facto jen o jinou podobu konzumní a industriální společnosti se všemi sociálními a **duchovními důsledky**, které to přináší. ["... what we have here is simply another form of the consumer and industrial society, with all its concomitant social, **intellectual, and psychological consequences**."] (1999, 4: 229; 1991: 131)

(5) Základním nástrojem tohoto sebeuvědomění společnosti je její kultura. Kultura jako konkrétní oblast lidské činnosti, ovlivňující – byť často velmi zprostředkovaně – **obecný stav ducha** a zároveň tímto stavem neustále ovlivňovaná. ["The main instrument of society's self-knowledge is its culture: culture as a specific field of human activity, influencing the **general state of mind** – albeit often very indirectly – and at the same time continually subject to its influence."] (1999, 4: 83; 1991: 63)

(6) Mým prezidentským programem je proto vnášet do politiky **duchovnost**. ["My presidential program is to bring into politics a **sense of culture**."]

In example (4), the translator avoids "spiritual" altogether and opts instead for the phrase "intellectual and psychological." Similar excerpts from other essays and speeches yield a translation via "intellectual" alone: *duchovní rozvoj* ("intellectual advancement"), *duchovní impotence* ("intellectual impotence"), *duchovní investice* ("intellectual investment"). A similar strategy (with a different verbal resolution) is used for a portion of a 1997 speech (Forum 2000 conference) where the phrase *duchovní proudy* is translated as "currents **of thought**."[45]

In (5), we see another translation path, with *duch* being rendered as "mind."[46] The phrase *obecný stav ducha* occurs fairly often in Havel's writings, and it clearly proves problematic for the translator. In "Dear Dr. Husák," this phrase occurs twice, and the translator renders it differently each time, first by "general state of mind" (as in the example above) and then by the expression "intellectual community." Translation of *duch* via "mind" is also the most frequent recourse in *Letters to Olga*.

Example (6) illustrates a third path of translation: *duchovnost* as "culture." This particular translation occurs only twice.[47] Passages from other speeches, however, yield variant translations for *duchovnost* that signal an affinity with the psychologized understanding of *duchovní* noted above. Thus, *druhem své* ***duchovnosti*** is rendered as "[through] the nature of his **mind and spirit**," *rozvoj naší* ***duchovnosti*** is "the development of our **minds**," and ***duchovnost*** *a politika* is translated by "the **intellect** in politics."

It is clear from these examples that the meanings of Czech *duchovní* and English "spiritual" cannot be considered equivalent. In most contexts, the translation is more or less automatic: that is, the translator takes the path of least resistance. In some cases, however, the translator is obliged to choose a different path, either because the word "spiritual" is not semantically adequate or, perhaps, because it evokes something inappropriate given the original Czech context.

These examples from Havel's writings suggest a number of different avenues for ethnolinguistic analysis, and I will explore several of these. As Bartmiński (2010: 216) has, however, noted, comparative ethnolinguistic analysis is most problematic when it comes to concepts related to "spiritual culture," at least in part because they are specific to a given culture and therefore untranslatable, and perhaps also because their meaning is not always stable across individuals within a given culture. The comparison of *duchovní* and "spiritual" offered here is an analytical sketch inspired by and grounded in the use of the word in Havel's texts, but it by no means represents the final word on the topic.

First and foremost, both Czech *duchovní* and English "spiritual" relate in some fundamental way to religious sensibility. It would not, however, be incorrect to claim that the English term implies a stronger association with the religious than the Czech term, which at the very least leaves conceptual space for other considerations. In the OED's entry for "spiritual," almost all the listed meanings are closely tied to religion. The only meaning that does not necessarily imply some kind of relationship to religion, illustrated by the phrase "spiritual home," is specially marked in the dictionary for the lack of just such an implication. In contemporary North American English, "spiritual" is often defined in opposition to "religious." It is common to hear people say that they are "spiritual, but not religious," although stating this is liable to cause some degree of awkwardness or even embarrassment.[48]

With Czech *duchovní*, religious connotations are present, but less strongly felt. Dictionaries list the primary meaning of the word as "relating to *duch*" or as implying in some unspecified way an opposition to the material (*hmotný*) or bodily (*tělesný*), and the suggested synonym is *duševní*.[49] Direct associations with religion are listed as secondary senses. This is not to say that *duchovní* does not suggest religious feeling, or that "spiritual" absolutely must relate to religion, but that the hierarchy of meanings in each expression seems to be reversed. At the very least, the semantic emphasis in each language is differently placed. My task is not to explore the reasons for this difference in emphasis (although it most certainly has much to do with the secular nature of Czech culture in contrast to the Anglo context, particularly in the United States), but rather to note that this difference plays an important role not only in how *duchovní* and related words are translated, but also in how these terms are understood in Czech and English respectively.

The various derivational possibilities in Czech seem to correlate differently to religious sensibility. *Duchovnost* in the abstract is the most closely related, and when Havel uses this term in reference to religion, *spirituality* is inevitably the translation, although even with *duchovnost* we have seen contextualized translations ("minds," "culture," "intellect") that go against this tendency. The adjective *duchovní* is less tied to religious sensibility and clearly leaves space for other relationships. As we have seen, English translations of the adjective require specification because the Czech word has a wider semantic range. At least in Havel's extended sense, *duchovní*, like *klid*, seems to span experiential domains

– not only the domain of religious sensibility, but also the domain of human feelings in general as well as of the mind and the intellect, and the exact same cannot be said for the meaning of English "spiritual." The least religious of the derived words seems to be *duch,* which has a strong association in Havel's writings with the phrase *duch doby* or German (and also, not incidentally, English) *Zeitgeist*. Taken together, these considerations suggest that the Czech terms leave relatively more space for a general understanding of spirituality or for a spirituality that is not automatically defined in terms of (or in opposition to) religion.

Two examples from Havel will illustrate what is at stake in this distinction. In one speech (Vratislav 1992), Havel describes a university as a *významné duchovní středisko* (important "spiritual" centre). This is not a common way in Czech to refer to an institution of higher education, but Havel's extension of *duchovní* to this context is made plausible by the word's semantic range. At the very least, the extension is relatively more plausible in Czech than the much more religiously oriented English phrase "spiritual centre" would be; indeed, in the translation we find the more appropriate English rendering "intellectual center." In this respect, it is also clear why Havel's translator renders *obecný stav ducha* as "general state of mind": using English "spirit" here would completely exclude mental processes concerned with thought and reason that the Czech phrase is intended to evoke.[50]

In another of Havel's speeches (Asahi 1992), we come across the argument that *svět politiky by měl být zlidštěn a zduchovněn*, which represents a running theme throughout Havel's body of work. Not surprisingly, the translator is confronted with the problem of how to render *zduchovněn*. The word *zduchovněn* is a past participle of the verb *zduchovnět* ("to spiritualize"), and the path-of-least-resistance (i.e., the literal) translation of this phrase would be "The world of politics should be humanized and spiritualized." In the American sociopolitical context, however, this evokes something radically different from that which Havel intends. "Spiritualization of politics" or a "spiritualized politics" would mean a politics of religion, which is a marked political form in the contemporary United States. Havel is unconsciously relying on the meaning of Czech *zduchovnět* in a sense that is broader than a merely religious one. The translator, realizing this, cautiously renders the phrase as "politics should be widely humanized and its intellectual and spiritual dimension cultivated."[51]

There is indirect (and naive) evidence for the assertion that English "spirituality" has more direct connections to religion than Czech *duchovnost*, and this comes from a comparison of the respective Wikipedia entries for the terms.[52] The naive understanding of "spirituality" in English is captured by the image on the page for the English entry – a photograph of the Helix Nebula, which is also called the Eye of God. The association here is explicitly religious, and there is an implication that "spirituality" represents a focus on a kind of transcendence that is primarily vertical. That is, the concern is with an individual's relationship with a divine being, one naively assumed to be localized in the heavens. The Czech entry provides no visual image associated with *duchovní transcendence*, and we might suggest that the meaning of the Czech term does not, in fact, privilege vertical transcendence, or rather that it does not exclude a kind of horizontal transcendence that is suggested by its associations with the mind and intellect, education, and culture.

There is a hint of the distinction between vertical and horizontal transcendence in a passage from Havel's letter to Husák:

> Jsme schopni rozvinout svou tvořivost a fantazii, **duchovně a mravně se vzepnout k nečekaným činům**, bojovat se za svou pravdu a obětovat se pro druhé ["We are capable of unleashing our imagination and creativity, of **rising spiritually and morally to unexpected heights**, of fighting for the truth and sacrificing ourselves for others"]. (Havel 1991a: 82 and 1999, 4: 107)

The Czech verb *vzepnout se* ("to rear/rise up," with the verbal prefix *vz-* denoting upward motion) implies verticality, but in the original Czech context the verticality has human dimensions. It is the physical verticality needed to prepare oneself to engage in *nečekané činy* (literally, "unexpected actions" or actions that are of and in the human world). The spiritual and moral components of these unexpected actions have a horizontal dimension, because the actions that result from our "rising up" will presumably affect the world in which we live. The translation of this passage evokes, however, an alternate image, namely, the metaphorical image of vertical motion that is associated with English spirituality. We rise up to "unexpected heights." This distinction is a matter of textual detail, but there is a hint here that, at least in English, "rising up spiritually and morally" is more compatible with an emphasis on vertical, and not horizontal, transcendence.[53]

Of direct relevance here is the distinction between vertical and horizontal construals of spirituality suggested by Johnson, who makes a distinction between a traditional understanding of spirituality in terms of vertical transcendence and what he terms embodied horizontal transcendence:

> *Human spirituality is embodied.* For many people, their sense of spirituality is tied to notions of transcendence – of the soul, of spirit, of value, of God. The traditional notion of transcendence is what I call "vertical transcendence," because it requires rising above one's embodied situation in the world to engage a higher realm that is assumed to have a radically different character from that of the world in which we normally dwell ... By contrast, if we are inescapably and gloriously embodied, then our spirituality cannot be grounded in otherworldliness. It must be grounded in our relation to the human and more-than-human world that we inhabit. It must involve a capacity for horizontal (as opposed to vertical) transcendence, namely, our ability both to transform experience and to be transformed ourselves by something that transcends us: the whole ongoing, ever-developing natural process of which we are a part. Such a view of embodied spirituality may well support an environmental, ecological spirituality, but it is hardly likely to satisfy anyone for whom the only acceptable answer to our finiteness is the infinite. (Johnson 2007: 14)

The conventional semantics of English "spirituality" tend strongly towards the vertical construal, even to the extent that "spiritual" questions, which refer implicitly to the otherworldly, may lose their relevance for practical or everyday life.[54]

Other evidence for the association between *duchovnost* and a kind of in-the-world horizontal transcendence comes from a consideration of the term's scope of relevance, especially in comparison with "spirituality." Havel's collocations with the adjective *duchovní* in his speeches clearly point outward to the larger social implications of the term. Just a partial listing of the nouns that *duchovní* modifies confirms its association with values that are shared by people either historically (e.g., "spiritual traditions") or contemporaneously across a geographical space (e.g., "European spiritual identity"): *duchovní klima* ("spiritual climate"), *duchovní dimenze společnosti* ("spiritual dimension of society"), *duchovní stav společnosti* ("spiritual state of society"), *duchovní rozměr života společnosti* ("spiritual dimension of the life of society"), *duchovní občanské hodnoty* ("spiritual civic values"), *duchovní prostředí* ("spiritual milieu"), *duchovní tradice* ("spiritual traditions"), *duchovní prostor* ("spiritual space"), *duchovní dědictví národa* ("spiritual inheritance of the nation"), *duchovní východiska demokracie* ("spiritual roots of democracy"), *duchovní bohatsví lidstva* ("spiritual wealth of society"), *duchovní proudy* ("spiritual sources"), *duchovní étos* ("spiritual ethos").[55] There is a strong tendency for *duchovní* to collocate in some way with the noun *společnost* ("society"): the Czech word conveys not just a focus on one individual's spirituality but also on the spirit (*duch*) of society as a whole. This is reinforced by adjectival collocations with *duchovní* that tend to emphasize societal associations that transcend individualized concerns. Common adjectives that co-occur with *duchovní* in Havel's writings are *politický* ("political"), *mravní* ("moral"), *kulturní* ("cultural"), *sociální* ("social"), *společenský* ("societal"), *občanský* ("civil"), *civilizační* ("civilizational"), *evropský* ("European"), *národní* ("national"), *univerzální* ("universal"), and even *hospodářský* ("economic").

In his 1994 speech upon receiving the Philadelphia Liberty Medal, Havel makes clear that in-the-world transcendence may in fact be the only way for us to save ourselves:

> It logically follows that, in today's multicultural world, the truly reliable path to coexistence, to peaceful coexistence and creative cooperation, must start from what is at the root of all cultures and what lies infinitely deeper in human hearts and minds than political opinion, convictions, antipathies or sympathies. It must be rooted in self-transcendence. Transcendence as a hand reached out to those close to us, to foreigners, to the human community, to all living creatures, to nature, to the universe; transcendence as a deeply and joyously experienced need to be in harmony even with what we ourselves are not, what we do not understand, what seems distant from us in time and space, but with which we are nevertheless mysteriously linked because, together with us, all this constitutes a single world; transcendence as the only real alternative to extinction.

It should be noted here that the original Czech for "self-transcendence" in the passage above is the more outwardly focused *lidská transcendence* ("human transcendence"), which implies, as the rest of the passage reinforces, the expansion of the individual outward in horizontally transcendent terms. Armstrong offers a complementary way of understanding horizontal transcendence that resonates strongly with Havel's (not to mention Johnson's). She notes that transcendence is built into everyday life and the human condition in that every act of meaningful cognition requires us to go beyond ourselves, to "reach beyond the prism of selfhood" (2009: 283).

Another aspect of each term's relative scope of relevance is hinted at through a translation detail in a speech given by Havel in 1999 (Forum 2000). In this speech, the phrase *ohnisko* ***duchovního a kulturního*** *života* is translated as "focus of **cultural and spiritual** life." The key here is the change in word order and the relative importance of the terms. In Czech, *duchovní* precedes *kulturní,* which implies that *duchovní* has a broader semantic scope; the "spiritual," at least in a Czech understanding, encompasses the cultural but is not limited to it. Havel's translator has reversed this hierarchy. In English, the "cultural" encompasses the "spiritual," which has a decidedly more limited scope of conceptual relevance.

Indeed, English "spirituality" is arguably a much more personal concept than the corresponding Czech term. This is not to say that Czech *duchovnost* excludes the personal, but rather that the emphasis does not fall heavily on the personal or that the personal aspect of the meaning of the concept is not profiled at the expense of a broader understanding. I will not argue this point at any length, except to note that there is ample circumstantial evidence to support the claim. Armstrong, for example, has written about Western spirituality in precisely these terms, claiming that a rift between spirituality and theology in the fourteenth and fifteenth centuries resulted in a re-orientation of the spiritual towards personal comfort. Individual good feelings became a sign of God or the ultimate focus of a spiritual life, but the goal of genuine spirituality ought to be the community and an individual's contribution to it (Armstrong 2009: 154). The modern American focus is aimed at "spiritual experiences" that are discrete and separable from normal, everyday life, and these become akin to experiential or spiritual products that we consume to promote our own individual "spiritual wellness" (Armstrong 2009: 283). In this understanding, spirituality is largely associated with forms of "self-realization."[56]

Perhaps another way of putting this is that there is a strong tendency not just to consumerize but also psychologize the spiritual, to make it a matter of an individual's own feelings and mind.[57] In a 2009 op-ed in the *New York Times*, Gordon Marino raises this very point in suggesting that modern psychology has mistakenly conflated psychological and spiritual disorders – that is, on one hand, clinical depression that could be profitably treated by drugs and, on the other, existential despair. Genuinely spiritual despair has been medicalized: "These days, confide to someone that you are in despair and he or she will likely suggest that you seek out professional help for your depression" (Marino 2009).

Marino's point is that despair is a spiritual attitude and not a feeling – that is, unless you happen to live in a culture where the "spiritual" has been, to a significant degree, psychologized and consumerized.

I do not mean to suggest that a tendency to consumerize and psychologize the spiritual is entirely absent from the Czech cultural context. Indeed, this is arguably a modern phenomenon writ large, and it is precisely in reaction against this creeping tendency that Havel directs his prose. Havel's broad argument is that all human activity has a spiritual dimension and that "spirituality" is not something we can choose to associate ourselves with or not, nor is it something that ought to be consumed for our own personal benefit. In Havel's sense, then, spirituality is much less a matter of something that we as individuals *have* or are able to *use* than it is a matter of what and who we *are*. To misunderstand spirituality – to equate it with religious dogma, to consumerize it, to psychologize it – results in a fundamentally distorted understanding of human identity.

There is a final component of a comparative ethnolinguistic discussion of Czech *duchovní* and English "spiritual" that bears directly on reading Havel in translation, and it involves the degree of reverence that each term evokes in its respective culture. "Spirituality" is taken less seriously than *duchovnost*. The English concept is often the butt of teasing and jokes because it is associated with a certain level of hokeyness (mawkishness, corniness, phoniness) that does not apply to *duchovnost*. In short, Americans tend to make fun of "spirituality" and of people who proclaim themselves "spiritual." Perhaps this is the result of an associative connection between "spirituality" and contrived "spiritualism," with the latter undermining the seriousness of the former.[58]

Possibly related to this point is one particular passage in Havel's 1994 Philadelphia Liberty Medal speech in which the word *duchovní* in the Czech original is simply left out of the English version of the text:

> A rozhlížejíce se **po nejpřirozenějším duchovním zdroji** tvorby nového světového systému, zcela samozřejmě upínají svůj pohled k oblasti, která je tradičním základem moderní spravedlnosti a velkou vymožeností novověku, totiž k souboru hodnot, které byly – mimo jiné – poprvé deklarovány v této budově.
>
> ["And in searching **for the most natural source** for the creation of a new world order, we usually look to an area that is the traditional foundation of modern justice and a great achievement of the modern age: to a set of values that among other things were first declared in this building."]

Did the translator purposefully ignore "spiritual" in this passage because it might have suggested – to the American audience in attendance – a level of hokeyness that would have been decidedly at odds with Havel's eloquent statement regarding the status of democracy in the modern world?

In summing up the status of *duchovnost* as a Havelian keyword, we are now in a position to answer the question of whether translation via English "spirituality" provides the same conceptual starting point. We have seen that the terms *duchovní* and "spiritual" have different semantic resonance in their respective languages. While considerable overlap exists in the meanings of the terms, considerable differences in semantic range (how does each term relate to religious sensibility?), semantic scope (to what extent does each term profile the personal?), and semantic value (how seriously do people take the concept?) all do so as well. In these respects, English "spiritual" falls short as an adequate semantic substitute for Czech *duchovní,* and the sense in which Havel uses the Czech word is not always the sense conveyed by the English term. As we saw with "conscience" and "home," Havel's familiar starting point is a kind of "spirituality" that does not exist in conventional English. For this reason, Havel's translator is often obliged to pursue different paths for translation.

We would do well to keep this in mind when considering Havel's fixation on *duchovnost* as a key part of the solution that he proposes to the existential crisis that confronts us in the modern world. In my own experience teaching a monograph course on Havel's writings in translation over the past decade, American students marvel at Havel's keen analysis of the problems faced by humanity in the late twentieth and early twenty-first centuries. While they readily accept much of Havel's description of the modern-day existential crisis, they become easily frustrated – and sometimes even angered – by what they perceive as Havel's refusal to propose concrete ways to solve this crisis. Much of their frustration undoubtedly stems from their expectations of pragmatic, policy-oriented solutions to this crisis; their frustration is grounded in a belief that the crisis represents a classic case of a technical problem that we need to "solve" somehow. Havel, however, mainly focuses on the underlying cause of the crisis – its existential roots – and not as much on the symptoms of the crisis, which are those that might lend themselves to technical, policy-oriented solutions. For Havel, the root cause of humanity's crisis is "spiritual" in nature, and the "solution" that he consistently offers across genres and time periods necessarily involves reflecting on the meaning of *duchovnost*.

In this regard, we have already seen that Havel urges a "spiritualization" of global politics, and this is one way in which he phrases his proposal for a solution to the global crisis. Another way is his insistence upon the need for a "new spirit" (*nový duch*) or "new spirituality" (*nová duchovnost*) through which we will be able to transcend the limitations of the modern hyperrational *Zeitgeist* that is itself at the root of our existential and moral – that is, spiritual – dilemma. Calls for a "new spirituality" become particularly insistent in Havel's later speeches (from 1997 onward), and the speeches as a whole could be read as explorations in the realization of just such a new human spirit. Havel's proposal, then, is not a traditionally "practical" solution in the sense of a political or economic program that consists of a set of concrete policy initiatives. Rather, it is an existential solution that revolves around the cultivation of a new sense of human "spirituality" that also suggests a new understanding of human meaningfulness in the world. Only this, Havel insists, can address the true cause of our modern dilemma.

The conventional meaning of English "spirituality" proves, in this connection, to be an obstacle to understanding Havel's argument, while the meaning of *duchovnost* in Czech provides more fertile ground for it. The cultivation of a new *duchovnost* or new human *duch* as a solution to humanity's existential crisis is somewhat less of a blind leap of faith for readers of Havel in Czech than a new "spirituality" may well be for readers of Havel in English translation.

Conclusion

Havel's translator Paul Wilson has written about the "intimacy" that he developed with Havel in the course of working on the translations. Good translators, Wilson implies, establish a deep connection with the author's mind along with a sense of the author's ideas as living things (Wilson 1999: 22). Wilson developed this sense in translating Havel from Czech to English, but readers of Havel, and particularly readers of Havel in English, must also cultivate a feel for Havel's ideas as living entities and "translate" these ideas into terms that they can, based on their own personal histories and experiences in the world, understand.

This chapter has presented case studies in translating four words in Havel's core vocabulary that represent key concepts for making sense of Havel's larger project. In each case, we explored the differences, some overt and some subtle, in the burdens of meaning carried by the Czech words and their English counterparts. In contrasting the basic meanings of Czech *(ne)klid*, *domov*, *svědomí*, and *duchovnost* with their English counterparts, I suggested that the Czech words highlight more vividly the relationship between an individual's existence and the totality of Being. They enact, in this respect, an *understanding* mode of thinking about – and of being in – the world. I make this suggestion at the risk of overstating the case, and a more cautious way of saying it might be that this conceptual overtone is felt more in the meaning of the Czech words than in the meaning of the English ones, and it is part of the elusive nature of the difference in construal and resonance. Havel's treatment of each concept, as we have seen, follows the trajectory of the Czech meanings.

The import of these concepts cuts across socio-historical -isms. These words not only tell us something about human identity within a post-totalitarian context, but ought also to tell us, who live outside of that context, something about ourselves. In reading Havel, we come to understand that all of these words embody something essential about modern human identity, but that the nature of this insight is in danger of being drowned out in the noise of modern consumer-industrial society. By better imagining our relationship to Havel's keywords, we can better understand the nature of Havel's appeal. Thinking more explicitly about the differences in the meaning of the words in the original Czech and in English activates our sense of what these words mean to us personally.

In a particularly lyrical passage in his post-presidential memoir, Havel writes:

> The beauty of language is that it can never capture precisely what it wants. Language is disconnected, hard, digital as it were, and for that reason, but not only for that reason, it can never completely capture something as connected as reality, experience, or our souls. (Havel 2007a: 347 and 2006: 246)

In this chapter I contended that the meanings of Havel's keywords in Czech are comparatively less "disconnected" and less "hard" than the meanings of their English counterparts. In contrast to the English words, all four of the Czech words evoke a similar feeling; they all have an air of the philosophical about them that is reminiscent of Havel's description of the "transcendental breeze [*závan transcendence*]" that ruffles the surface of our souls and that we cannot, even if we wanted to, ignore (1991a: 122 and 1999, 4: 212).[59]

English tends to concretize and specialize, and in this regard it may well be the consumer-industrial, scientific, and bureaucratic language par excellence (Goatly 2007), but this runs directly counter to the current and spirit of Havel's thinking. In his subtle extensions and expansions of the meaning of his keywords, Havel grounds himself in the air of transcendence that the Czech words suggest. This strategy is consistent with Havel's larger project of metaphysical reconstruction, the aim of which is to restore a sense of, and respect for, the transcendent in everyday human experience – to activate our spiritual restlessness in order to expand our understanding of home and awaken the slumbering potential of our human conscience.

The privileging of the understanding mode in these Czech words finds affinity with Havel's early poetics. According to Kosatík (2006), Havel developed his early aesthetic views under the influence of, and partly in contrast to, the poetics of his literary mentor, Jiří Kolář. Kolář purposefully left out of his poetry references to subjective, inner states and left in only what he considered to be objective, external observations. Havel, however, countered this with a synthesis:

> According to Havel, it would be more accurate to acknowledge the duplex nature of reality [*dvojjedinost skutečnosti*]: we know that it exists outside of us and without us, but at the same time we are incapable of apprehending it except subjectively. A poet should therefore convey, and not evade, reality's two faces. (Kosatík 2006: 150)

The meanings of *(ne)klid*, *domov*, *svědomí*, and *duchovnost*, in contrast to the meanings of their English counterparts, hint more strongly at reality's *dvojjedinost*. Their meaning is carried along by the current of Havel's transcendent breeze.

Conclusion: Havel's Legacy as Appeal

For me, the notion of some complete and finite knowledge that explains everything and raises no further questions is clearly related to the notion of an end – an end to the spirit, to life, to time and to Being. Anything meaningful that has ever been said in this matter (including every religious gospel) is on the contrary remarkable for its dramatic openness, its incompleteness. It is not a confirmation so much as a challenge [*výzva*] or an appeal [*apel*] ...

– Václav Havel,
Letters to Olga[1]

Shortly after finishing my doctoral degree in Slavic Languages and Literatures with a dissertation on Czech, I found myself teaching at a private American university. Near the end of my first academic year there, a professor of Political Science who had heard of my background in Czech studies invited me to be the final reader of an undergraduate thesis about Václav Havel. Knowing Havel's writing well and having become an avid follower of his post-1989 political career, I eagerly agreed to join the committee. At that late stage in the process, the thesis had already been completed; I read it through and prepared my question for the thesis defence, which I went to at the appointed day and time. When it was my turn to question the author of the thesis, I asked about something that, to my great surprise, had not been addressed in the thesis itself, which had been entirely devoted to the question of whether Havel fit Max Weber's model of a charismatic leader (the conclusion was that he did). My question struck a different note: "*In study-*

ing Havel as a charismatic leader, do you feel that he has something to say to us about American society and American democracy? In researching and writing this thesis, did Havel teach you something about yourself?" To my embarrassment, the question was met with nervous silence on the part of the author of the thesis, who had evidently not been thinking about Havel – and had not been encouraged to think about him – in quite this way.

Throughout this book, I have argued for an approach to reading Havel that puts us in a better position to address the questions that I raised at the thesis defence. It is a framework for thinking about Havel that promotes an open – not a closed, totalizing, or fixed – reading of Havel in which the determination that he was indeed a charismatic leader becomes not an end point in and of itself, but rather the starting point for a larger discussion. How might Havel's exploration of the form/meaning nexus across his various incarnations as writer and political figure help us make sense of our own lives? Can human meaning be reduced to a matter of *explaining*? What is the moral lesson that the post-totalitarian East has to offer the post-1989 world? What power do words exert over our identity? In the approach to Havel that I have both outlined and enacted, we do not read him from a safe and comfortable distance; instead, we break the glass in the museum display-case by allowing ourselves to be read, and perhaps also to be changed, by the very act of reading. We make Emersonian use of the strategies and tools that Havel offers us in order to make better sense of who we are.

This is a perspective on Havel that has the potential to render him meaningful to us in Arendt's sense of the word. Unlike approaches to Havel that focus on contextualization, mine makes accessible the core of Havel's intellectual project. It is a project that is aimed at understanding modern human identity across various sociopolitical –isms, and one that is ultimately geared towards metaphysical reconstruction in the service of spiritual renewal and existential awakening. Without a revolution in spirit, Havel argues, humanity will not be able to confront adequately the civilizational crisis that it faces.

At the heart of Havel's project lies the appeal, and a central motif of this book has been to extend the concept of the appeal to Havel's oeuvre in general. A programmatic strategy in Havel's dramatic style, the appeal goes beyond the merely theatrical. In his early essays devoted largely to criticism of literature and film, art itself is viewed through the lens of the appeal, and artistic devices like the cinematic gag function as coded messages hinting at ways to achieve existential catharsis; Havel's *Anticodes* from the 1960s are visual appeals to the extent that we cannot make sense of them without accessing our own experience of the world to endow them with a less schematically abstract and more personally embodied meaning; Havel's philosophical essays are replete with rhetorical questions directed at their readers, "activating" them to grapple with the difficult questions that the essays raise; *Summer Meditations* is an appeal to his fellow citizens to consider a larger moral and spiritual vision in which to imagine the socioeconomic and political details of Czechoslovakia's future; his letters from prison are appeals in the forms of personal philosophizing inviting us to cultivate a deeper sense of ourselves through our everyday experiences; and Havel's engagement as a politician, which includes the speeches and the memoir that emerge from it, provokes us to rethink politics and power, thereby setting the stage for the kind of metaphysical reconstruction that may well be a necessary precondition for genuine cultural change.

The four chapters in this book have also described forms of Havelian appeal. The key conceptual threads that run throughout Havel's thinking – his restlessness of transcendence, his orientation towards *understanding*, his conviction that humanity is in the process of transitioning to a new age, his wariness of words – are all anchored in the appeal form to the extent that they simultaneously serve as tools for making sense of human identity in the modern world. The ways in which Havel structures his literary and political engagement become crucial components of the message and meaning of his larger project.

In relation to the appeal, it is instructive to refer to the epigraph to this conclusion, which is excerpted from one of Havel's letters from prison (1983a and 1983b: letter 92), in which he suggests that anything useful that has ever been said on the question of the meaning of life has the nature of a call, challenge, or appeal. Over the course of the letter, Havel uses two Czech words to denote the "appeal," the second of which is the word *apel*, familiar to us from theatre of the appeal (*divadlo apelu*). The first word he uses is *výzva*, the meaning of which is, in Havel's usage, roughly synonymous with the meaning of *apel*, but which has a broader range of usage in everyday Czech than the more abstract and domain-specific *apel*. Like the words analysed in the preceding chapter, we can consider *výzva* a keyword in Havel's thinking; it forms a motif in the prison letters and becomes a frequent touchstone in his presidential texts. We may profit from considering the meaning of this keyword in Czech alongside the meaning of its English translation. In fact, multiple paths exist for translating the Czech word into English, and exploring these paths will contribute to an understanding of the appeal as both dominant strategy in Havel's oeuvre and a central component of his legacy.

According to Fronek's Czech-English dictionary (Fronek 2000), *výzva* has five contextual equivalents in English. These emphasize different aspects of Havel's understanding of the word and its relationship to meaning, and his understanding seems to have its conceptual roots in the intersection of all five of the English senses that Fronek lists. A *výzva* is a literal "call" (e.g., a call to begin boarding a plane), an "appeal" or "plea" (in the sense of a public appeal), a "summons" (in the bureaucratic sense), a "prompt" (on a computer screen), and a "challenge" (as in the phrase *výzva na souboj* or "challenge to a duel").

The last word in particular is a frequent path for translation, given the way in which Havel exploits the word's meaning. An example of *výzva* as "challenge" is taken from Havel's 1993 address at George Washington University:

> I think we must not understand post-communism merely as something that makes life difficult for the rest of the world. I certainly did not understand communism that way. I saw it chiefly as a challenge [*výzva*], a challenge [*výzva*] to think and to act. To an even greater extent, post-communism represents just that kind of challenge [*výzva*] ... It seems to me that the challenge [*výzva*] offered by the post-communist world is merely the current form of a broader and more profound challenge [*výzva*] to discover a new type of self-understanding for man, and a new type of politics that should flow from that understanding.

Another possible path for translation that we encounter in Havel's usage, but that Fronek does not mention, is via the English word "opportunity," as in the following passage concerning the floods that devastated the Czech lands in 2002: "I have one idea related to the floods. Many ugly buildings, badly and expensively constructed and in the wrong place, were destroyed. A flood is an opportunity [*výzva*] for us to give our country a slightly improved appearance here and there" (Havel 2007a: 103 and 2006: 74).

As Havel's emphasis on *výzva* as both "challenge" and "opportunity" implies (and as Fronek's other possible English translations, each in its own way, confirm), the meaning of the Czech word profiles a focus on someone's response to the appeal. A *výyza*, in other words, expects an appropriate *odezva* ("response," "echo"). Contexts in which Havel uses *výyza* often, therefore, contain the preposition *k* ("to," "toward," "for") followed by a specification of the response. Havel also sometimes uses *výzývat/vývzat* ("to call out"), the verbal form associated with *vývza*, which gives the appeal a more active shape.[2] In the following example from Havel's post-presidential memoir, we see the verbal form combined with the *k* construction:

> This year didn't begin well, either for the world or for me. Its beginning was foreshadowed by the waves of a tsunami. You had to ask yourself: was the planet trying to tell us something, to warn us of something, challenge us to take some action [*k něčemu nás výzvat*]? (Havel 2007a: 56 and 2006: 45)

If the appeal component of a Havel play is designed to activate its audience to engage in some form of reflection that may ultimately lead to personal catharsis, then Havel seems to read the world around us in the same way. Like an artistic object, the world is replete with signs that we should understand as "prompts" for serious reflection and sometimes even urgent action, and our response to these signs imbues our lives with a kind of transcendent, and perhaps even cathartic, meaning.

This interpretation of *vývza* and *vývzat* is consistent with the etymology of both words. The words derive from the root *zva-* ("call") in combination with the prefix *vy-* ("out"), and the resultant meaning is one of "calling out."[3] It is as if Havel's voice of Being is calling us out, activating our sense of conscience and responsibility, and this call necessarily points towards something (*k něčemu*) that we – both as individuals and as the only meta-aware species living on the planet – must strive to achieve. Indeed, the meaning of *vývza* in Havel's writings is closely bound up with the meanings of two other words that often collocate with *výzva* in his presidential texts: *poselství* ("message," "legacy") and *poslání* ("mission," "calling"). As participants in Being who are also privileged with an awareness of our role as such, we should understand our response to the world's appeal as our human mission and human calling. We should understand it as that which endows a human life with its transcendent message and meaning and as that which forms the essence of our personal and collective legacy.[4]

In understanding *výzva* in this way, we have circled back to Havel's letter from prison in which he associates meaning itself with *vývza* and *apel*. An appeal, as Havel additionally explains, is characterized by its dramatic openness and incompleteness (*nehotovost*). It is

> ... something that is living, something that overwhelms us or speaks to us, obliges or excites us, something that is in concord with our innermost experience and which may even change our entire life from the ground up but which never, of course, attempts to answer, unambiguously, the unanswerable question of meaning. (Havel 1983a and b: letter 92)

In his explanation of the meaning of *výzva*, he cites the Czech philosopher Josef Šafařík on the difference between information and truth. While the former is concrete, objective, discrete, and freely transmittable, the latter is more complicated and more elusive. Conceiving of truth as consisting of discrete bits of information that simply need to be transmitted to other people, Havel asserts, has been one of the most dangerous currents in human history. Authentic human meaning is not informational: it is not transferable, not objective, not concretizable, not discrete. It is not, in Havel's words, a stopping point that exists beyond or apart from life (not "a full stop at the end of life"), but rather a starting point – a call, challenge, opportunity, summons, prompt, appeal, plea – for a deeper experience of life. Meaning is not what we conventionally think it is; it is "not a confirmation so much as a challenge [*výzva*] or an appeal [*apel*]" (Havel 1983a and b: letter 92).

It is not incidental that this very same prison letter devoted to the centrality of the appeal for human meaning begins with a discussion of the Speaker in Ionesco's *The Chairs*. If the Speaker's purpose, Havel writes, is really to inform the gathered public of the meaning of life

> ... then it seems to me that his attempt failed because, among other things, the meaning of life is not, as people often think, just an item of unfamiliar information that can be communicated by someone who knows it to someone who doesn't, somewhat the way an astronomer would tell us how many planets the solar system has, or a statistician how many of us are alcoholics. The mystery of Being and the meaning of life are not "data" and people cannot be separated into two groups, those who know the data and those who don't. (Havel 1983a and b: letter 92)

The meaning of life is "in no way finite or complete," and any attempt to comprehend it "merely raises questions about what exactly is being offered as the alleged meaning." We can never, then, unambiguously answer "the unanswerable question of meaning (answer in the sense of 'settling the matter' or 'sweeping it off the table')"; rather, our attempts to answer "always [tend] to suggest a certain way of living with the question." Living with the question means, in Havel's view, constantly "responding" to it and "constantly hearing a faint echo of it." This is not an end to the problem of human meaning, but rather "an even closer coexistence with it." He concludes these reflections by stating: "I don't know any other way of dealing with the question of 'the meaning of life' except by undergoing the experience personally and attempting to report on it."

In regard to Havel's legacy, Paul Wilson has written: "In the ledger of history, Václav Havel may well be remembered more for what he said than what he managed to accomplish, at least in visible political terms" (Wilson 1999: 29). How better to understand this statement than in terms of Havel's stance on meaning as appeal as proposed in letter 92? His legacy will, after all, depend largely on the response (*odezva*) that his words prompt in his present and future readers. His lasting relevance is not so much a matter of historicizing (or otherwise contextualizing) his literary and political contributions as it is of understanding them as meaningful in some essential way to our own present and our own future. The audience of Havel's *poselství* – both his message and his legacy – consists of those who, in reading Havel, are also eager to let themselves be read by him.

Notes

Introduction: Approaches to Reading Havel

1 The citation is from Edmundson (2004: 7).
2 Rocamora 2004 is a thorough documentation of Havel's career as a playwright. More discussion of Havel as a playwright will appear in chapters 1 and 2 of this book.
3 For a cultural history of Czechoslovak normalization, see Bren (2010), while Šimečka (1984) is an insider's account of the same period. Bolton (2012) traces the development of the dissident movement in a "normalized" Czechoslovakia with a particular focus on Charter 77 and the community of writers, intellectuals, and cultural figures that comprised it. Suk 2013 is a historical account of Havel's life and activities from 1975 to 1989.
4 For a dramatic first-hand account of the Velvet Revolution in Prague, see Garton Ash (1993). Suk (2013) provides the most detailed historical account of the revolution in the context of Havel's life. The Czechoslovak president was elected by a parliamentary vote, and Havel's unanimous rise to power was the result of an agreement negotiated by the Civic Forum with representatives of the Communist Party.
5 Chief among these global initiatives was the foundation Forum 2000 with its annual conference of the same name (see http://www.forum2000.cz).
6 This does not exhaust the list of Havel's genres; see chapter 1 for a fuller sketch.
7 Havel invoked mosaic and collage images frequently in his writings. He also made use, particularly in his presidential speeches, of a "fabric" metaphor to describe the coherence of various domains of human experience (for example, society as a fabric woven together from distinct

threads). In a certain light, all of these images represent variants of the same basic structural principle: a whole that is, in some way, greater than the mere sum of its parts and whose integrity depends on the (at least potentially) coherent relatedness of its parts. In the course of this book, I will primarily make reference, as Havel himself did, to the mosaic image, but will also invoke the other images where relevant. A more focused discussion of the mosaic image and its import for reading Havel (and reading ourselves) is offered at the end of chapter 1.

8 In practice, biographical and historical readings tend to overlap. For an English biographical (and fragmenting) account of Havel's life, see Keane (2000). Tucker 2001 is an intellectualizing account of Havel's thought. More recent Czech biographical accounts are Suk (2013), Putna (2012), and Kaiser (2009). The first is a sophisticated example of historical biography that largely avoids the trap of fragmenting but at the same time does not offer a framework for reading Havel that transcends a certain historical, cultural, and sociopolitical context (and, to be fair, that is not its goal). The second Czech account examines the intellectual and spiritual influences on Havel throughout his life and provides a strong critique of Havel's presidency. The last book is intended as a "political biography" (Kaiser 2009: 7) that focuses on Havel's actions (*činy*) while programmatically avoiding discussion of his writings; in doing so, it offers an extreme example of the pitfalls of fragmenting and compartmentalizing Havel's various faces.

9 As any of his historically themed presidential texts confirms, Havel himself read history in just this way. See, for example, his written text commemorating the Czechoslovak war-time president Edvard Beneš ("Dilemmas of a European Politician," April 2002). Havel understands Beneš's story as a "great drama of modern times." Every drama, he writes, "is also a challenge to the human race," and how we "read this challenge and what conclusions we shall draw from it for ourselves" and in relation to our historical present are matters for our own conscience. Translations of many of Havel's presidential texts, organized chronologically, are available online at http://old.hrad.cz/president/Havel/speeches/index_uk.html.

10 See also Edmundson (1995).

11 A course description and other information on the course, including a sampling of student reactions to reading Havel, are available online at http://havelcourse.tumblr.com.

12 Examples of English-language scholarship that takes Havel's appeal seriously include Goldfarb (1991, 1998, 2006); Isaac (1998); Pontuso (2004); and Popescu (2012). In his or her own way, each of these scholars makes

a case for reading Havel beyond the confines of his own historical and sociopolitical frame.

13 In Ionesco's play, an Old Man and an Old Woman, who are nearing death, hire a professional Speaker to sum up the meaning of their life together for them. The couple invites a host of guests to the Speaker's oration, but the Speaker arrives on scene to find only a room full of empty chairs. He nonetheless proceeds with his oration, but all that emerges from his mouth are inarticulate and almost inhuman sounds. Havel wrote about Ionesco's play twice: once in a letter from prison (1983a and b: letter 92) and two decades later in a presidential address (Janáček Academy of Performing Arts, 2001).

1. The "restlessness of transcendence": Havel's Genres

1 Citations from Havel will be made first by reference to the English translation (where available) and then to the Czech original. This citation is from Havel (1991a: 71 and 1999, 4: 93). This chapter represents a revised and expanded version of Danaher 2013b, which appeared in Czech. Note that Havel 1999 is a multi-volume collected works, and citations will include the volume number.

2 Josef Čapek was the older brother of Karel Čapek, a rather better-known figure in much of the world, and another Czech cultural figure with the same genre-crossing profile. The translations here are mine.

3 This statement is generally valid for non-Czech commentators on Havel. Czech scholars of Havel (for example, Putna [2012] and Suk [2013]) are less likely to fall into this trap; Kaiser (2009), who programmatically attempts to isolate Havel as man-of-action from Havel as writer, is a glaring exception. For an extended discussion of how Havel's faces or incarnations have generally been fragmented and the misreading of Havel that results from this approach, see Danaher (2007a).

4 I do so not to propose a formal and definitive typology of Havel's works, but rather by way of surveying the versatility of Havel's engagement.

5 For introductions to Russian Formalist thought, see Erlich (1980) and Steiner (1984). We revisit the meaning of the Czech word *zvláštní* – the root of the Czech equivalent of defamiliarization – in chapter 2.

6 The first half of this volume contains Havel's juvenilia poetry, a genre that I do not consider in this survey.

7 The dramatic tension inherent in many of the *Anticodes* was noted by Chris McKim, a student in my monograph course. For his final project in the course, he reimagined several of the poems in the form of theatrical shorts.

8 Although they seem simple, it is in fact rather difficult to write (or type out) a good anticode. Of course, in the modern era of computer graphic design, Havel's typograms have an archaic feel, a technical point that ought not to undermine their thought-provoking qualities.

9 For book-length studies of Havel-as-playwright, see Rocamora (2004) in English and Štěrbová (2002) in Czech. Published translations of his plays into English include Havel (1994) and Havel (2012a–d). Czech originals are found in volume two of Havel (1999) and in Havel (2007b). Havel also directed a film version of his last play *Leaving* (2012b and 2007b), which may be considered yet another one-off genre in its own right.

10 For a specialized study of the small-form theatre movement in Czechoslovakia, see Beck (1996).

11 After the events of Prague Spring and the national tragedy of the Soviet invasion, the post-1968 regime under Gustáv Husák promoted sociopolitical "consolidation" and "normalization" of conditions in Czechoslovakia that included a return to a "quiet life" (*klidný život*). For a first-hand discussion of normalization, see Šimečka (1984). Bren (2010) and Bolton (2012) are cultural histories of normalized Czechoslovakia.

12 Samizdat – from the Russian word literally meaning "self-published" – was a form of dissident activity in which banned publications were typed up and passed from reader to reader by hand. Skilling (1989) is a comprehensive account of the samizdat phenomenon in Czechoslovakia.

13 Rocamora (2004) is a detailed account of Havel's career as a playwright, and provides a thorough treatment of the performances of his plays, along with their reception, in Czechoslovakia and abroad. On the popularity of Havel's plays abroad, Trensky notes that when they were staged in the West, "it was immediately realized that the experience of socialist man and of Western man is in fact not so totally dissimilar" (1978: 102). He goes on to say that despite an "idiom peculiar to the totalitarian regimes of the East, the Western audiences easily found parallels to their own existence, and the plays were perceived more as tragicomic commentaries on the predicament of modern man than as political allegories" (1978: 102).

14 Rocamora (2004: 35) sees Vyskočil's influence on Havel in terms of teaching that the "purpose of text was to 'appeal to the audience, to engage and involve them, to make them think and feel'." In a conversation with Žák (Žák 2012: 61ff.), Havel describes theatre of the appeal in similar terms as a non-ideological dramatic style designed to raise questions and prompt the audience to (self-)reflection.

15 Older English translations of the Vaněk plays are found in Havel (1994) and newer ones in Havel (2012a). The Czech titles of *Audience* and *Protest*

are the same as the English, while the middle play's original title is *Vernisáž*. For discussion of these plays, see Goetz-Stankiewicz (1987) and Pontuso (2004) (chapter 4).

16 This is a concrete case of Grossman's principle concerning the theatre of the absurd that "every grotesque gag is based on a real-life gesture" (1999: 92).

17 In the original Czech, the standard definition of *audience* is the first, although it can be assumed that the meaning of the word as it relates to theatre-goers and observers would also be understood.

18 This has led to a range of English translations for the title *Vernisáž*, which have included *Private View*, *Exhibition*, *Unveiling*, and even *Varnishing Day* (see Schamschula [1980]).

19 Vaněk's adoption of the foreman's role is more strongly emphasized in the Czech original. Until the twist at the end, Vaněk has spoken literary Czech, and the foreman has teased him for doing so. In saying the foreman's line, he drops the literary style.

20 I once saw an English-language production of *Audience* in which the actor playing Vaněk could not sit still in his chair. He was jittery and fidgeted nervously as if under interrogation from the foreman. The foreman was also overplayed as a drunken bully who would loudly knock over his chair every time he got up to go to the bathroom (which is a repeated motif in the play). Needless to say, these performances undermined the play as a form of appeal. See Sloupová (1997: 100) for a brief discussion of *neherectví* as a key feature of staging a Havel play.

21 It would certainly be possible to categorize Havel's essays into sub-groups and even, as an anonymous reviewer of this book has suggested, to investigate in this regard the Czech cultural particularities of the essay style. These worthwhile projects fall outside the scope of the present work.

22 For the Czech original, see Havel (1999: vol. 4). An English translation is available in Havel (1991a) (and widely available in pdf form on the internet). See Bolton (2012) for a thorough historical and cultural contextualization of "Power of the Powerless" and a provocative inquiry into the meaning(s) of "dissent."

23 The Communist Manifesto begins: "A specter is haunting Europe – the specter of communism. All the powers of old Europe have entered into a holy alliance to exorcise this specter ..." For thoughts on this parody, see Bolton (2012: 1).

24 In the later genre of presidential speeches, Havel often reverts back to questioning the conventional frame associated with "dissent" by referring to the "so-called dissidents" of the pre-1989 period.

25 Havel defamiliarizes and reframes the meaning of a whole host of terms, not just "dissent" and "power," as the essay progresses. These include "totalitarianism," "dictatorship," "opposition," "ideology," "law," "democracy," and "politics."

26 Scholars from different disciplines use different terms to refer to the pre-1989 sociopolitical order in East and Central Europe, and one's choice of term ("consumer socialism," "communism," "totalitarian," "post-totalitarian," and so on) may even reflect one's attitude toward the subject. Suk (2013) largely uses *diktatura* ("dictatorship"), and that choice has been questioned (see Tabery [2013]). Popescu (2012) (chapter 2) offers an extensive and provocative discussion of Havel's "post-totalitarian" coinage. Since "post-totalitarian" seems best to capture Havel's understanding, I will largely stick to this term when referring to Havel (and this despite the fact that Havel himself was not consistent in this regard).

27 See Danaher (2008a: 41) for a discussion of metaphors for ideology in "Power of the Powerless" and other texts.

28 There is a second story in the essay about an earnest brewer who comes into conflict with his brewery bosses. For a discussion of the brewer's tale in "Power of the Powerless," see Bolton (2012: chapter 6).

29 For details on Havel's imprisonment, see Kaiser (2009: 160ff.) and Suk (2013: 164ff.).

30 See Havel (1983a and 1983b). This volume is not part of Havel's collected works (Havel 1999).

31 A volume titled *Letters from Olga* (I. Havel et al. 2011), representing the other voices in the dialogue, has recently been published in Czech. For an extended contextualization of Havel's letters from prison and Havel's relation to the intellectual group known as Kampademie, see Putna (2012: chapter 6). For a brief history of Kampademie, see Kroupa (2010).

32 Not all readers of Havel admit the importance of *Letters to Olga* for Havel's thought. Kaiser (2009: 161), for example, suggests that the letters occupy the same place in Havel's oeuvre that Ingmar Bergman's films do in world cinematography: they may enjoy a strong reputation, but few people are actually fully acquainted with them. Hejdánek, on the other hand, sees Havel's reflections in the letters as forms of appeal that ought to be duly considered by all thinking people (Hejdánek 2009: 56).

33 We ought to consider some of these words core words in Havel's vocabulary even beyond the letters, and I will analyse some of them as such in chapter 4.

34 The Czech original appears in volume 4 of Havel (1999), and the English translation is Havel (1991b). The English title has a double meaning: "disturbing the peace" is also what "dissidents" actually set out to do.

35 The book is in volume 6 of Havel (1999), and its translation is Havel (1993b).

36 The latter half of Suk (2013) provides a detailed account of Havel's involvement in the Civic Forum and its negotiations with representatives of the state apparatus.

37 Havel was a vocal proponent of a nation-wide referendum that would decide the question of dissolution. When dissolution was agreed upon and the details worked out behind the scenes by Czech and Slovak politicians, Havel felt that he could not in good conscience remain in office.

38 One of the presidential texts that could be considered a separate genre in its own right – Havel's radio program entitled *Hovory z Lán* ("Conversations from Lány": Lány is the Czech president's country estate) – will not be considered here; see Putna (2012: 281ff.) for a brief discussion. Recordings of these programs are available via the website of the Václav Havel Library (http://www.vaclavhavel-library.org/). Annotated transcripts of the programs will be published gradually; see Havel (2013) for transcripts of the programs from 1990.

39 Almost all of Havel's presidential speeches, arranged chronologically by year, are available online at http://old.hrad.cz/president/Havel/speeches/index.html (for the Czech versions) and http://old.hrad.cz/president/Havel/speeches/index_uk.html (for the English versions); to cite one of his speeches, then, it will suffice to give the name of the speech and the year it was given. Of his 313 presidential speeches, only slightly over half have been translated into English and made available on the website of Prague Castle (the seat of the Czech president).

40 For a review of the memoir in English, see Danaher (2008b). For reviews in Czech, see Chuchma (2006) and Šlajchrt (2006).

41 In this connection, it is worth noting Jiří Kolář's influence on Havel as an artist (Kosatík 2006: 42). As noted earlier, Kolář was a poet and visual artist who served as an artistic mentor to the young Havel, and he was as famous for his work in collage, with which he began to experiment in the late 1930s, as he was for his literary output. According to Kosatík (2006: 49), Havel was fascinated with Kolář's work in collage and montage.

42 Other scholars have compared Havel's ideas to Arendt's; in this regard, see particularly Popescu (2012), who makes extensive and productive use of Arendt in her analysis of Havel and who notes that, at times, "Havel seems to be engaged in a dialogue with Arendt, responding to some of her

concerns" (2012: 85). I also read Havel through Arendt in both the second and third chapters of this book.

43 Actively positing a disjuncture usually results in praise for Havel as a successful "dissident" and criticism of him as a failed post-1989 politician. Mlejnek (2006) illustrates this approach, and the gist of his argument is contained in the article's subtitle, which reads in English: "Václav Havel's dramatic works are world-class and retain their appeal while his political trajectory has come to a very sad end." Pontuso (2004: chapter 6) takes on the question of Havel as failed president and refutes well-known critics of Havel's politics (Keane [2000] and Tucker [2001]). I return to the theme of the assumed or hypothesized disjuncture between pre- and post-1989 incarnations of Havel in chapter 3.

44 See Wilson (2006: 15) on Havel's "unconventionality" in this regard.

45 Lewis Lapham, the American writer and former editor of *Harper's Magazine*, wrote the following of his surprise upon reading one of Havel's presidential speeches: "The man apparently was trying to tell the truth, and because I had never heard an American president try to tell the truth, the effect was both violent and shocking, as if somebody's anarchist cousin had fired a pistol in the midst of a cocktail party meant to raise funds for the New York Public Library" (Lapham 1999: 92).

46 The importance of framing in critical thinking cannot be overemphasized. Scholars in cognitive science and discourse generally agree that a frame serves to establish a mental landscape. When we shift to another frame, we reimagine our conceptual topography: "[F]rames are not quite rooms, but it can be helpful to think of a frame metaphorically as a place rather than a set of ideas" (Feldman 2007: 9).

47 Masaryk was a philosopher, scholar, and politician who was instrumental in founding the first Czechoslovak Republic, and he served as its president from 1918 until his death in 1937. Beneš was Masaryk's second-in-command and his Minister of Foreign Affairs; Beneš became president after Masaryk's death, and had the unfortunate duty of serving as such both during the 1938 Nazi invasion of Czechoslovakia and the 1948 Communist *coup-d'état*. Dubček, a Slovak Communist politician, served as leader of Czechoslovakia during the late stages of Prague Spring and briefly as a figurehead following the Soviet invasion of the country in August 1968.

48 I analyse *(ne)klid* more fully in chapter 4.

49 Putna was referring here specifically to Havel's analysis, in his early literary-critical period, of Walt Whitman's poetry. Putna's portrait as a whole, however, testifies that this mosaic-like ability was an intellectual motif throughout all of Havel's life.

50 Although a collage and a mosaic have similar conceptual structuring, there are some key differences between them that suggest that our principle for reading Havel should be oriented toward the latter. One of these differences lies in the fact that a mosaic is much less suggestive than a collage. The mosaic's whole is clearer in that we actually see the final pattern or image, which we do not need to hypothesize or imagine – as in a collage – almost entirely on our own. In this respect, the mosaic principle is more appropriate for Havel, who did not tend to leave us guessing about the pattern or image represented by the whole.

51 See Kornblatt (2001) for a similar analysis of the form/meaning or context/content relationship in the writings of the Russian religious philosopher Vladimir Solovyov. Solovyov's emphasis on integral knowledge is, according to Kornblatt, consistent with "an interest in the integration of discourses," and in his philosophy and fictional prose "neither matter nor manner are divorced from spiritual truth" (302). Form and meaning remain, to borrow from Solovyov's own religious vocabulary, "undivided, yet unmerged" (302).

52 Havel often used a structural variant of the mosaic image in which he imagined, as he does here, a meaningful whole as a single fabric woven from interconnected threads. If you try to pull one thread out and isolate it, the whole piece will begin to ravel. In his 1996 speech "Europe as Task," for example, Havel imagines Europe in exactly these terms.

53 For a later philosophical meditation on the order of Being as a mosaic, see Havel's 1995 Hiroshima speech. Havel also adopted a mosaic approach to theatre and theatrical performance in the prison letters and some of the speeches (see, in particular, the untranslated AMU speech in 1996). In a small but significant way, every dramatic performance always enacts the meaningfulness of theatre as an art form, and, in doing so, manages to capture, at a micro-level, something of the very skeleton of Being.

2. *Explaining* and *Understanding*: The "Weirdness" of Havel's Plays

1 Havel (1991b: 195 and 1990: 169).

2 Havel (1994) contains the classic English translation by Vera Blackwell. A newer translation by Paul Wilson, which is titled simply *The Memo*, is Havel (2012c).

3 In my experience, this reaction to Havel's plays is not limited to undergraduates studying communication. When fellow academics have found out that I research and teach Havel, more than a few have told me that they love Havel's writing – those essays and post-1989 political texts that they have happened to read – except that they find the plays rather

odd. When pressed, they have for the most part admitted to having only read one or two of them, and to never having seen any of them staged.

4 Admittedly, there is also a better way to capture this contrast than by resorting, as my student did, to a distinction between "objective" and "subjective," and I will return to this point soon enough.

5 As Rocamora (2004: 312) tells us, Havel referred to the *Garden Party*'s "liquidation office" in his resignation speech as Czechoslovak president just prior to the Velvet Divorce between the Czech Republic and Slovakia in saying that he refused to be the country's "Liquidation Secretary."

6 In addition to being married to two women simultaneously, Macheath is also in love with a prostitute.

7 I am grateful to Jonathan Bolton for this observation.

8 Havel expressed his views on theatre primarily in three sources: *Letters to Olga* (Havel 1983a and b), *Disturbing the Peace* (Havel 1991b and 1990), and certain presidential speeches. In the first book, the letters in which Havel develops his metaphysics of theatre are the following: 31, 32, 37, 52, 56, 58, 62, 67, 71, 80, 92, 102 through 107, 112, and 114 through 117. Freimanová (2012) is a collected volume of Havel's views on the theatre; see also Žák (2012).

9 The very word "theatre" comes from Greek *theatron*, which means "place for seeing or watching."

10 This is a speech that Havel gave as president. Almost all of Havel's presidential speeches, arranged chronologically by year, are available online at http://old.hrad.cz/president/Havel/speeches/index.html (for the Czech versions) and http://old.hrad.cz/president/Havel/speeches/index_uk.html (for the English versions). Hereafter, speeches are indicated by the name of the speech and the year it was given.

11 As I noted in chapter 1, the Czech word for defamiliarization is *ozvláštnění*, which has *zvláštní* – provocative "weird" – as its root.

12 This line is delivered by Fistula, an enigmatic devil-like character in Havel's occult-themed play *Temptation*. Fistula tempts the play's main character, Dr Foustka (the "little Faust"), and goads him into action that leads to his petty downfall. For an interpretation of the play, see Neubauer (1990).

13 We might study Havel's theatre of the appeal in conjunction with approaches to theatre other than Boal's. For example, Havel's appeal-oriented absurdism has much in common with Bertold Brecht's *Verfremdungseffekt* (see Brecht [1964], "Alienation Effects in Chinese Acting") as well as with the distinction that Brecht made between "epic" and "dramatic" theatre (see Brecht [1964], "The Modern Theatre Is the Epic

Theatre"). Havel and Brecht seem to have used different triggering effects to accomplish the goal of implicating the audience in the meaning of the performance; a detailed study of the similarities and differences between Havel and Brecht in this regard falls outside the scope of this study. (I am grateful to Dijana Mitrovic Longinovic for a discussion of Brecht's *Verfremdungseffekt*.)

14 I am not suggesting that Havel knew of Johnson's work (or Johnson of Havel's), but merely that Johnson's account of meaning is useful in helping us understand better Havel's approach to meaningfulness. Johnson is, of course, not the only philosopher to promote an embodied view of meaning. It is, however, likely that Havel knew something of Dewey and the American pragmatic school of philosophy, if only through Karel Čapek (2000 [1918]).

15 Material in this paragraph is taken from Havel's 1996 speech to the Czech Academy of Performing Arts (DAMU), which is devoted to the meaning of theatre and its relationship to both human spirituality and politics. This speech has not been translated into English, and the translations here are mine.

16 This is an essential point about Havel's dramatic style that my two communication undergraduates viewing *The Memorandum* were unprepared to understand, and the provocative aspects of the "weirdness" of the experience proved, as a consequence, inaccessible to them.

17 While it is certainly true that Havel's essays are far more accessible to scholars outside of the Czech Republic than staged performances of his plays are, it does not follow from this that scholars are unable to access the critical literature on Havel as a playwright and integrate its insights more directly into their reading of the essays. Given Havel's profile as a playwright, it would, at the very least, seem reasonable to make the attempt to do so.

18 The Czech equivalent for "explain" is *vysvětlovat*, which breaks down into the prefix *vy-* ("out") and the root *svět* ("light"). The etymology gives us a meaning identical to English "elucidate" (i.e., "to shed light on something").

19 For an ethnolingusitic analysis of Czech *lidský* – "human," "humane," "personal" – as a Havelian keyword, see Danaher (2010b).

20 It is not surprising that the phrase "intuitive understanding" works well, but "intuitive explanation" seems like a contradiction.

21 The online translation of this speech is awkward, and I have modified it stylistically where necessary.

22 Following up on an observation from chapter 1, we might call this speech "The Anatomy of Waiting." I have again somewhat modified the existing translation.

23 See, for example, Havel's 2002 speech nominating Eliška Wagnerová to the Czech constitutional court, as well as his address from the same year upon receiving an honorary degree from the University of Malta. The latter, but not the former, has been translated.
24 Havel devoted a number of his more important speeches to this theme. See, for example, his 2000 speech to the European parliament and his 1996 speech "Europe as Task."
25 I will return to the role played in "Politics and Conscience" by "conscience" (Czech *svědomí*) in chapter 4.
26 The citation is to be read as volume 1, paragraph 220.
27 Crittenden 2009 (20) suggests another pair of words in ancient Greek, *chronos* and *kairos*, that also fall in line with the opposition between *explaining* and *understanding*. The former referred to logical or quantitative time – specific chronological ordering that was mechanistic and objectively impersonal. The latter embodied a qualitative and personal or human relationship to the passage of time, and was oriented toward specific events and the meaning of these events for people. Crittenden's study focuses on "meta-temporal drama," and one of the playwrights that he examines in this regard – and in terms of *kairos* – is Havel.
28 Bergen points out that Arendt's views on the *explaining / understanding* opposition were never fully clarified (Bergen 1998: 38), and certainly not with regard to the question of totalitarianism. As we will see in the next chapter, Havel answers, in his own way, Arendt's question regarding how to *understand*, and not merely *explain*, (post-)totalitarianism.
29 In a similar characterization, Fromm stresses Eichmann's bureaucratic mentality – he was merely doing his job as an organizer – and his profound, inhuman indifference to everything else; this attitude, Fromm goes on to argue, characterizes modern man, and as a result, "there is a bit of Eichmann in us all today" (Fromm 2005: 28). See also Goldfarb (1991: 14ff.), who discusses Arendt's Eichmann analysis in proposing the idea that totalitarianism redefined the relationship between reason and violence, and Popescu (2012: chapter 4), who treats Havel's approach to human responsibility largely through a discussion of Eichmann.
30 This is not to imply that the technical details of frame analysis ought not to be applied to making sense of individual texts by Havel or elements of those texts. For example, Goffman asserts that frames have what he terms a "directional track" that regulates the interactions in the given frame – for example, punctuation in written language (1974: 210). Because it is not often essential to the message, material from the directional track is itself typically not profiled in an interaction;

the directional track can, however, sometimes "contaminate" the main text. This is exactly the case with one well-known element in Havel's play *The Garden Party*, in which Hugo's parents occasionally receive telegrams from a highly placed bureaucratic official who is meant to help Hugo with his career. The telegrams are strange (in the *zvláštní* sense) because they transmit both the contents of the telegram itself – the main text or the true message of the telegram – as well as seemingly extraneous material from the directional track present when the telegram was being dictated. These latter elements consist of conversational asides made by the boss to his secretary during the dictation that expose their affair. In the telegrams to Hugo's parents, then, the directional track ends up "contaminating" the main text, and the audience is forced to attend to this track in order somehow to make sense of the telegram's larger message. Indeed, it could be argued that the larger message of *The Garden Party*, if not also of the majority of Havel's plays, involves just such an appeal to the audience to focus attention on – in Goffman's terms, to stop "disattending" – the directional track behind everyday forms of communication. Havel's telegrams in *The Garden Party* represent a clever and humorous framing strategy for making this point.

31 Here (1974: 311) he offers the example of a dramatic real-life misframing that he took from a newspaper account: a women on a trolley in San Francisco who was actually having a brain hemorrhage was believed by the trolley driver and other passengers to be merely drunk, and the police took her to a drunk tank in the local jail where she received no medical care and died.

32 Havel the politician concurs: "I want to stress that even minor decisions are better made within a framework of ideas [*na pozadí určité rámcové koncepce*]; without such a framework, it's all random groping and an opportunity for lobbyists and con men" (2007a: 161 and 2006: 113). See also Pontuso's discussion of the anchoring citation (2004: 41).

33 See, for example, his 1999 and 2000 New Year's Addresses. *Domov* is a keyword in Havel's thinking, and translation via English "home," while inevitable, is inadequate; see chapter 4 for a comparative semantic analysis of these terms.

34 Havel is reproducing here a statement made in *Disturbing the Peace* (Havel 1991b and 1990). I have somewhat altered Wilson's translation of the phrase (2007a: 161 and 2006: 113) "vše, co se vymyká řádu a co ho problematizuje," which reads (2007a: 161 and 2006: 113), "everything that escapes order and makes it problematic."

35 Havel gave the speech upon acceptance of the St Adalbert prize (in Czech, Adalbert is Vojtěch). I have somewhat modified the online translation as needed.

36 The online translation has, instead of my "trouble-maker," the more literal translation "unsettler."

37 Etymologically, the word *klid* derives from the Old Czech verb *kl'uditi*, which was used in reference to clearing land, or putting the land in order, for the purposes of farming (Machek 1968: 256). The modern word, depending on the context in which it occurs, could be translated into English by any of the following words: "peace, quiet, calm, order, rest, repose, composure, tranquility, serenity." See chapter 4 for a more detailed analysis of the meaning of this Havelian keyword.

38 I have also asked my students who could tell me with absolute certainty that there is an electrical or telephone pole visible outside of their bedroom window. In five years of asking this question, only one student has ever raised her hand: she was absolutely certain that there is an electrical pole outside of her window, but only because it had been hit by lightning one night in a thunderstorm.

39 "Keying" means transposing events, activities, and entities that are already meaningful in some primary framework into another framework. Examples of keying include playful make-believe, contests, ceremonies, dry-runs, or rehearsals. In this regard, Goffman claims that the theatrical frame is "something more than a simple keying" (1974: 138).

40 On this very point, note Andrej Krob, who directed both the original staging of *The Beggar's Opera* in 1975 as well as an anniversary performance at the Žižkovské divadlo in November 2005: "I am glad to serve a good script, and I don't want to dress it up or make it somehow cheaply accessible. With their perfect composition and construction, Havel's plays stand on their own. When you add in comic effects, you ruin Havel's own delicate and wise humor" ("Je to třicet let ..." 2005).

41 As we have seen, many of Havel's plays have open-ended conclusions that either return the play to the beginning of its cycle (*Audience, Unveiling, The Memorandum*) or send a direct appeal to the audience ("Go home!" is the last line, directed at the audience, in the English translation of *The Garden Party*). The last line of *The Beggar's Opera* essentially does both at the same time.

42 Pontuso's thorough treatment of the Heidegger/Havel relationship comprises chapter 2 of his book (Pontuso 2004).

43 We are reminded here of some of Havel's anticodes.

44 In my experience, productions of Havel's plays tend to fail because either the actors do not successfully execute the precisely timed movements or the directors do not respect the choreographic tension and overact the choreography for farcical effect.

45 See, for example, Rhonda Blair's 2008 book that examines ways in which actors and directors can benefit from discoveries in cognitive science to achieve more effective performances. Amy Cook discusses mirror neurons in her 2010 book on Hamlet's mirror, in which she suggests that "perhaps the rehearsal of actions and feelings that [watching a play] generates allows us to respond to current or future experiences *as if* we had experienced them before, even though only a few of our neurons *actually have* experienced this before" (Cook 2010: 136).

46 Mirror neurons are part of recent discoveries in cognitive science that demonstrate how imagining (or engaged watching) can actually change the structure and function of our brains (see Doidge [2007]).

47 Cook (2010) has used blending theory to analyse the image of the mirror in Shakespeare's *Hamlet*. Cook argues that Hamlet's mirror is a complex conceptual blend as well as a conceptual compression that serves as a figurative nexus for the play as a whole.

48 Stoppard makes use of the same personal/sociopolitical compression in Max's lesson about *amachanon* love.

49 As suggested in chapter 1, the Vaněk trilogy plays a significant role in Havel's intellectual chronology in that the plays serve as companion pieces to "Power of the Powerless": the first two plays (*Audience* and *Unveiling*) were written before the essay, and the third (*Protest*) was written more or less at the same time as the essay.

50 Cook notes that this is true in general of blends: their power is not primarily *semantic*, but *conceptual* (2010: 30).

51 See Havel (1983a and b) (letter 117) for this citation and fragments from the rest of this paragraph.

3. Understanding East and West: The World in Existential Crisis

1 Havel (1990: 145 and 1991b: 168).

2 Suk references the reframing largely as a matter of historical record regarding Havel's writing of "Politics and Conscience" and Havel's correspondence at the time with the Czech philosopher-in-exile Václav Bělohradský (Suk 2013: 276ff.). In his own analyses of this essay and others, Suk limits himself to the domestic level. He does, however, admit

that we must consider the crisis of modernity to be the traditional starting point of Havel's thought (2013: 252).

3 In fairness to Judt, his article was about the dissident movement throughout Central/Eastern Europe, and not devoted exclusively to Havel; he also notes that not even all dissident intellectuals agree with Havel's argument (Judt 1988: 234ff.). Judt's article was written in 1988, and it may not be wrong to suggest that Judt might have reconsidered Havel's East/West reframing, especially given the content and tone of Judt's last book (Judt 2010). Other scholars who are similar to Kaiser and Judt in this regard are discussed at a later point.

4 Goldfarb (1991 and 2006), Isaac (1998), and Popescu (2012) represent the best examples. Popescu explicitly states that Havel's writings have two audiences, East and West, and that the "stream that runs under both post-totalitarianism and Western liberal democracy is modernity" (2012: 62); this is, according to Popescu, the main source of Havel's continued relevance (2012: 138). Falk acknowledges Havel's contributions in this regard by writing that the "failure of the Western European imagination is that it cannot see post-totalitarianism for what it in fact is ... It is much more ideologically convenient to cast East Europe as the anti-democratic 'other,' the opposite of its achievement rather than a logical extension of its excesses" (Falk 2003: 227–8); she does not, however, explore the implications of them. Pontuso (2004) largely assumes the general validity of Havel's reframing without making an explicit argument in support of it.

5 In this respect, we could interpret Havel's strategy here along lines similar to those suggested by Bolton (2012: chapter 4). Bolton argues that Havel's description of the mid-1970s trial of the Plastic People of the Universe, which misrepresented key aspects of the trial itself and both distorted and simplified the actual history of the Czech musical underground, functioned as a mythological narrative that was used by Havel and others to cultivate interest in and support for Charter 77. Even though it was not exactly true, Havel's narrative of the trial, as a kind of poetic appeal, became a focal point for the call to action embodied in the Charter.

6 Bolton (2012: chapter 4) argues that it was largely the Czech musical underground that influenced Havel and the signatories of Charter 77 to adopt an approach that bridged the divide between East and West in that the underground promoted "a critique of consumerist culture that did not distinguish between communism and capitalism" (2012: 118). As far as Havel is concerned, it might be more accurate to say that the musical underground's views reinforced his own thinking. The plays written in

the 1960s (not to mention the anticodes) offer evidence to suggest that the East/West reframing was strongly rooted in Havel's mind well prior to his encounter with the musical underground.

7 On the other hand, it is true that few of my students pick up on this line of argumentation on a first reading. In most cases, they do not actively see Havel's reframing of the East/West dynamic until it has been pointed out to them.

8 This leads Popescu (2012: 135ff.) to suggest that, for Havel, the West is Dorian Gray and the East is Dorian Gray's picture.

9 Indeed, Isaac has argued that Arendt saw totalitarianism as a phenomenon that is a *consequence* of the modern existential crisis faced by humanity, not a *cause* of it (1998: 63). Like Havel, Arendt also understood that the "pressing concerns of human freedom and indeed human survival were best served by detaching them from the dualistic framework of Cold War thinking" (1998: 66). See also Judt (2010), who makes the argument that our twentieth-century "morality tale of 'socialism vs. freedom' or 'communism vs. capitalism'" is deeply misleading (2010: 145). Havel's reframing of Cold War dualism is hardly a radical thought.

10 In this regard, Pontuso points to Heidegger's influence on Havel's thinking. Havel agreed with Heidegger in seeing (post-)totalitarianism in the East as an offshoot of Western rationalism: "Both liberal democracy and Marxist totalitarianism rest on the notion that human responsibility can fully comprehend and control Being" (2004: 65).

11 Other intellectuals have made similar claims. The Canadian writer John Ralston Saul, for example, has emphasized the strong structural and ideological affinities among Marxism, fascism, and capitalism. If, he asks, we defeated corporate fascism in World War II and Marxism in the Cold War, then "why do we cling to the basic corporatist belief in group legitimacy and the basic Marxist belief in economic determinism? I've said elsewhere, at least half seriously, that the only true Marxists functioning today teach in the Chicago School of Economics and manage our large corporations. I could add that these same people are the true descendants of Benito Mussolini" (Ralston Saul 1997: 120). This is also, and not incidentally, the very lesson that Eleanor teaches Max in Stoppard's *Rock 'n' Roll*.

12 Bren is a case in point here, because her main interest as far as Havel is concerned is the greengrocer in "Power of the Powerless."

13 Other presidential texts in which Havel invokes the East/West reframing include the following: a 1991 speech at the University of California in which he discusses the hubris of Marxist ideology and its

relation to humanity's global spiritual (and ecological) crisis; his 1992 speech to the French Academy of Humanities and Political Sciences, the theme of which is existential waiting (discussed in chapter 2), and at the end of which he suggests that impatient people in Czechoslovakia probably think that Godot has arrived post-1989, but that this would be as grave a mistake as it was to think of communism as Godot; a 1997 piece published in the Czech newspaper *Mladá fronta dnes* that discusses ideological forms of "destructive collectivism" that bridge both East and West as well as the 1989 divide; a 1999 address to the French Senate in which he considers the East/West divide and the revolutions of 1989 against the larger background of a world in existential crisis; a 1999 speech in Warsaw on the anniversary of the founding of the Polish newspaper *Gazeta Wyborcza* that speculates on how the East can repay the West for its post-1989 help; a 2001 speech to a conference about political culture in a united Europe in which he repeats and extends the theme of the *Gazeta Wyborcza* address; a 2001 address to a conference titled "Europe's New Democracies: Leadership and Responsibility" in which he examines the cultural and semiotic implications of the East/West Cold War divide; and his 2002 New Year's address, in which he makes a direct reference to the existence of certain "modern, refined 'normalizers'," powers-that-be who would like to pull the strings, hidden behind the scenes, of the country's sociopolitical and economic institutions, and who thereby undermine authentic democracy. This does not represent an exhaustive list of speeches in which the reframing is invoked.

14 The Czech phrase for "poor failure" that Havel uses here is *chudý odpadlík*. Bolton (2012: 178) has noted that the word *odpadlík* was used in Czechoslovakia's anti-Charter campaign to describe signatories to the Charter: they were labeled as renegades, apostates, people who had (literally) "fallen away" from society's mainstream. In "Power of the Powerless," Havel used this word, perhaps with the anti-Charter in mind, in his ironic description of "dissidents," and it is quite possible that he is mindful of that context and usage here.

15 This address has not been translated.

16 This speech has not been translated. Translations are mine.

17 Havel evidently believed his whole adult life that the twentieth century represented an age of transition for humanity. Evidence for an early commitment to this belief comes in correspondence from the 1950s (see Kosatík [2006: 30]).

18 In this connection, it is interesting to note that absurdist theatre has been characterized as an ideal form for a transitional age:

> Ours being, more than most others, an age of transition, it displays a bewilderingly stratified picture: medieval beliefs still held and overlaid by eighteenth-century rationalism and mid-nineteenth-century Marxism, rocked by sudden volcanic eruptions of prehistoric fanaticisms and primitive tribal cults. Each of these components of the cultural pattern of the age finds its own artistic expression. The Theatre of the Absurd, however, can be seen as the reflection of what seems to be the attitude most genuinely representative of our own time. The hallmark of this attitude is its sense that the certitudes and unshakable basic assumptions of the former ages have been swept away, that they have been tested and found wanting, that they have been discredited as cheap and somewhat childish illusions. (Esslin 2001: 22–3)

19 For example, in his 1999 address upon receipt of the Saint Adalbert (in Czech, Svatý Vojtěch) Prize, Havel introduces the idea of an age in transition with the phrase "As we all know ..." (in Czech, *Jak známo ...*).

20 Frankl characterizes this longing in terms of an "existential vacuum" and the haunting experience of an "inner emptiness" or "void" (see Frankl [2006: 105ff.]).

21 Another culminating work in this line of thinking is Havel's 1985 play *Temptation*. Neubauer (1990) analyses it in terms that evoke the grand hypothesis of humanity in an age of transition. If Goethe's German Faust was a symbol of scientific civilization who prophesizes the rise of science and warns about its dangers (Neubauer 1990: 11), then Havel's Czech Foustka (literally, the "little Faust") signals the end of the Modern Age: "Faust is a character at the dawn of the Renaissance who stands at the border between the Middle Ages and the Age of Science. In Foustka, however, we see the contemporary breaking point that represents the end of the Modern Age" (Neubauer 1990: 13; translation mine). Much of Neubauer's book explores Havel's implicit criticism of (in our terms) the *explaining* mindset of the Modern Age.

22 For the moment, I have left out a key part of the Harvard address that concerns Havel's proposed solution to the global crisis, and I will return to it toward the end of this chapter.

23 In this regard, I am reminded of the Czech philosopher Erazim Kohák's discussion (Kohák 1989) of the relationship between the "world of

everydayness" and philosophy. The former "blindly takes a framework of intelligibility for granted" (1989: 19), is preoccupied with its own ambitions, and thus holds the latter in contempt. In Kohák's wording, "the world in its mundane doings will fear and hate the philosopher because, in projecting a vision, he places the world's self-justifying preoccupations in question, challenging their justification" (1989: 19). Although this statement is too forceful to apply in all respects to the discussion here, it is nonetheless clear that Havel is on the side of the philosopher.

24 My goal here is to summarize Toulmin's argument as it relates to Havel's hypothesis of the end of the Modern Age, and my summary will obviously not do full justice to Toulmin's study.

25 For historical details of the reach of the Newtonian cosmopolis in sociopolitical terms, see Toulmin (1990: 132ff.).

26 Ralston Saul characterizes this as elevating reason to an ideology: "I am not attacking reason *per se*. I am attacking the dominance of reason. Reason as an ideology. Sensibly integrated with our other qualities, reason is invaluable. Put on its own as a flagship for society and for all of our actions, it quickly becomes irrational" (1997: 100).

27 The speech was given in Prague on 12 June 1991 to attendees at a gathering devoted to the idea of European confederation. It has not been translated, and translations are mine. Palouš's book titled *1969: Hypotéza o konci novověku, ba o konci celého eurověku a o počátku světověku* (in English, *1969: A Hypothesis about the End of the Modern Age, If Not Also about the End of the Whole European Age and the Beginning of the World Age*) appeared in samizdat in 1985, and I have used this version. Translations from this book are also mine.

28 The common root of the Czech terms is *věk*, which means "age." The root *staro-* means "old," *středo-* is "middle," and *novo-* means "new." Palouš's proposed *světověk* is a combination of the words for "world" (*svět*) and "age" (*věk*).

29 As with my discussion of Toulmin, my goal is not to provide an exhaustive account of Palouš's book, but rather to summarize his arguments insofar as they are relevant to my discussion of Havel's views.

30 The word "spiritual" (*duchovní*) is not only key to Palouš's discussion, but also functions as a keyword in Havel's thinking. The Czech term resonates in different ways from its usual English translation equivalent, and I analyse the differences in the next chapter.

31 In Palouš's view, historical periodization has its origins in religious thought (1985: 4ff.), and its methodological grounding in spiritual transcendence is thereby reinforced.

32 As noted in chapter 2, Crittenden (2009) views Havel as a "metatemporal" dramatist whose focus is *kairos*.
33 This frames yet another possible reading of Havel's anticode "Forward" that was discussed in chapter 1.
34 For Palouš, the three initial ages of humanity were Eurocentric in that they were geographically centred in or around Europe and its offshoots. The World Age marks the end of Eurocentricity: it is an age that emerges from European sources but is not Eurocentrically chauvinistic (1985: 26).
35 As it happens, this shift in understanding has been described by astronauts themselves, and has come to be known as the Overview Effect (see http://en.wikipedia.org/wiki/Overview_effect); I am grateful to Tom McCarthy for drawing my attention to this. The American astronaut James Irwin visited President Havel in 1990 and described both what it was like to be on the moon and how the experience affected him spiritually; Havel was deeply moved by the visit and conversation (Havel 2013: 117).
36 There is much in Palouš's argument that evokes the image of a mosaic, and we examined the importance of this image for Havel in chapter 1.
37 Radim Palouš (R. Palouš 1997: 175) understands Havel's existential revolution to represent a radical renewal in "human consciousness [*lidské vědomí*]," which entails a relationship to the "human order" in general that includes, but is not limited to, the political order. Without a revolution at the level of consciousness, nothing can change for the better.
38 See also Goldfarb (1991), which proposes a sophisticated and nuanced framework for rendering the post-totalitarian experience "meaningful" in the post-1989 world.

4. "Metaphysical reconstruction": Translating Havel's Keywords

1 Havel (1991a: 387 and 1999, 4: 1139).
2 To my knowledge, this question has not been systematically raised before.
3 For applications of the "keyword" approach to culture, see Wierzbicka (2006, 1997, and 1992). Vaňková (2010) contains a useful discussion of and commentary on Wierzbicka's understanding of the term. Note also Edmundson on the role of keywords in philosophical thinking: "[I]t is not surprising that to every philosopher of consequence we attach a word list, a central vocabulary. We think of the words and phrases they have invented or those that they have bent themselves over for long periods, minutely shaping and polishing, like expert gem cutters" (1995: 13).

4 To be clear, I do not intend to suggest that this is a question of the translations themselves, and I am certainly not casting doubt on the skills of Paul Wilson, whose work is exemplary. As we will see, the translator usually has only a limited choice, if any choice at all, in how to render Havel's keywords into English, but this does not preclude the existence of palpable differences in the "burdens of meaning."

5 For a discussion of Havel as a crypto-semanticist, see Danaher (2007a: 36ff.). Note also Jan Trefulka's stance that Havel took words seriously even at a time when most thought that they did not matter (Trefulka 1997: 20–1). Grounding himself in a discussion of the term "civil society" in the context of post-1989 Central and Eastern Europe, Goldfarb 1998 (81ff.) notes that intellectuals have tended to provide democratic societies with their political vocabulary, which is another reason that words do matter.

6 I noted in chapter 1 that Havel defamiliarizes and reconceptualizes the meaning of a whole host of words in the course of the essay, and these include "dissent," "power," "dictatorship," "opposition," "ideology," "law," "democracy," and "politics." In addition to "post-totalitarianism," Havel also coins the term "life-in-truth" in order to give linguistic embodiment to a concept or idea that does not exist in our collective consciousness but that we would arguably benefit from having.

7 Parts of this chapter have been taken from Danaher (2013a) ("conscience"), Danaher (2010a) ("restlessness," "home," and "conscience") and Danaher (2010b) ("spirituality"). The last article also presents an analysis of another Havelian keyword, *lidský* ("human, humane"), which I will not consider here.

8 A number of interrelated and largely complementary methodological approaches to ethnolinguistic analysis exist, and sources that theorize, describe, and/or apply these various methodologies include the following: Bartmiński (2010), Deutscher (2010), Underhill (2011, 2009), and Wierzbicka (2010, 2006, 1999, 1997, 1996, 1992). A recent volume of papers devoted largely to Bartmiński's approach is Głaz et al. (2013). For ethnolinguistics as practiced in the Czech context, see Vaňková (2007) and Vaňková et al. (2005). For an enlightening discussion of the interrelationships among culture, language, and literature, see Vaňková (2013).

9 Note also the cognitive linguist George Lakoff's view of words:

> What are words? Words are neural links between spoken and written expressions and frames, metaphors, and narratives. When we hear the words, not only their immediate frames and metaphors are activated, but also all the high-level worldviews and associated narratives – with

their emotions – are activated. Words are not just words – they activate a huge range of brain mechanisms. (Lakoff 2007: 70)

10 At the same time, however, I have made an effort to avoid technical details associated with this approach. My goal here is not to provide exhaustive comparative analysis of Havel's keywords, but rather to detail those aspects of their meaning in Czech and English that prove especially relevant to Havel's attempts at "metaphysical reconstruction."
11 The prefix *ne-* means "un-," "dis-," or "not."
12 Wilson's "disquiet" here is a rendering of *zneklidňovat*, another verb derived from the root *(ne)klid*.
13 Another illustration of a translator's difficulties in dealing with the semantic range of *klid* is also this passage from Havel in which he speaks about his yearning for *klid* amidst a dissident's necessarily *neklidný* life: "... zvolil jsem si dost **neklidný** život a sám pořád někde **zneklidňuji** – a přitom po ničem netoužím víc než po **klidu**" (Havel 1990: 176). The English translations of the three *klid* words here, which I have bolded, are completely different: "I have chosen a rather **agitated** way of life, and I myself am always **ruffling the surface** somewhere, yet I long for nothing more than **peace and quiet**" (Havel 1991b: 203).
14 These suggestive and mutually reinforcing metaphors begin in earnest from page 72 in Havel (1991a) and from page 95 in Havel (1999: 4).
15 For a thorough treatment of *pohoda*, a Czech keyword that shares semantic affinities with *klid*, see Vaňková (2010).
16 Kaiser (2009) completely misses the transcendent element in Havelian *neklid*, criticizing Havel for engaging in *zneklidňování* ("disturbances" or the activity of promoting *neklid*) merely for its own sake (Kaiser 2009: 75). As a result, he cannot grasp the implications of the concept for Havel's understanding of human responsibility and human identity, although perhaps this is not surprising in a biographical work that programmatically avoids engagement with Havel's writings in a misguided attempt to isolate Havel as "man of action."
17 For a discussion of circles of home as frames for identity, see Danaher (2007a).
18 See in particular letters 52 and 53 (Havel 1983a and b), in which he writes about *domov* in terms of concrete and absolute horizons of Being.
19 As I mentioned earlier, the meaning of Czech *země* exhibits a similar range in that it means both "country" and "earth."
20 Bartmiński notes that the same is true for the meaning of the Polish word *ojczyzna*. He analyzes this concept in terms of seven concentric

circles, with the definition of "fatherland" occupying the outermost circle (Bartmiński 2010: 168). For a thorough ethnolinguistic analysis juxtaposing the meanings of Czech *domov* ("home") and *dům* ("house"), see Vaňková (2012).

21 In the original Czech of this passage, the word *kruh* ("circle") is used once in the lead phrase "concentric circles." In the extended discussion that follows, Havel uses only *vrstva* ("layer") or *vrstvy* ("layers"), and he does so twelve times. Wilson's translation of these terms is nearly evenly split among "circle," "aspect," and "stratum."

22 Indeed, the harmony of diachrony and synchrony in questions of human identity at both personal and societal levels is a running motif in Havel's presidential texts.

23 The interview was conducted by Jiří Lederer on 29 April 1975 and appeared as part of the samizdat volume *Jiří Lederer: Czech Conversations, 1975–76* (issue number 177). The volume was published by Edice Petlice.

24 See also Havel's 2002 "Státní svátek" address.

25 Needless to say, these connotative associations can become quite complicated, and one's sense of *domov* need not be straightforward. For some contemporary Czechs, for example, the country layer of their *domov* – that is, the country of their childhood or young adulthood – may well be not the Czech Republic as much as it is (or was) Czechoslovakia.

26 In one passage, for example, Havel insists on a distinction between the Czech words *bydliště* and *domov*: "Jde ... o to, aby člověk na této zemi neměl jen bydliště, ale i domov," which in English reads "... it's important that man have a home [*domov*] on this earth, not just a dwelling place [*bydliště*]" (Havel 1991b: 15 and 1990: 18).

27 Several years ago, I attended a conference at which one of the keynote speakers – Joe Grady, a cognitive linguist who had become a language consultant for non-profit organizations seeking to brand or market their missions in more effective ways – directly confirmed the conclusion of the OED in regard to the meaning of "home." In a project he was working on for an arts organization in a mid-sized American city, he initially intended to develop a promotional campaign for the arts centred on the distinction between "house" and "home" – in much the same way that Havel insisted on the difference between *bydliště* and *domov*. The idea was to suggest that a city without the arts was a house but not a home. Grady field-tested the idea with focus groups, and to his surprise discovered that most people did not see a strong difference between the two concepts. Americans, in other words, tended to focus on "house," and "home" suggested merely a "house" that was decorated or materially outfitted in a comfortable (or

luxurious) way. Grady was forced to drop the idea and opt for a different promotional strategy. This is not, of course, to suggest definitively that every native speaker of English has a commodified understanding of "home," but rather that the trend toward such an understanding is strong.

28 The word *svědomí* does occur in the play *Temptation* in the ironic phrase *vědecké svědomí* ("scientific conscience"). See Neubauer (2010: 29) for a brief discussion.

29 In detailing the development of Havel's thought with regard to *svědomí*, I will for the most part use, for ease of reading the English text, the word "conscience" instead of the original Czech term.

30 Ralston Saul is another intellectual who has written on this theme. His concern is with the modern obsession with the unconscious and the consequences of this for society:

> In this century, dominated by mass ideologies, all-inclusive structures and technological revolution, it is as if the Western individual has taken refuge in the search for something that no one can take away – their own unconscious. Therapy ... thus becomes yet another ideology ... But this flight into the unconscious has gone far beyond formal therapy into the general Western myth of what an individual is and – more importantly – what properly should interest an individual. The answer? Himself. Herself. Not society. Not civilization. (1997: 51)
>
> Our retreat into ourselves means that personal fulfillment has replaced responsible citizenship: "It is as if our obsession with our individual unconscious has alleviated and even replaced the need for public consciousness." (1997 54)

31 See Pontuso (2004: 63ff.) for a similar argument, but made through a comparison of Havelian and Heideggerean views on "conscience." See also Popescu (2012: 97), who views Havel's dialogic understanding of "conscience" as filling in gaps in Arendt's thinking on the same theme.

32 The question of Havel's belief in God, which is one possible interpretation of the "voice of Being" or "higher authority" that *svědomí* instantiates, is a complicated one. For the most part, he seems to use purposefully vague language that does not invoke a specific version of God (language that is spiritual but not religious, a phrase that we will return to shortly), but that also does not exclude a religious interpretation. For more on Havel's faith, see Balabán (2009), Pontuso (2008, 2004), and Putna (2012 [especially 217ff.], 2010). For an (unnuanced) evangelical Christian perspective on Havel, see Sires (2001).

33 See, for example, the speeches given at Asahi Hall in Japan in 1992 and George Washington University in 1993.
34 The English version of this speech online has a serious mistranslation, rendering the original Czech *politika, které předchází svědomí* as "politics that precede conscience," which is the exact opposite of Havel's intended meaning.
35 This speech has not been translated, and the translation here is mine.
36 Note in particular the dramatic statement in his Harvard University address (1995): "Our conscience must catch up to our reason, otherwise we are lost."
37 This citation is taken from a November 1995 interview that appears with Havel's speeches on the website of the Czech presidency. The translation is mine.
38 Indeed, the adjective *lidský* (along with the derived noun *lidskost*) represents another keyword in Havel, especially in his post-1989 texts. In the presidential speeches, Havel uses this adjective in combination with more than one hundred different nouns. Translating *lidský* into English is not as straightforward as it might seem, since its meaning subtly blends the meaning of the two separate (although obviously related) English words "human" and "humane."
39 The translation is mine. One wonders if a mechanized understanding of "conscience" – a "conscience" controllable by an exercise of will – might also help to explain the case of Adolf Eichmann, the Nazi war criminal discussed in chapter 2 in the context of Hannah Arendt's study.
40 Both Wierzbicka's focus on a "rational ethics" and the notion that English "conscience," in opposition to Czech *svědomí*, might be understood more as a mechanism or ability raise the question of whether reason itself is also a mechanism or ability. It can be and, of course, has been (or conventionally is?) construed as such, but this may very well also be a culturally grounded understanding. For a persuasive counter-argument in the cognitive-linguistics tradition, see Johnson (2007).
41 Garton Ash also cites a Polish priest who described Solidarity, in an alternate but compatible metaphor, as a "forest of awakened consciences" (1990: 60). English "conscience" misses the forest for the trees, while Havel's *svědomí* focuses on an understanding of conscience as a moral ecosystem.
42 Putna has also noted Havel's frequent use of the adjective "in all manner of collocations" (2012: 14). The adverb *duchovně* also occurs in Havel's writings, although infrequently. Derived verbs with the root *duch* will also, where relevant, be considered.

43 *Duchovnost* is mentioned, in some form, in nearly half of Havel's more than three hundred presidential speeches; in more than a few cases, it is the main theme of the speech.

44 Analysis of Havel's use of *duchovnost*, *duchovní*, and *duch* (and their renderings in English translation) is based on selected essays ("Dear Dr. Husák," "Power of the Powerless," "Politics and Conscience," "Thriller") as well as *Letters to Olga*, *Disturbing the Peace*, *Summer Meditations*, and the presidential texts.

45 In the course of the book *Disturbing the Peace* (Havel 1991b and 1990), *duchovní* is used more than twenty times, and in almost half of these contexts the translation reads "intellectual." Eight instances are translated as "spiritual," and the remaining uses have both "intellectual and spiritual" as their English equivalents.

46 The adjective is sometimes translated as "mental," for example, in letters 134 and 141 (from *Letters to Olga*) where the phrase *před-duchovní* is rendered as "pre-mental."

47 The second time is from the year 2000 in the opening address to the Forum 2000 conference, where the phrase *Jeho tématem je vzdělanost, duchovnost, moudrost, duchovní dimenze společenského života*, translated as "The topic of our Forum is 'Education, **Culture**, Wisdom and Spiritual Values'," is found.

48 A Google search for the phrase "spiritual but not religious" resulted in almost one million hits, and the phrase itself, as a mantra in popular culture, has its own Wikipedia entry. Rifkin has noted, based on an annual survey that tracks shifting attitudes toward religion and spirituality world-wide since 1981, that the number of "Americans who say they are 'spiritual but not religious' has increased by 10 percentage points since 1999," and that as many as forty percent of American adults described themselves in these terms as of 2006 (Rifkin 2009: 461).

49 The word *duchovní* derives from *duch* ("spirit") while *duševní* derives from *duše* ("soul"). The latter is not a full synonym for the former, and the differences in usage, which I have not investigated in detail, would be interesting in terms of the argument presented here.

50 Of course, English "mind" is also not an adequate equivalent for Czech *duch*, because it profiles reasoning at the expense of other psychological processes. For a general discussion of aspects of this problem, see the chapter on the words "mind," "heart," and "soul" in Wierzbicka (1997).

51 There is, in the same speech, another context with the word *zduchovnění*, which is a deverbal noun. Contemporary politics, Havel writes, needs a new impulse *v podobě určitého zduchovnění*. The translator

renders this, again cautiously and as if intentionally to avoid the word "spiritualization," as an impulse "that would add a badly needed spiritual dimension" to politics.

52 Entries on Wikipedia frequently change, and these pages were last accessed on 27 April 2011. The Czech page was for *spiritualita*, which was indicated to be a synonym for *duchovnost*.

53 I am grateful to Daniel Vojtěch for discussing this passage and its translation with me. Any misinterpretations remain my responsibility.

54 An advertisement that I happened to see on the Boston metro for a lecture series sponsored by a local church reads: "The sermons are **practical** and **relevant** – and yet still spiritual." The relevance of spirituality to practical life, at least in Boston, must be argued in boldface.

55 Translations are given here more or less literally to highlight Havel's use of *duchovní* and the strangeness of English "spiritual" in at least some of these phrasings.

56 American interpretations of "spirituality" and of Havel's concept of "life in truth" run parallel to one another. My students often understand the latter idea in wholly personal or individual terms, that is, as referencing a privatized kind of truth, along with a life that fulfills an individual's "spiritual" quest. This is obviously not what Havel suggests by the term at all.

57 In this respect, "spirituality" is similar to "conscience."

58 Fromm has this to say on the difficulties of using the words "religious" and "spiritual" in English: "As a result, almost everybody reacted to the word 'religious' as he would react to the concept of God. One could bypass this difficulty using the phrase 'spiritual' instead of 'religious', and I shall do so sometimes. (And needless to say, the word 'spiritual' has associations to 'spiritualism', which also tend to vitiate it)" (Fromm 2005: 133).

59 Havel is referring here to the souls of those imprisoned under Article 203, but the point can easily be generalized.

Conclusion: Havel's Legacy as Appeal

1 Havel (1983a and b: letter 92).

2 In his analysis of Ivan Jirous's legendary manifesto on the meaning of the Czech musical underground in the 1970s, Bolton mentions Jirous's frequent use of the verb *oslovovat* ("to address," "to speak to," "to connect with"); according to Bolton, Jirous's *oslovovat* was meant to emphasize "neither the artist nor the listener but that mystical space of communion in between the two" (2012: 127). This is obviously similar to Havel's later use

of *vyzývat*, although it might be suggested that Havel's appeal engages the world beyond the mystical space of artistic communion.

3 This sense is perhaps most evident with the verb in its passive form, as in the phrase *být vyzván*, meaning "to be called out."

4 We might shift etymological gears for a moment and note that English "calling" is related to the Greek words *kalein* ("to call") and *kalos* ("beautiful" and "morally good"). In Havel's treatment of the world's *výzva*, then, we see a strong echo of the spiritual dimensions of the Greek words. (I am grateful to Jeffrey Perkins for a discussion of the spiritual dimensions of "calling.")

Bibliography

Arendt, Hannah. 1968. *The Origins of Totalitarianism*. New York: Harcourt, Brace, Jovanovich.

Arendt, Hannah. 2006. *Eichmann in Jerusalem: A Report on the Banality of Evil*. New York: Penguin.

Armstrong, Karen. 2009. *The Case for God*. New York: Knopf.

Balabán, Milan. 2009. *Víra (u) Václava Havla*. Prague: Oikoymenh.

Bartmiński, Jerzy. 2010. *Aspects of Cognitive Ethnolinguistics*. London: Equinox.

Beck, Dennis. 1996. "Divadlo Husa na Provázku and the 'Absence' of Czech Community." *Theatre Journal* 48 (4): 419–41. http://dx.doi.org/10.1353/tj.1996.0077.

Bergen, Bernard. 1998. *The Banality of Evil: Hannah Arendt and the "Final Solution."* Lanham: Rowman & Littlefield.

Blair, Rhonda. 2008. *The Actor, Image, and Action: Acting and Cognitive Neuroscience*. New York: Routledge.

Boal, Augusto. 1998. *Legislative Theatre*. New York: Routledge.

Bolton, Jonathan. 2012. *Worlds of Dissent: Charter 77, the Plastic People of the Universe, and Czech Culture under Communism*. Cambridge: Harvard University Press. http://dx.doi.org/10.4159/harvard.9780674064836.

Boyd, Brian. 2009. *On the Origin of Stories: Evolution, Cognition, and Fiction*. Cambridge: Harvard University Press.

Brecht, Bertolt. 1964. *Brecht on Theatre*. Edited and translated by John Willett. New York: Hill and Wang.

Bren, Paulina. 2010. *The Greengrocer and His TV: The Culture of Communism after the 1968 Prague Spring*. Ithaca: Cornell University Press.

Čapek, Karel. (1918) 2000. *Pragmatismus čili filosofie praktického života*. Olomouc: Votobia.

Carey, Phyllis. 1999. "Havel's *The Memorandum* and the Despotism of Technology." In *Critical Essays on Václav Havel*, edited by M. Goetz-Stankiewicz and P. Carey, 173–83. New York: G.K. Hall.

Ceplina, Jerrie. 2009. "Václav Havel's Presidential Speeches as Hybrid: Reconciling Havel the Dissident and Havel the President." Unpublished paper.

Chuchma, Josef. 2006 (6 May). "Havel na hranici možného," *Mladá fronta dnes*, A8.

Cook, Amy. 2010. *Shakespearan Neuroplay*. New York: Palgrave Macmillan. http://dx.doi.org/10.1057/9780230113053.

Crittenden, Cole. 2009. *Theater in Time: The Meta-Temporal Drama of Chekhov, Vvedensky, and Havel*. Saabrücken: VDM.

Danaher, David. 2007. "Framing Václav Havel," *Slovo a smysl / Word and Sense* 8, 25–47.

Danaher, David. 2008a. "Teaching Havel." In *Between Texts, Languages, and Cultures (A Festshrift for Michael Henry Heim)*, edited by C. Cravens, M. Fidler, and S. Kresin, 35–42. Bloomington: Slavica.

Danaher, David. 2008b. "Review of Václav Havel's *Prosím stručně / To the Castle and Back*." *Czech Language News* 29: 10–12.

Danaher, David. 2010a. "Translating Havel: Three Key Words," *Slovo a slovesnost* 71: 250–95.

Danaher, David. 2010b. "An Ethnolinguistic Approach to Key Words in Literature: *lidskost* and *duchovnost* in the Writings of Václav Havel." In *Ročenka textů zahraničních profesorů* 4, 27–54. Prague: Charles University.

Danaher, David. 2013a. "Ethnolinguistics and Literature: The Meaning of *svědomí* 'conscience' in the Writings of Václav Havel." In *The Linguistic Worldview: Ethnolinguistics, Cognition and Culture*, edited by A. Głaz, D. Danaher, and P. Łozowski, 93–113. London: Versita.

Danaher, David. 2013b. "*Neklid transcendence*: žánry Václava Havla," *Česká literatura* 1: 29–50.

Deutscher, Guy. 2010. *Through the Language Glass: Why the World Looks Different in Other Languages*. New York: Henry Holt.

Dewey, John. 2005. *Art as Experience*. New York: Penguin.

Doidge, Norman. 2007. *The Brain That Changes Itself*. New York: Penguin.

Dubský, Ivan. 1997. Untitled text in Freimanová 1997, 10–11. Prague: Lidové noviny.

Edmundson, Mark. 1995. *Literature against Philosophy: Plato to Derrida*. Cambridge: Cambridge University Press. http://dx.doi.org/10.1017/CBO9780511552755.

Edmundson, Mark. 2004. *Why Read?* New York: Bloomsbury.

Erlich, Victor. 1980. *Russian Formalism*. Amsterdam: Walter de Gruyter.

Esslin, Martin. 2001. *The Theatre of the Absurd*. New York: Vintage Books.

Falk, Barbara. 2003. *The Dilemmas of Dissidence in East-Central Europe: Citizen Intellectuals and Philosopher Kings*. Budapest: Central European University.

Fauconnier, Gilles. 2001. "Conceptual Blending." In *The Encyclopedia of the Social and Behavioral Sciences*, edited by N. Smelser and P. Baltes. Oxford: Elsevier.

Fauconnier, Gilles, and Mark Turner. 1998. "Conceptual Integration Networks." *Cognitive Science* 22 (2): 133–87. http://dx.doi.org/10.1207/s15516709cog2202_1.

Fauconnier, Gilles, and Mark Turner. 2003. *The Way We Think: Conceptual Blending and the Mind's Hidden Complexities*. Chicago: Basic Books.

Feldman, Jeffrey. 2007. *Framing the Debate*. New York: Ig Publishing.

Fish, Stanley. 2009. "Conscience vs. Conscience." *The New York Times*, April 12.

Frankfurt, Harry. 2005. *On Bullshit*. Princeton: Princeton University Press.

Frankl, Viktor. 1986. *The Doctor and the Soul: From Psychotherapy to Logotherapy*. New York: Random House.

Frankl, Viktor. 2006. *Man's Search for Meaning*. Boston: Beacon Press.

Freimanová, Anna, ed. 1997. *Milý Václave ... Tvůj: Přemýšlení o Václavu Havlovi*. Prague: Lidové noviny.

Freimanová, Anna, ed. 2012. *Václav Havel o divadle*. Prague: Václav Havel Library.

Fromm, Erich. 2005. *On Being Human*. New York: Continuum.

Fronek, Josef. 2000. *Velký česko-anglický slovník*. Prague: LEDA.

Gaddis, John Lewis. 2006. *The Cold War: A New History*. New York: Penguin.

Garton Ash, Timothy. 1990. *The Uses of Adversity: Essays on the Fate of Central Europe*. New York: Vintage.

Garton Ash, Timothy. 1993. *The Magic Lantern: The Revolution of '89 Witnessed in Warsaw, Budapest, Berlin, and Prague*. New York: Vintage.

Garton Ash, Timothy. 1999. "Prague: Intellectuals and Politicians." In Goetz-Stankiewicz and Carey 1999, 57–71. New York: G.K. Hall.

Głaz, Adam, David Danaher, and Przemysław Łozowski, eds. 2013. *The Linguistic Worldview: Ethnolinguistics, Cognition, and Culture*. London: Versita.

Goatly, Andrew. 2007. *Washing the Brain: Metaphor and Hidden Ideology*. Amsterdam: Benjamins.

Goetz-Stankiewicz, Marketa, ed. 1987. *The Vaněk Plays: Four Authors, One Character*. Vancouver: University of British Columbia Press.

Goetz-Stankiewicz, Marketa. 1999. "Variations of Temptation – Václav Havel's Politics of Languages." In Goetz-Stankiewicz and Carey 1999, 228–40. New York: G.K. Hall.

Goetz-Stankiewicz, Marketa, and Phyllis Carey, eds. 1999. *Critical Essays on Václav Havel*. New York: G.K. Hall.

Goffman, Erving. 1974. *Frame Analysis: An Essay on the Organization of Experience*. Boston: Northeastern University Press.

Goldfarb, Jeffrey. 1991. *Beyond Glasnost: The Post-Totalitarian Mind*. Chicago: Chicago University Press.

Goldfarb, Jeffrey. 1998. *Civility and Subversion: The Intellectual in Democratic Society*. Cambridge: Cambridge University Press. http://dx.doi.org/10.1017/CBO9780511581717.

Goldfarb, Jeffrey. 2006. *The Politics of Small Things: The Power of the Powerless in Dark Times*. Chicago: Chicago University Press.

Grossman, Jan. 1999. *Texty o divadle (I)*. Prague: Pražská scéna.

Havel, Ivan, et al. 2011. *Dopisy od Olgy*. Prague: Knihovna Václava Havla.

Havel, Václav. 1983a. *Dopisy Olze*. Prague: Atlantis.

Havel, Václav. 1983b. *Letters to Olga*. Translated by Paul Wilson. New York: Henry Holt.

Havel, Václav. 1984. "Anatomy of the Gag," translated by Michal Schonberg. *Modern Drama* XXIII (1): 13–24.

Havel, Václav. 1987. "Light on a Landscape." In Goetz-Stankiewicz 1987, 237–9. Vancouver: University of British Columbia Press.

Havel, Václav. 1990. *Dálkový výslech (rozhovor s Karlem Hvížďalou)*. Prague: Melantrich.

Havel, Václav. 1991a. *Open Letters*. Translated by Paul Wilson et al. New York: Knopf.

Havel, Václav. 1991b. *Disturbing the Peace: A Conversation with Karel Hvížďala*. Translated by Paul Wilson. New York: Vintage.

Havel, Václav. 1993a. *Antikódy*. Prague: Odeon.

Havel, Václav. 1993b. *Summer Meditations*. Translated by Paul Wilson. New York: Vintage.

Havel, Václav. 1994. *The Garden Party and Other Plays*. Grove Press.

Havel, Václav. 1999. *Spisy*. 7 vols. Prague: Torst.

Havel, Václav. 2001. *The Beggar's Opera*. Translated by Paul Wilson. Ithaca: Cornell University Press.

Havel, Václav. 2006. *Prosím stručně*. Prague: Gallery.

Havel, Václav. 2007a. *To the Castle and Back*. Translated by Paul Wilson. New York: Knopf.

Havel, Václav. 2007b. *Odcházení*. Prague: Torst.
Havel, Václav. 2012a. *Vaněk Plays*. Translated by Jan Novák. New York: Theater 61 Press.
Havel, Václav. 2012b. *Leaving*. Translated by Paul Wilson. New York: Theater 61 Press.
Havel, Václav. 2012c. *The Memo*. Translated by Paul Wilson. New York: Theater 61 Press.
Havel, Václav. 2012d. *Increased Difficulty of Concentration*. Translated by Štěpán Šimek. New York: Theater 61 Press.
Havel, Václav. 2013. Václav Havel: Hovory v Lánech 1990 (1). Prague: Václav Havel Library.
Hejdánek, Ladislav. 2009. *Havel je uhlík*. Prague: Václav Havel Library.
Hiršal, Josef. Introduction to *Antikódy*, by Vaclav Havel, 5–9. Prague: Odeon.
Humphrey, Nicholas. 1999. *A History of the Mind: Evolution and the Birth of Consciousness*. New York: Copernicus.
Huxley, Aldous. 1959. *"Preface" to Collected Essays*. New York: Harper.
Iacobini, Marco. 2009. *Mirroring People: The Science of Empathy and How We Connect with Other People*. New York: Picador.
Isaac, Jeffrey. 1998. *Democracy in Dark Times*. Ithaca: Cornell University Press.
"Je to třicet let, co policie rozehnala premiéru Havlovy Žebrácké opery." 2005. *Mladá fronta dnes*, 29 October, p. B1.
Johnson, Mark. 2007. *The Meaning of the Body: Aesthetics of Human Understanding*. Chicago: Chicago University Press.
Judt, Tony. 1988. "The Dilemmas of Dissidence: The Politics of Opposition in East-Central Europe." *Eastern European Politics and Societies* 2 (2): 185–240.
Judt, Tony. 2010. *Ill Fares the Land*. New York: Penguin.
Kaiser, Daniel. 2009. *Disident: Václav Havel 1936–1989*. Prague: Paseka.
Keane, John. 2000. *Václav Havel: A Political Tragedy in Six Acts*. New York: Basic Books.
Kohák, Erazim. 1989. *Jan Patočka: Philosophy and Selected Writings*. Chicago: Chicago University Press.
Kornblatt, Judith. 2001. "The Truth of the Word: Solovyov's *Three Conversations* Speaks on Tolstoy's *Resurrection*." *Slavic and East European Journal* 45 (2): 301–21. http://dx.doi.org/10.2307/3086331.
Kosatík, Pavel. 2006. *"Ústně více": šestatřicátníci*. Brno: Host.
Kroupa, Daniel. 2010. *Dějiny Kampademie*. Prague: Václav Havel Library.
Lakoff, George. 2007. "What Orwell Didn't Know About the Brain, the Mind, and Language." In *What Orwell Didn't Know: Propaganda and the New Face of American Politics*, edited by András Szántó, 67–74. New York: Public Affairs.
Lapham, Lewis. 1999. "Play on Words." In Goetz-Stankiewicz and Carey 1999, 91–7. New York: G.K. Hall.

Machek, Václav. 1968. *Etymologický slovník jazyka českého*. Prague: Czechoslovak Academy of Sciences.

Macura, Vladimír. 1993. *Masarykovy boty a jiné semi(o)fejetony*. Prague: Pražská imaginace.

Marino, Gordon. 2009. "Have We Lost the Distinction between Psychological and Spiritual Disorders, between Depression and Despair?" *New York Times*, 29 October.

Mlejnek, Josef. 2006. "Politická postava k podpírání: dramatické dílo Václava Havla je světové a zůstává výzvou, kdežto jeho politická dráha se sesula k hodně smutným koncům," *Mladá fronta dnes*, February 25: E6.

Nejedlá, Miroslava. 2001. "Sémantické pole lexémů VĚDOMÍ a SVĚDOMÍ." Master's thesis, Charles University, Prague.

Neubauer, Zdeněk. 1990. *Faustova tajemná milenka: k faustovskému mýtu nad Havlovým Pokoušením*. Prague: Artforum.

Neubauer, Zdeněk. 2010. *Výzva k transcendenci: Consolatio philosophiae hodierna (k šesnácti dopisům Václava Havla)*. Prague: Václav Havel Library.

Nunberg, Geoffrey. 2007. *Talking Right*. NY: Public Affairs.

Palouš, Martin. 1997. "Politika a moc: Je Václav Havel vůbec politikem, a jestliže ano, pak jakým?" In Freimanová 1997, 132–46. Prague: Lidové noviny.

Palouš, Radim. 1985 [in samizdat publication]. *1969: Hypotéza o konci novověku, ba o konci celého euroveku a o počátku světověku*. Prague: Nové cesty myšlení.

Palouš, Radim. 1997. "Filozofování s Havlem." In Freimanová 1997, 162–87. Prague: Lidové noviny.

Peacock, Molly. 2010. Conversation in *Poetry in Person: Twenty-Five Years of Conversation with America's Poets*, edited by A. Neubauer, 191–205. NY: Knopf.

Peirce, Charles S. 1931. *The Collected Papers of Charles Sanders Peirce*. Edited by C. Harsthorne and P. Weiss. Cambridge: Harvard University Press.

Pistorius, Luboš. 1997. Text in Freimanová 1997, 102–15. Prague: Lidové noviny.

Pontuso, James. 2004. *Václav Havel: Civic Responsibility in the Postmodern Age*. Lanham, MD: Rowman & Littlefield Publishers.

Pontuso, James. 2008. "An Interview with Václav Havel." *Society* 45 (1): 9–11. http://dx.doi.org/10.1007/s12115-007-9039-3.

Popescu, Delia. 2012. *Political Action in Václav Havel's Thought: The Responsibility of Resistance*. Lanham: Lexington Books.

Purdy, Jedediah. 2010. *A Tolerable Anarchy: Rebels, Reactionaries, and the Making of American Freedom*. New York: Vintage.

Putna, Martin. 2010. "The Spirituality of Václav Havel in Its Czech and American Contexts: Between Unitarianism and New Age, T.G. Masaryk and Kampademia." *Eastern European Politics and Societies* 24 (3): 353–78. http://dx.doi.org/10.1177/0888325410368560.

Putna, Martin. 2012. *Václav Havel: Duchovní portrét v rámu české kultury 20. století*. Prague: Václav Havel Library.

Ralston Saul, John. 1997. *The Unconscious Civilization*. New York: The Free Press.

Rifkin, Jeremy. 2009. *The Empathic Civilization: The Race to Global Consciousness in a World in Crisis*. New York: Penguin.

Robertson, James. 1999. Preface to *Small Is Beautiful: Economics As If People Mattered*, by E.F. Schumacher, xi–xii. London: Hartley & Marks.

Rocamora, Carol. 2004. *Acts of Courage: Václav Havel's Life in the Theater*. Hanover: Smith & Kraus.

Roth, Philip. 1990. "A Conversation in Prague (with Ivan Klíma)." In *Writings on the East: Selected Essays on Eastern Europe from the New York Review of Books*, edited by Rea Hederman, 101–31. New York: New York Review of Books.

Sayer, Derek. 1998. *The Coasts of Bohemia*. Princeton: Princeton University Press.

Schamschula, Walter. 1980. "Václav Havel: Between the Theater of the Absurd and Engaged Theater." In *Fiction and Drama in Eastern and Southeastern Europe*, edited by H. Birnbaum and T. Eekman, 337–48. Columbus: Slavic Publishers.

Schiff, Stephen. 1999. "Havel's Choice." In Goetz-Stankiewicz and Carey 1999, 75–89. New York: G.K. Hall.

Shklovsky, Victor. 1990. *"Art as Device."* In V. Shklovsky, *Theory of Prose*, translated by B. Sher, 1–14. Elmwood Park, IL: Dalkey Archive Press.

Šiklová, Jiřina. 1997. "Havlovi k šedesátinám." In Freimanová 1997, 128–31. Prague: Lidové noviny.

Šimečka, Milan. 1984. *The Restoration of Order: The Normalization of Czechoslovakia*. Translated by A.G. Brain. Verso Books.

Sires, James. 2001. *Václav Havel: The Intellectual Conscience of International Politics*. InterVarsity Press.

Skilling, Gordon. 1989. *Samizdat and an Independent Society in Central and Eastern Europe*. Columbus, OH: Ohio State University Press.

Šlajchrt, Viktor. 2006. "Sám sobě Havlem: bývalý president psát nezapomněl." *Respekt* 19 (9–14 May):22.

Sloupová, Jitka. 1997. "Loutky, herci, lidé: dokument o 'havlománii'." In Freimanová 1997, 86–101. Prague: Lidové noviny.

Steiner, George. 1989. *Real Presences*. New York: Faber and Faber.

Steiner, Peter. 1984. *Russian Formalism: A Metapoetics*. Ithaca: Cornell University Press.

Steiner, Peter. 2001. Introduction to *The Beggar's Opera*, by Václav Havel, translated by Paul Wilson, ix–xxxi. Ithaca: Cornell University Press.

Steiner, Peter. 2008. "The Power of the Image: Václav Havel's Visual Poetry." In *Between Texts, Languages, and Cultures: A Festschrift for Michael Henry Heim*, edited by C. Cravens, M. Fidler, and S. Kresin, 209–22. Bloomington: Slavica.

Stoppard, Tom. 1997. *Tom Stoppard in Conversation*. Edited by Paul Delany. Ann Arbor: University of Michigan Press.

Stoppard, Tom. 2006. *Rock 'n' Roll*. New York: Grove Press.

Štěrbová, Alena. 2002. *Modelové hry Václava Havla*. Olomouc: Palacký University.

Suk, Jiří. 2013. *Politika jako absurdní drama: Václav Havel v letech 1975–1989*. Prague: Paseka.

Tabery, Erik. 2013. Interview with Jiří Suk ("'Byl vizionář, svoji vizi ale neprosadil'"), *Respekt* May 20–6: 40–5.

Taylor, Brandon. 2004. *Collage: The Making of Modern Art*. New York: Thames & Hudson.

Toulmin, Stephen. 1990. *Cosmopolis: The Hidden Agenda of Modernity*. Chicago: Chicago University Press.

Trefulka, Jan. 1997. "Havlovský paradox." In Freimanová 1997, 20–1. Prague: Lidové noviny.

Trensky, Paul. 1978. *Czech Drama Since World War II*. New York: Columbia Slavic Studies.

Tucker, Aviezer. 2001. *The Philosophy and Politics of Czech Dissidence from Patočka to Havel*. Pittsburgh: University of Pittsburgh Press.

Uličný, Oldřich. 1999. "Hlas svědomí a mluvní akty," *Prace filologiczne* 44: 529–33.

Underhill, James. 2009. *Humboldt, Worldview and Language*. Edinburgh: Edinburgh University Press.

Underhill, James. 2011. *Creating Worldviews: Metaphor, Ideology, and Language*. Edinburgh: Edinburgh University Press.

Vaňková, Irena. 2007. *Nádoba plná řeči: člověk, řeč a přirozený svět*. Prague: Karolinum.

Vaňková, Irena. 2010. "Bud'te v pohodě! (*Pohoda* jako české klíčové slovo.)" In *Obraz člověka v jazyce*, edited by I. Vaňková and J. Pacovská, 31–57. Prague: Charles University Philosophical Faculty.

Vaňková, Irena. 2012. "*Dům* i *domov* v češskoj jazykovoj kartine mira." In *Wartości w językowoj kartine mira Slowiań i ich sąsiadów*, edited by M. Abramowicz, J. Bartmiński, and I. Bielińska-Gardziel, 49–68. Lublin: Wydawnictwo Uniwersytetu Marie-Curie Skłodowskiej.

Vaňková, Irena. 2013. "What Words Tell Us: Phenomenology, Cognitive Ethnolinguistics, and Poetry." In *The Linguistic Worldview: Ethnolinguistics,*

Cognition, and Culture, edited by A. Głaz, D. Danaher, and P. Lozowski, 77–91. Amsterdam: Versita.

Vaňková, Irena, Iva Nebeská, Lucie Saicová-Římalová, and J. Šledrová. 2005. *Co na srdci, to na jazyku: kapitoly z kognitivní lingvistiky*. Prague: Karolinum.

Wierzbicka, Anna. 1992. *Semantics, Culture, and Cognition: Universal Human Concepts in Culture-Specific Configuration*. New York: Oxford University Press.

Wierzbicka, Anna. 1996. *Semantics: Primes and Universals*. Oxford: Oxford University Press.

Wierzbicka, Anna. 1997. *Understanding Cultures through Their Key Words*. London: Oxford University Press.

Wierzbicka, Anna. 1999. *Emotions across Languages and Cultures*. Cambridge: Cambridge University Press. http://dx.doi.org/10.1017/CBO9780511521256.

Wierzbicka, Anna. 2006. *English: Meaning and Culture*. Oxford: Oxford University Press.

Wierzbicka, Anna. 2010. *Experience, Evidence & Sense: The Hidden Cultural Legacy of English*. Oxford: Oxford University Press.

Wilson, James. 2000. Rhetorical Inventions and Interventions: Václav Havel and Civil Society. PhD diss, University of Pittsburgh.

Wilson, Paul. 1999. "Václav Havel in Word and Deed." In Goetz-Stankiewicz and Carey 1999, 21–30. New York: G.K. Hall.

Wilson, Paul. 2006. "Notes from the Underground." *Columbia (The Magazine of Columbia University)*, Fall, 12–15.

Woodruff, Paul. 2008. *The Necessity of Theater: The Art of Watching and Being Watched*. Cambridge: Oxford University Press.

Young-Bruehl, Elisabeth. 2006. *Why Arendt Matters*. New Haven: Yale University Press.

Žák, Jiří. 2012. *Hovory s V. H.: Autentické svědectví o divadle, o kultuře, o letech šedesátých*. Prague: XYZ.

Index

www.ingramcontent.com/pod-product-compliance
Lightning Source LLC
LaVergne TN
LVHW090154080826
844660LV00013B/805/J

* 9 7 8 1 4 4 2 6 4 9 9 2 7 *